Duties and Responsibilities of Islamic People

Duties and Responsibilities of Islamic People

By

Masood Ali

2008

CYBER TECH PUBLICATIONS
4264/3, Ansari Road, Daryaganj, New Delhi-110002 (India)
Ph.: 011-23244078. Fax: 011-23280028
E-Mail: cyberpublicationsdelhi@yahoo.com

DUTIES AND RESPONSIBILITIES OF ISLAMIC PEOPLE

Masood Ali

First Edition 2008

Published by :

G.S. Rawat for **Cyber Tech Publications**
4264/3, Ansari Road, Daryaganj, New Delhi-110002 (India)
Ph.: 011-23244078. Fax: 011-23280028
E-Mail: cyberpublicationsdelhi@yahoo.com

Printed at : **Amit Enterprises**, Maujpur, Delhi, (9810878184)

Preface

Islam, as a philosophy, a way of life and of course as a faith, has served like a lighthouse for the whole world. It has, as a force, influenced all civilizations. Be it education, social fabric or science, Islam has left its impact in all the spheres. In fact, Islam is basically a scientific and progressive religion.

This book is based on authentic sources and material, available in libraries, institutes and some private collections, as well. A rich bibliography, along with references is provided with each volume to prove the authenticity of the work and in order to guide the scholars and readers for further studies. This modest work should prove to be of worth for those, who are kind enough to peruse it and may desire to make use of it for their academic enrichment.

Hopefully, this book would be able to satisfy the urge of all those who desire to know about real Islam and also to create a new awareness, regarding this religion, as a radical discipline, based on reason and opposed to fundamentalism and dogmatism. Though, a small effort, yet its rational treatment and radical approach make it different from other works on the same or related subjects.

—*Author*

Contents

1

Concept of Social Relations

SOCIETAL VALUES

Relations between individuals in an Islamic community can be harmonious if certain rules are adhered to. These consist, firstly, of duties toward others, secondly, cultivating essential personal characteristics, and thirdly, avoiding bad personal characteristics.

Duties toward Others

- Speech is an important element and an important means of social relations. It is therefore essential that what is said and how it is said are wisely considered.
- Honesty makes a person likeable and helps in building and strengthening social bonds. It is also an essential attribute of a good Muslim.
- Amiable facial expressions during conversation are of great importance and should be understood as part of a person's duty towards others.
- A Muslim should judge people by their deeds. He should treat well those who treat him well. No man knows another's hidden intentions and feelings - those are for God to judge. But he who shows evil, is not to be trusted, even if he expresses good intentions.
- Relations with others should be based on respect and kindness.
- A Muslim should make sure before making a promise that he can keep it. He should not break promises by making excuses, thinking this will be enough. To think

that others' acceptance of his excuses is the end of the matter leaves a bad effect on him.

- Care should be taken not to make many promises at one time or to many people, lest one is unable to keep them.
- Among social duties towards others is to visit them if they become sick and to attend the funerals of their dead.
- 'He who does not thank people does not thank God' (Hadith). The best way for a Muslim to thank a person for doing good to him is to say: Jazak Allah Khayran (May God reward you well).
- A Muslim should help anyone who seeks his help, unless he asks for something forbidden or undesirable. He should not hesitate to do good to others, especially when asked to do so.
- It is a duty to accept invitations; an important one not to be turned down is to a wedding ceremony.
- It is a Muslim's duty not to displease others with unpleasant odours from his clothes, body or mouth such as that caused by onions or garlic.

INDIVIDUAL QUALITIES

Generally speaking, there is no goodness better than a good character. The best people are those with the best character, and the worst people are those with an evil character. The following are some aspects of a positive character which should be aspired to. A Muslim should:

- Be humble and should not boast to others.
- Fulfil his trust when put in a position of trust.
- Speak the truth always, and carry out his actions in accordance with it.
- Show mercy and tenderness to others, Muslims and non-Muslims alike.
- Supply help to one who needs help, and aid the distressed, even though he is not asked to do so.
- Forgive when in a position of power and authority.
- Harbour good thoughts of others.

- Be disposed in friendship to others, and treat them in a friendly way.
- Advise sincerely when consulted by others.
- Leave alone and never speak about what does not concern him.
- Never ask others for anything unless it is urgent or necessary.
- Keep his appointments.
- Restrain his anger and refrain from negative reactions.
- Attach special importance to his relationship with those who practise Islam.
- Be patient always.
- Greet whom he has quarrelled with previously.
- Guarantee the well-being of his family and kin.
- Be modest.
- Be satisfied and contented with what is given to him by God.
- Put trivialities aside, concentrate on important things.
- Be wise when dealing with evil people.
- Exchange gifts with others.
- Guide those towards good deeds who want to perform good deeds.
- Mediate between disagreeing parties.
- Contemplate his actions before performing them.
- Be kind to others.
- Keep secret that which others have confided to him or he has discovered about others.
- Ask forgiveness if he has committed a deed affecting a Muslim's honour.
- Forgive someone who has treated him badly, as though he were a close friend.
- Meet others with a cheerful countenance.
- Mix with others, if they are good; if not, then solitude is better for him.

- Defend others who are absent when they are slandered in his presence.
- Direct someone who has lost his way, especially some one who has bad eyesight.
- Be uncomplicated but not naive.
- Be generous, but without extravagance.
- Show gentleness toward the weak and affection toward his parents.
- Not take revenge on someone who reviles or reproaches him for something he knows about him, by reproaching that person for something he knows about him.

NEGATIVE ASPECTS

To be successful in developing social relations, it is necessary to avoid some negative characteristics and just as necessary to practise some positive ones. The following are a list of negative characteristics. A Muslim should avoid:

- Being nervous, highly strung or liable to sudden anger.
- Bad relations with others.
- Speaking about what does not concern him.
- Arrogance, especially if it comes from a poor person, who considers himself to be great but is in fact, not so in the eyes of others.
- Slandering anybody.
- Listening to other people's talk when they do not want him to hear, or they are trying to avoid him.
- Being two-faced.
- Reviling other people's genealogies.
- Displaying pleasure at a fellow-Muslim's misfortune.
- Boasting about ancestors who have died or who are of high rank.
- Seeking out others' faults in order to expose them.
- Avoiding a Muslim for more than three days, if he has had difficulties with him.
- Being a mischief-maker, spreading slander.
- Saying something about a Muslim which he or she

dislikes even if what he says of him or her is true.

- Being suspicious of others.
- Being inquisitive about others.
- Spying.
- Bidding against another in order to raise the price of a commodity.
- Envying others.
- Hating other Muslims.
- Speaking evil of others behind their back.
- Ridiculing others; laughing, scoffing or jeering at them.
- Acting dishonestly toward others, deceiving and misleading them.
- Self-deception or self-delusion.
- Being avaricious and miserly.
- Being a coward, unable to control his fear and running away from danger.
- Grumbling and complaining and never being satisfied with anything.
- Drawing attention to his own helpfulness, charity, or generosity.
- Being selfish, thinking chiefly of and being interested in his own needs and welfare without care for others.
- Withholding help, when he is able to offer it to others.
- Praising and flattering somebody in his presence.
- Showing undue respect to those of a sinful nature, or those who are wealthy or have a high position.
- Speaking loudly.
- Being harsh or rude to others.
- Praising himself or overestimating himself.
- Lying.
- Talking and Listening.

The Conversation : Talking is an important means of communication, it is also an extension and expression of a person's personality.

- Moderation in speech is an excellent quality, which a good Muslim should cultivate. A Hadith says that one should either speak good or keep silent.
- A Muslim should not talk just for the sake of talking because he thinks it is a shortcoming to be silent. The shortcoming lies in talking badly and talking too much. His duty is to say what is good or to keep silent. While being silent is a good characteristic, it should not be overdone to the extent of annoying others.
- A Muslim should adhere to the truth and speak it whether pleased or displeased. He should speak the truth, even if it is bitter.
- A Muslim should think carefully before speaking, and avoid saying something that he might regret and for which he would have to apologize.
- Simplicity and clarity should characterize speech; enunciating over-carefully and speaking gutturally should be avoided. Using strange archaic words, in an attempt to demonstrate linguistic ability or to show that one is more knowledgeable than others, is forbidden.
- Looking pleasantly at others when speaking to them is required as a courtesy.
- There is a specific topic related to every occasion. Decorum, appropriateness, should exist between the topic discussed and the occasion concerned.
- A Muslim should be sure of the truthfulness and accuracy of what he says.
- If those listening to a person cannot follow him and need to have his words repeated, it is courteous to repeat them.
- One should not speak hurriedly. It is better to speak neither too slowly nor too quickly, neither too loudly nor too softly, for such ways of speaking may tire the listener. Nor should words be interspersed with long pauses, as this will bore the listener.

SIGNIFICANCE OF LANGUAGE

- Colloquial and slang words and expressions should be avoided as much as possible.

- Foreign words and terms should be avoided.
- One should try to attain to a pleasant, agreeable and moral mode of expression.
- It is not fitting for a Muslim to be given to cursing. He must never invoke God's curse, God's anger, or Hell on another.
- A Muslim should not be given to using bad or objectionable language and should guard against speaking slander and abuse. Being of those whom others leave alone for fear of their ridicule or ribaldry casts a bad light on one's personality and character.
- Reviling the dead is bad conduct, and is forbidden to the same degree as reviling the living.
- Objecting to his destiny and attributing injustice to God ill-befit a Muslim and must be avoided.
- It is a bad thing to express an overpermissive attitude toward others, especially Muslims, or to life in general.
- Calling down evil upon himself, his children, his servants, etc. is forbidden to a Muslim.
- Certain expressions that contradict the basic tenets of Islamic faith - for example, expressions that seem to ascribe partners to God - must be avoided. A Muslim should never say: 'What God Wills and so-and-so wills'; rather he should say: 'What God alone wills' or 'What God wills and afterwards so-and-so wills.' He must never say: 'I have no supporter but God and you', but rather say: 'I have no supporter but God and afterwards you.' He should never say: 'I swear by so-and-so.'
- To revile the wind, rain or other natural phenomena is forbidden, for these are under God's command. Instead of reviling the wind or rain, one should say: 'O God, make it a blessing and not a punishment.' Also, the rooster should not be reviled, for he wakes people for the dawn prayer.
- A woman must not become the intimate of another woman and then describe the latter to her husband.
- A Muslim should not try to display superior knowledge of a topic discussed; he should avoid overuse of the pronoun 'I'.

- It is better to be gentle when blaming others for something they might have done and to avoid doing so before other people.
- However good a Muslim may be, he should not disgrace or revile another's beliefs or character directly or indirectly.
- A Muslim should be careful not to say anything that might give offence or be passed on, and perhaps misquoted. Subjects that might lead to embarrassment should be avoided.
- Just as a Muslim should not disgrace or revile others in his speech, he also should not disgrace or revile himself.
- A Muslim should never praise another in his presence. If he cannot avoid it, he should be moderate in his expression; it is for God to declare anyone pure.
- It is a Muslim's duty to stop anyone who continually criticizes others.
- Discussing personal and family secrets with others should be avoided; it is better to keep such things to oneself.
- A Muslim should never allow others to tell him bad things about some third person, for it is better to meet and mix with others with no ill-feelings. If he hears people talking unjustly about others, it is his duty to defend the person spoken about.
- After having done something a Muslim should not express the wish that he had not done it or had done it another way.
- Speaking for too long is a bad characteristic. Being moderate when speaking is better.
- A Muslim should avoid talking about things which do not concern him.
- Eavesdropping on the private conversation of others should be avoided.
- The term 'brother' should be confined to fellow Muslims.

- Calling a Muslim an infidel or accusing him of unbelief is completely forbidden.
- Inquiring about something from someone should be preceded by greeting the person first, taking into consideration what he is engaged in at that moment, and then confining oneself to the necessary matter.
- It is a part of courtesy that when a Muslim mentions the Prophet or when he is mentioned in his presence he should invoke a blessing on him by saying: Sallal-Lah alayhi wa sallam (Allah's blessing and peace be upon him).
- A Muslim may not use absolute and assertive terms about future events without referring to God's will by saying: insha Allah (If God wills).
- A Muslim should not abuse or revile another person or speak of his faults, even if that person abuses and reviles him and even though he speaks of his faults.

Listening : A Muslim should:

- Try to listen to others as politely as possible.
- Avoid interrupting others when they are speaking.
- Face the person he is speaking to and show interest in what he is saying, even if he is not interested in the topic being discussed, try to control himself, unless the topic is directed against Islam, its principles or the Prophet, in which case he should either try to put an end to it or leave.
- Avoid getting involved in a pointless argument with someone who expresses views with which he does not agree.

Swearing

- As far as possible, swearing and taking an oath should be avoided.
- A Muslim should swear by Allah, one of His attributes or names, only. He is not allowed to swear by something else, such as the Prophet, Prayer, the Kaaba, the Quran, etc.

- Swearing in Allah's name, unfaithfully, is considered a great sin.
- Using the colloquial expression 'by God' should be avoided.
- If a Muslim swears to do something or to refrain from doing something, and afterwards he finds doing something else is better, he is recommended not to carry out his oath and to make proper atonement.
- It is a Muslim's duty to fulfil his oath. Therefore, he must be sure before swearing that he has the means to carry out his promise.
- Using the threat: 'If you don't do this or that, I will divorce my wife', is distasteful and unbecoming to a Muslim. Marriage must not be referred to in such a trivial and childish manner.
- Swearing oaths should be avoided in certain cases, for example, in business or financial transactions.
- Breaking an oath must be avoided. If a Muslim breaks his oath then he must make atonement by providing food for a meal for ten poor people or providing each of the ten with one article of clothing. If he is not financially able to do this, then he must fast three, successive days.
- If a Muslim vows to do something forbidden in Islam, such as to take something which does not belong to him, then it is his duty to break his oath.
- If a Muslim vows to do something not recommended by Islam, then he is advised not to fulfil his oath and to make atonement.

Nadhr (to connect a vow with the fulfilment of a wish)

- To vow, in return for a favour from God to oneself, to do some specific thing for the sake of God, is permitted but is not recommended.
- Vowing to oneself to do a certain thing should be done only for the sake of God.
- A Muslim must fulfil his vow pledged for the sake of God, and may avoid fulfilling it if pledged for the sake of someone else.

- It is not permissible for someone who has made a vow to slaughter an animal for the sake of Allah, to eat anything of it unless his initial intention included the stipulation that he would eat some.

Laughter

- There are many reasons for laughing, such as seeing a pleasant thing, hearing good news or a joke.
- To laugh because other people laugh is not recommended; there should be a reason for laughter.
- Laughter should not be characterized by loud or unpleasant sounds.
- A broad smile, such as makes the back teeth visible, is better than laughing.
- It is better always to control the sounds of laughter; excessive noise should be avoided.
- It is not fitting for a Muslim to make people laugh for the sake of laughter, especially if that leads to lying.
- One should not sit with people amongst whom is a person trying to make them laugh at any expense.
- Laughing in ridicule of another person must be avoided.

Weeping

- Weeping should be spontaneous and for a good reason.
- It is not unmanly to cry because emotions should not be suppressed. Yet it should be done with restraint and not with excessive or loud sounds.

Jokes

- It is good to share jokes with others, because always being serious is burdensome.
- When making jokes, it is better to avoid using impolite or hurtful terms, directly or indirectly.
- Over-seriousness and excessive joking should both be avoided because they will lessen self-esteem and risk hurting others' feelings.
- Attention should be given to the context in which the joke is told so as to avoid hurting others' feelings.

- A joke should not be accompanied with excessive gestures or bodily movements.
- One should not take what belongs to others while joking.
- To terrify others, in jest, is forbidden.
- Lying is not allowed even for joking purposes.

Behaviour when Meeting Others : A Muslim should observe the following:

- He should smile, for a smile is the key to a successful meeting. However, he should not smile at people because of their material wealth.
- He should be first to salute other Muslims.
- He should not bow to any person when saluting, no matter who he is and whatever the occasion.
- When meeting others and after saluting, he should extend his right hand and shake hands; this enhances mutual respect.
- He should not shake hands with anyone for whom it might be a nuisance.
- If his hand is dirty and someone wants to shake hands with him, he should politely excuse himself, explaining the reason.
- He should not feel upset about shaking hands at every meeting.
- Men shake hands with men, women with women. If a woman wants to shake hands with a man or vice versa, he/she should excuse himself/herself.
- Too many questions about the family, etc. when meeting is a time-wasting activity and is likely to lead to boredom, so he should avoid it.
- If anyone meets him and begins a conversation before saluting him, he has the right not to speak to him.
- If he is seated, it is not necessary for him to stand up to shake hands. Although there are certain occasions when he may stand up, such as meeting someone who has returned from a journey.
- There is no objection to him kissing the hand of a Muslim scholar or of his parents. However, this gesture

is forbidden in the case of a wealthy or powerful person. In the first case it is allowed on condition that kissing the hand does not replace shaking hands.

- When a meeting is finished he should extend his hand to shake hands once again, saying: Assalamu alaikum (Peace be upon you).
- He should not shake hands with someone who has a contagious disease.
- It is not sunnah for him to shake hands after praying, saying: Taqabbal Allah (May God accept our prayer).

Manners of Greeting

- The habit of greeting is of great importance for it increases friendship and acquaintance. It is also an act of kindness and courtesy.
- A person who is riding should greet one who is walking, a person who is walking should greet one who is sitting, and a small group should greet a larger one. The young should greet the old. If two people of more or less the same age and both walking meet each other, either may greet the other first.
- Flexibility should characterize observance of the above-mentioned rules, for the best of people are those who do not hesitate to greet others.
- Others should be greeted by saying: Assalamu aliykum (Peace be upon you).
- Using other expressions of greeting, such as 'good morning', 'good evening', 'hello', are allowed only after saying: Assalamu aliykum.
- Politeness requires that a salutation be returned in the same or better way. Required, at least, is that one says: Wa aliykum assalam (Upon you be peace) and the ideal and perfect form is: Wa aliykum assalam wa rahmatullah wa barakatuh (Upon you be peace, God's mercy and His blessings).
- It is a Muslim's duty to respond to a salutation by returning it without delay, unless there is a good reason for delay.

- When a Muslim greets others or is greeted by others, his greeting or response to the other's greeting should be done audibly.
- If a Muslim thinks that the other did not hear his greeting for some reason, then it is his duty to greet him another time, even for a third time, but not more.
- If meeting others is repeated within a certain period of time, it should not be thought boring or monotonous to greet them again.
- Greeting others by making a gesture with the fingers, with the palm of the hand, or with the head must be avoided.
- A Muslim should greet both those whom he knows and those whom he does not know. This increases the number of his acquaintances and friends. He cannot, however, in certain cases, such as at markets or on crowded streets, give salutations to everyone he passes or meets.
- If passing a company of people, a Muslim should not greet some of them by mentioning their names or titles. Politeness requires him to greet them all in general terms, so that everyone is greeted.
- When greeted by a company of people the salutation should be returned with a general greeting and without specifying anyone in particular.
- If someone passes a Muslim, and he is in doubt of his greeting, he is not required to respond to him.
- If someone greets a company of people, and his greeting is returned by a member of this company then this is enough, though it is recommended that all members respond.
- It is a Muslim's duty to respond to another's greeting whether he is a Muslim or non-Muslim.
- If a Muslim meets someone and he is in doubt whether he will return his greeting, it is nonetheless his duty to greet him.
- Though greeting others is recommended there are certain cases where salutations should be avoided, such as

greeting someone who is in the act of relieving himself, or sleeping, or drowsing.

- If a Muslim passes a mixed company of Muslims and non-Muslims, he should greet them by saying: Assalamu alaikum (Peace be upon you).
- If a Muslim is greeted while relieving himself, he should not respond until he leaves the lavatory.
- A Muslim should not neglect to greet members of his family upon returning home.
- If passing children, it is better to greet them, even though they are supposed to greet one first.
- If someone has sent another person to a Muslim with a message which includes a greeting, he must greet both of them by saying: Assalamu alayka wa alaiyhi (Peace be upon you and upon him).
- If sending a message to a non-Muslim, he may be greeted by writing: Assalamu ala man ittabaa al-huda (Peace be upon who follows the right path).
- When approaching a group of people or meeting a person, a salutation should be given. When parting, a salutation should again be given at the end of the meeting. It is of particular importance to greet when parting; especially in the case of two parties who may have argued or disagreed during their conversation, for the greeting implies that there are no hard feelings and that both attach value to a continuing good relationship.
- When greeting other Muslims, whether orally (on the telephone) or by writing (letters, etc.), one should start and finish with: Assalamu alaikum.
- It is not un-Islamic to greet non-Muslims, but a Muslim should not use: *Assalamu alaikum*.

Asking Permission to Enter Another's House

- A Muslim may not enter another's house before asking permission to do so. Politeness requires such permission, even from those who are very close to him, such as his parents, for people in their homes may be in a state of dress or of mood in which they do not wish to be seen.

This is especially important in regard to women who must have time to arrange themselves, to cover their hair, and so on.

- It is forbidden to glance into someone else's house when the door is opened to greet one.
- The visitor must greet whoever answers the door before asking permission to enter. The manner of asking permission to enter should be thus: *Assalamu alaikum,* may I enter?', or '*Assalamu alaikum,* may (mention your name) enter?' Refusal of permission to enter is justified in the absence of a greeting first.
- If the visitor is asked to give his identity before the door is opened to him, he must give it. To say merely: 'It is me', is insufficient and not approved.
- The request to enter, if permission is not granted, may be repeated three times. If permission is still not granted, the visitor should leave. If the caller does not have an appointment, then the person he wants to visit is not required to receive him. Therefore, he should not take offence if he informs him that he is busy and would rather not receive guests at this time.
- Knocking at the door or ringing the bell is not a substitute for giving a greeting and asking permission to enter.
- Knocking at the door should be done gently, for there might be someone asleep or ill inside the house. If after knocking at the door three times there is no response, the caller should leave.

At a Friend's House : Exchange of visits strengthens relationships between individuals and is valued as one of the main elements in a healthy social life. It eradicates that social isolation which is not acceptable within Islam.

- It is a recommended Islamic procedure that a Muslim should inform his host of his intention to visit him. If he visits somebody without a previous appointment, and he is unwilling to receive him for one reason or another, he should not be upset.
- Appointments must be kept promptly. If there is just cause for changing or cancelling the appointment then either party should properly inform the other.

- Suitable times to pay a visit do not include night time, evening (after 'Isha' prayer) or the siesta hour.
- It is the duty of the host to receive the guest if there is an appointment.. Otherwise the host has the right to apologize for not being able to receive him. In this case the guest should not feel offended.
- Visits should be free of any personal interest or other selfishness. The aim of visiting should be to strengthen brotherly relations with other Muslims, for the sake of God.
- Men should not visit women whose husbands are away from home, unless they are mahrams to the women visited.
- A Muslim may not enter the host's house until he has his permission, and has greeted him, even if he has an appointment with him.
- A visitor should remember that he is in someone else's home. Therefore, he should try his best to fit in with the plans made by his host, even if he finds things a little boring.
- A Muslim should not limit his visits only to those who visit him.
- A guest must not lead a host in prayer or sit in the host's accustomed place without his permission.
- Social intercourse and mixing between men and women when visiting other families is forbidden. A guest is allowed to speak to the wife or daughters of the host if there is a need. The host's wife can serve the guests provided she dresses and behaves correctly.
- A woman may not visit others if her husband objects.
- Open violation of Islamic teachings by the host or members of his family should cause the guest to leave. Such behaviour is unacceptable and intolerable to good Muslims. The host in this case is requested to show understanding toward the guest's behaviour.
- If a Muslim wants to stay as a guest with someone then he should not expect his hospitality to continue for more than three days. Anything beyond that, he receives as

charity. A guest should not stay so long as to make himself an encumbrance.

- It is impolite for a guest to refuse what a host offers him unless there is a medical reason, or he is fasting. In this case he must apologize and explain the reason to him.
- If a visitor wants to relieve himself he should first inform the host. He should not leave his place until permission is given.
- When visiting others, it is not proper to stay long unless requested to do so. Becoming a nuisance by remaining too long and overstaying as a guest is not proper Islamic conduct.
- When the time comes to leave, a visitor should thank the host for his entertainment. He should ask permission to leave, and not move until permission is given. He should bid the host farewell.
- If a Muslim intends to fast while staying with others as a guest, then it is polite to inform the host of his intention.
- If a friend or relative does not visit him, a Muslim should not accord him the same treatment. He should call on him and not wait for him to return his visit.
- A Muslim should not limit his visits to only special occasions. As mentioned above, exchange of visits between individuals is always beneficial.

Receiving Guests

- A Muslim host should receive his guests heartily and with a welcoming smile. To honour and entertain a guest is an Islamic duty.
- It is the host's duty to keep all sources of annoyance away from his guests.
- It is impolite to ask the guest to perform any service.
- The guest needs no invitation to come and stay for a number of days, though it is better if the visitor can inform the host in advance of his arrival. The guest can stay three days and then should leave.

- If a guest comes to visit a Muslim, it is his duty, if he is able, to be hospitable and generous by offering him food and drink, whether or not he receives the same treatment when he visits him.
- When the visit is ended and the guest is about to leave, the host should accompany him to the outside door and give him a good farewell.

Inviting Others to Dine

- Inviting others to dine is recommended, provided a Muslim's intention is not to boast about his own achievements.
- Invitations to a banquet should not be confined to the rich and influential, the poor and needy should be included too.
- Invitations to dine should be restricted to good Muslims, though inviting others is not forbidden. Priority should be given to Muslims, however, since a result of dining together is a strengthening of friendship and brotherhood and this aim should be reserved for fellow Muslims.
- It is recommended that neighbours are among those invited to dine.
- Showing generosity to invited guests is an important matter, provided exaggeration and extravagance are avoided.
- The manners of receiving a guest, should be adhered to.
- Although the guests may begin eating as soon as the meal is served, it is nevertheless good conduct to indicate to the guests that they should begin by-saying: Bismillah (In the name of God).
- It is polite and considered a form of generosity to urge guests to eat and drink, but not to excess, and not to insist that they eat a certain kind of food.
- A Muslim should be careful when speaking not to praise his own generosity or his own table.
- Restricting invitations to dine only to special occasions is not recommended; an invitation may be offered at any time.

- A host should avoid giving his guests the impression that he is observing how much he eats or that he thinks he is eating too much.
- If a guest arrives unexpectedly, it is a Muslim's duty to see that he is adequately cared for.

When Invited to a Meal

- If a Muslim is invited to a meal, it is recommended that he accepts. It is obligatory to accept a wedding feast invitation (though not if it entails forbidden things).
- An invitation to a meal from anybody who is extending the invitation only out of personal interest should be declined.
- If a Muslim is invited by someone to a meal while fasting voluntarily, then he is free either to break his fast or to visit him and keep his fast.
- When going to a meal in somebody's house, a Muslim should not take anyone with him who has not been invited.
- If someone follows a Muslim and accompanies him without his consent when he is going to his hosts, it is his duty to inform the host of the situation. The host may accept or reject the uninvited guest, as he wishes.
- When the meal is served, it is not good manners to rush to the table. It is correct to follow the person who is to one's right.
- The invitations of people competing with each other to provide a feast for the sake of ostentation, should not be accepted.
- An invitation from a morally corrupt person should not be accepted merely because one does not wish to say no to him. The invitation may be accepted only if the intention is to bring him back to Islam, otherwise not.
- When sitting down to eat, proper table manners should be observed.
- If something among the dishes or drink offered to a Muslim is forbidden according to Islam, such as wine or pork, then he should inform the host of the necessity

of removing it, otherwise of his leaving, and if it is not removed he should leave immediately.

- A guest should thank the host for his invitation and ask God to bless him. The following dua may be recited: *Akala taamukum al-abrar, wa salla alaykum al- Malaika wa aftara indakum as-Saimun* (May the righteous eat your food, may the angels invoke blessings on you, and may those who have been fasting break their fast with you).

Visiting the Sick

- Visiting the sick is one way of expressing concern for them, and it helps them feel better. It also strengthens and develops social relations. So, the sick should be visited, not only among friends and relatives, but also those who are not immediate relations or acquaintances.
- Making an appointment to visit the sick is a good thing but not necessary. One should keep in mind the proper visiting times if the sick are in hospital, and comply with all regulations, including those prohibiting taking food and drinks.
- The kind of sickness determines the nature and length of the visit. Visitors may be prevented by doctors from seeing the sick person or they may be allowed a brief visit. If doctors permit, it is recommended to stay long enough for the sick person to feel that he/she is not neglected.
- A visitor should sit close to the sick person and ask how he/she feels.
- When visiting a patient one is recommended to pray for his/her recovery and that the sickness may be the cause of purification of sins. The Prophet used to say to the patients he visited: La bas Tahur insha *Allah* (No harm will come; it is a purification, if God wills).
- A visitor should select his consoling words with care; avoiding any mention of objection to destiny, describing the sickness as evil, or any words that might have a bad effect on the sick person. Instead, he/she should be

encouraged to accept the illness as something that God has planned and that one must think well of God.

- If the sick person has reached a hopeless state a Muslim may say: *Inna li-llah wa-inna ilayhi rajiun* (We belong to God and to Him we return).
- A Muslim should not deprive the sick person of his visits; he should make them as frequently as necessary, especially if the sick person feels close to him.
- Concern for the patient should not be limited to visiting him; one is also required to ask his family, from time to time, about his health.
- It is permissible to visit a non-Muslim who is sick if he happens to be a friend, neighbour or relative, or if one seeks to persuade him to become a Muslim.
- To stare at a leprous person or at others with similar diseases or deformities, should be avoided lest they feel looked down upon.

Group Meetings

- Socializing, just to kill time, should be avoided. Time is a precious asset not to be wasted. Rather, it should be spent on useful affairs. Also, friends should be selected carefully.
- Places for a gathering should be respectable, such as private houses and mosques, not pavements, markets, etc.
- Socializing, if one's body, clothes or mouth smell bad, should be avoided.
- After seeking permission to enter and greeting the house owner, a Muslim should next greet the people seated. He should shake hands with everyone, starting from the right and sit where he finds himself when he has finished.
- When joining a gathering, a person should sit where a place is made for him; otherwise he should sit in any vacant place.
- If someone offers his place to someone joining the gathering, he should apologize politely for not accepting

it and sit where he finds himself or where someone makes room without getting up, or where there is enough room.

- One should be careful not to oblige anyone to leave his seat, even a child, in order to take his place.
- It is not fitting to sit between two people unless permission is given, because they may be talking privately or expressing some intimacy.
- Care must be taken when sitting not to turn one's back on anyone, since this might be interpreted as a form of dislike or disrespect.
- If more people join the gathering, those already seated should make room for the newcomers.
- Someone joining a gathering should remember that those present do not have to stand up for him.
- If someone has left his seat intending to return, he has more right to his seat and others should be careful not to take his place.
- If the company consists of three people, any two of them must not talk privately in front of the third.
- If two people are talking privately when a newcomer arrives, he should not obtrude uninvited upon their conversation.
- If more than three people are present, then two of them may talk privately or intimately.
- It is polite to listen to others and not interrupt or let one's attention wander.
- A person's sitting posture should be humble and respectful of others.
- It is necessary that in any gathering people should remember God and invoke blessings on His Messenger Muhammad, peace be upon him.
- If a Muslim hears people talking about someone behind his back, he should politely try to stop them; if they persist he should excuse himself and leave.
- What is said or done in a sitting place should continuously be noted and judged in terms of the permissible and the forbidden.

- Any secrets that people exchange and divulge in private conversation are in confidence and should always be respected.
- Gatherings are not recommended after 'Isha' prayer unless necessitated for study purposes or for the sake of a guest.
- Those who sit in an assembly, gathering, meeting, etc., where there is much clamour or meaningless talk, are recommended, at the end of the gathering and before getting up to leave, to say the following dua: *Subhanaka Allahumma wa bihamdika ashhadu an la ilaha illa anta astaghfiruka wa atubu ilayka* (O Allah, I witness Your absolute transcendence, and praise You. I testify that there is no god except You; I ask Your pardon and turn to You in repentance).

Forms of Sitting

- Sitting should be respectful of others. Stretching legs out in front of others or sitting higher up than others should be avoided.
- Private parts should always be concealed in any sitting posture.
- Sitting with the left hand behind the back, while leaning on the other hand, should be avoided.
- A person should not sit with one part of his body in the sun and the other part in the shade.
- Sitting on the floor is the best posture for eating.

Women's Conduct Outside the Home

- A woman who has used incense, make-up, or has perfumed herself, should not leave her home until the make-up is removed and no scent of the perfume remains.
- A man may not spend the night in the house of a woman unless he is her husband or a mahram.
- A man and a woman are not permitted to be alone together unless the man is a mahram to the woman or, of course, her husband.

- If a man should, happen to look at a woman, he must turn his eyes away. An accidental glance is allowed, a second look is forbidden.
- Social intercourse or mixing of men and women is of two kinds:
  (a) That which is related to general public life and not confined to certain groups of people, but common to all people, such as in streets, markets and mosques. Mixing in this case is allowed, provided all the above-mentioned conditions are fulfilled.
  (b) Free mixing of men and women in places confined to particular groups of people, such as in school, university or work place, is forbidden, and separation of the sexes is required.
- Outside the home when a woman speaks to a man her speech should not be inviting, but should remain objective and crisp.
- Women are allowed to indulge in all business transactions allowed to men; a woman may also hold a job if it does not affect her main responsibility of the house and family, if her husband agrees, and if she is not required to mix with men. For instance, a woman may teach in a girls' school or be a women's doctor.
- When leaving work for home, a woman should remember to wear Islamic dress.
- Islam does not consider the house to be a woman's jail; she is allowed to leave the house, as long as there is a good reason for doing so.

Celebrations

- The most important rules governing celebrations are:
  (a) Mixing of men and women should be avoided.
  (b) Extravagant parties and wastefulness must be avoided even if a Muslim is financially able.
- Celebrating occasions foreign to Islam, such as Christmas, New Year, Mother's Day, Father's Day, Labour Day, wedding anniversaries, birthdays and the like, is an imitation of other cultures.

- Certain other celebrations have also been introduced into Islam from outside such as the Prophet's birthday, the Prophet's Isra' and Miraj (the Prophet's night journey from Mecca to Jerusalem and then to the seven heavens), the Prophet's emigration, etc.
- Instead of forbidden occasions, Muslims are encouraged to have meetings of individual villages, towns, or city districts, to discuss different economic, political and social issues relating to the present and future; or to discuss specifically devotional matters or to read the Quran and praise God.

Behaviour Toward Relatives

- Visiting relatives and being concerned about them is extremely important.
- There is no prescribed number of visits to relatives, but they should be frequent enough so that they do not feel neglected.
- Whenever he meets his relatives, a Muslim should ask and concern himself about their welfare.
- A Muslim should remember that he has a responsibility toward his poor and needy relatives. He should extend help to them and from time to time give them as a present some of the things they need.
- If a Muslim is breast-fed by a woman other than his mother, he should remember that he has another family and relatives in breast feeding.
- It is best not to wait for a visit from relatives before visiting them.
- It is not good to answer an offence from a relative with the same. It shows moral stature to refrain from answering in that way.
- A Muslim should treat his mother's sister as he treats his mother.
- A Muslim should treat his uncle as he treats his father.
- It is permitted for a woman to sit with male relatives (other than those she is forbidden to marry), provided:
  (a) That they act within the limits of proper decorum;
  (b) That she is not alone with one relative.

Behaviour Toward Neighbours

- The first rule governing behaviour toward neighbours is to avoid causing them any form of material or moral harm such as by raising one's voice or having loud, noisy celebrations, especially at night.
- Visiting neighbours is important for it helps establish amiable relations, especially on major occasions such as births, weddings, sickness and death, etc.
- Being generous to neighbours is in accordance with the Prophet's teachings. One should invite a neighbour to dine from time to time, and send him food at other times.
- Doing any ill to a neighbour's children should be avoided. Care should be taken not to let children's conflicts engender misunderstandings between their parents.
- A neighbour and his family have certain special privileges on a Muslim. Extending help to them when it is needed is Islamic behaviour.
- If a Muslim knows his neighbour to be in some financial difficulty, he should not wait for him to ask for help, rather he should offer help if he can.
- A Muslim should keep secrets confided in him by neighbours, or which he may have overheard.
- A Muslim should talk well of his neighbours, defend them if people talk ill of them, because his relations with them deserve his special attention and care.
- It is the housewife's responsibility to look after relations with women neighbours.
- If a neighbour is a relative, good mutual relations become all the more important.
- Good relations should not be confined to next-door neighbours but should also extend to those further away.

Gifts : Exchanging gifts between individuals is recommended by Islam, for it strengthens relations. Therefore, if a Muslim is financially able, he should try to present gifts to relatives and friends while observing the following rules:

- Giving presents to relatives has priority over giving presents to others.

- Spending a lot of money on extravagant gifts and a lot of time choosing them are bad habits that limit the exchange of gifts and might even lead to non-exchange of gifts.
- A gift should only be bought with money earned in a legal way.
- The purpose of giving others gifts must be to honour them and to strengthen relations. Giving gifts in the hope of material gain or personal influence, is bribery, which is strictly forbidden.
- On presenting a gift, discussing anything that might make the recipient sceptical about its purpose should be avoided.
- On receiving a gift, a Muslim should open it and look at it, show satisfaction, and express thanks for it. If the one who sent him the gift is present, then he should pray for him.
- Giving someone a present and then asking for it back is not polite nor, with the exception of gifts presented to children by their parents or their grandparents, is it permitted.
- It is an act of politeness to return the courtesy of a gift received by seeking an occasion to do so.
- A Muslim should not accept a gift from someone who intends to exploit him or profit from his authority or influence in any way. In fact, such a gift is in reality a bribe.
- When a parent gives presents to his children he should not favour one above another.
- It is most important to remember that giving presents is recommended, not obligatory. It is an error to believe that giving presents is required: such an error may hinder exchange of visits between people who, especially if they are not financially able, will seek to avoid such visits in order to avoid giving presents.

2

Social Duties

Religion is generally regarded as a matter of one's personal life. Islam, however is not just a religion, but a *Deen*. It encompasses the spiritual and material aspects of one's personal as well as socio-political life and provides a well-integrated code of human behavior as a whole.

The Quran and Hadith provide well-defined guidance concerning a Believer's obligations to Almighty Allah, and His Creations, particularly to fellow human beings. These obligations begin with one's family and then spread out gradually to cover the rest of humanity.

The Quran and Hadith also make it clear that social obligations in a way are more important than those towards Allah. If someone commits a personal sin against Allah and then turns to him with sincere repentance, Allah may forgive his sin.

This is because Allah is Oft-forgiving, Most Merciful and loves those who turn to Him with sincere repentance. If, on the contrary, a person commits a social crime and usurps the due rights of an individual, he will meet Allah on the Day of Judgement with the other person's claim upon him. Allah in this case will serve as a judge between the two and will not forgive the oppressor unless the other person forgives him. This is because Allah is Just and commands us to practice justice towards fellow human beings.

The Quran and Hadith have clearly defined the respective rights of various members of a community. We should acquire the proper knowledge of these rights and try our best to honour them.

TOWARDS NEIGHBOURS

The people closest to an individual outside the bonds of family are his neighbours. Often, the contact with a neighbour is more intimate and permanent than that with a family member. If each person takes care of the due rights of his neighbour, this will lead to the prosperity and security of the whole community. One of the reasons for the increased crime rate in the Western society is apathy towards neighbours. Islamic teachings give utmost importance to the rights of neighbours. Moreover, the rights of neighbours in Islam exist regardless of religious or other differences. It is for this reason that street crimes in a Muslim society are very rare. The Quran states:

> *Serve Allah, and join not any partners with Him; And do Ehsan with parents, kinsfolk, orphans, those in need, neighbours who are near, neighbours who are strangers, the companions by your side, the wayfarer (you meet), and what your right hand possesses (i.e. servants and slaves).* *(Nisa 4:36)*

The Prophet through his conduct and Ahadith gave supreme importance to the rights of neighbours. "Love thy neighbour as thyself" is just a sweet expression of the West. Ahadith, on the other hand, define the rights of neighbours in the most comprehensive and well-defined language. Based on these Ahadith, the *Fuqaha* (Jurists) have derived various rules pertaining to the legal rights of neighbour. No religion or system in the world comes even close to the noble teachings of Islam regarding the rights of neighbours. Following are a few related Ahadith.

Types of Neighbours and their Respective Rights: Hasan ibn Sufyan reported that Rasoolullah said: The neighbours are of three classes. A neighbour who has a single right, a neighbour who has double rights, and a neighbour who has triple rights. The neighbour who has three rights is a Muslim neighbour having a family relation. For him is the right of neighbourhood, the right of Islam and the right of family relations. As for the one who has double rights, he is a Muslim neighbour, who has the right of neighbourhood and the right of Islam. The one who has a single right is a polytheist neighbour. (Masnad of Bazar, Al Hulyah of Abu Noyeem)

Aishah asked Rasoolullah I have two neighbours. To whom of these two shall I send my present first? He answered:

To the one who is nearer to you in respect of your door. *(Bukhari)*

Importance of Neighbour's Rights : Aishah and also Abdullah ibn Umar narrated that Rasoolullah said:

Archangel Jibbrail kept on exhorting me about the rights of neighbours until I felt that they would be included in the category of heirs. *(Bukhari, Muslim)*

Archangel Jibbrail was the one who used to bring Allah's revelation to the Prophet. So whatever Jibbrail said to him concerning neighbours was a revelation from Almighty Allah. It appears from this Hadith that Jibbrail brought these messages so frequently and stressed the importance of the rights of neighbours so much that the Prophet thought that neighbours would be included among heirs. Abu Hurrayrah narrated that Rasoolullah said:

He who believes in Allah and the Last Day must not put his neighbour to inconvenience, and he who believes in Allah and the Last Day must speak beneficently or keep quiet. *(Bukhari, Muslim)*

Abdullah ibn Umar reported that Rasoolullah said:

The best companion in the sight of Allah is the one who is the best among all others to his companions, and the best neighbour in the sight of Allah is the one who is the best among all others to his neighbours. *(Tirmidhi)*

The First Dispute on the Day of Judgement : Uqaba bin Amer reported that Rasoolullah said:

The first two disputants on the Day of Judgement will be regarding the neighbours. *(Ahmad)*

THE CRITERION

Abdul Rahman ibn Abi Qorad narrated: One day the Prophet performed ablution. His companions started to anoint themselves with the water of his ablution. The Prophet asked them: What makes you do this? They answered: the love of Allah and His Messenger. Rasoolullah then said:

Let him who loves Allah and His Messenger and desires that Allah and His Messenger love him, should be truthful in his speech when he speaks, fulfill his trusts when he is trusted, and be good to those who are his neighbours. *(Baihaqi)*

This Hadith is a reminder to those who claim to love the Prophet of Allah. The love of the Prophet calls for a total commitment to all of his teachings. The above Hadith states only three of his noble teachings. One of these is to be good to our neighbours.

A Criterion of Iman : Abu Hurrayrah related that Rasoolullah said:

By Allah he does not believe! By Allah he does not believe! By Allah he does not believe!

He was asked: Who does not believe? Rasoolullah answered:

He whose neighbour is not secure from his mischiefs. *(Bukhari, Muslim)*

Abdullah Ibn Masud related that Rasoolullah said:

By Him in whose hands is my life, no man is a true Muslim, until his heart and tongue accept Islam, and he does not truly believe until his neighbour is safe from his mischiefs. *(Ahmad)*

These Ahadith give us one of the criteria of true faith and it is that one must be good toward one's neighbour. Anas ibn Malik narrated that Rasoolullah said:

He does not have faith in me (as Allah's Messenger), one who sleeps comfortably with his stomach full while his neighbour is hungry and he is unaware of it. *(Tibrani)*

The noble teachings of Islam call for caring for the basic needs of neighbour. The Hadith means that if a person is so careless of his social obligations that he takes his full daily meal and then goes to sleep at night without bothering to know that his neighbour is hungry, then he does not justify his faith in the Prophet as the Messenger of Allah. It should be noted that no distinction is made in this Hadith between a Muslim and non-Muslim neighbour.

A Criterion of Good Conduct : Abdullah ibn Masud related that a man asked: O Messenger of Allah! how could I know when I do something good and when I do something bad? Rasoolullah answered:

> *When you hear your neighbour saying: You have done good, you have then done good, and when you hear your neighbour saying: You have done bad, then you have done bad.* *(Ibn Majah)*

The person closest to an individual outside the bonds of family is his neighbour. The relations with neighbour are thus one of the most valid criteria of one's social conduct.

Rights due to Neighbours : Muawiyyah reported that Rasoolullah said:

> *Following are the rights of your neighbour upon you: If he is sick, visit him; if he dies, help in his funeral; if he is in need, give him loan; if he commits a bad deed, cover him up; if he is blessed with some good thing, felicitate him; if he meets a trouble, sympathize with him; do not raise the walls of your home so high that you may deprive his home of fresh air; when you cook something good at your home, take care that its aroma does not cause a sense of deprivation to your neighbour or his family, unless you send some of it to him.*
> *(Tibrani)*

The Hadith speaks of the beauty and blessings of Islamic teachings that call for supporting neighbours during their happiness and health and also during their adversity and sickness. It also instructs the rich in the society not to build such houses that may obstruct the supply of air and light to the houses of their neighbours. It goes to the extent of caring for the emotions of the neighbours as well. It is possible that a rich person may often have good food and its aroma may hurt his poor neighbour, especially his children. The Hadith clearly states to avoid it or to share the good food with the poor neighbour and his children. Abdullah ibn Amr ibn As reported that Rasoolullah said:

> *If you bring some fruits for your family, send some of them to your neighbour. If it may not be possible, then bring them secretly and do not let your children take*

them outside, lest the neighbour's children see them, and feel deprived and hurt. *(Kanzul Ammal)*

The Hadith reiterates the importance of sharing Allah's blessings with neighbours. If this may not be possible, the rich should care for the feelings of their neighbours. They should practice a certain level of modesty in their behaviour and avoid showing off intentionally or unintentionally.

Giving Presents to Neighbours : Abu Zar related that Rasoolullah said:

When you cook broth, increase its water and give some of it to your neighbours. *(Muslim)*

Abu Hurrayrah reported that Rasoolullah said:

O Muslim women! No female neighbour must hold in contempt her neighbour even if it consists of giving her a mere hoof of goat. *(Bukhari, Muslim)*

It is generally not possible for poor people to send expensive presents to their neighbours. The Hadith instructs the neighbours to exchange presents even if it is as insignificant a thing as the hoof of a goat.

Warning to those who Offend their Neighbours : Anas ibn Malik related that Rasoolullah said:

One whose neighbour is not safe from his mischief shall not enter Paradise. *(Muslim)*

Abu Hurrayrah narrated that a man asked: O Messenger of Allah! Such and such woman is reputed for much prayer, fasting and alms-giving, but she also offends her neighbours with her tongue. Rasoolullah said: She will go to Hell. The narrator then said: Such and such woman is not reputed for her fasting, alms giving and prayers, but she gives alms of the remainder of curd and she does not offend her neighbours with her tongue. Rasoolullah said:

She will go to Paradise. *(Ahmad, Baihaqi)*

The Hadith illustrates in a beautiful manner the essence of the teachings of Islam. Prayers and good deeds alone will not lead one to Paradise. It is equally important in Islam that one should fulfill one's social obligations as well. The Hadith, however, does not mean that the person who fails in his social obligations will never enter Paradise. It means that he will have to go first to Hell and suffer for his sins and then enter Paradise. Numerous Hadith state that the believers will eventually enter Paradise.

Most Valuable Possessions : Saad ibn Abi Waqqas reported that Rasoolullah said:

> *The most valuable possessions of a Muslim are: A comfortable home, a good neighbour and a pleasant means of conveyance.* *(Ahmad)*

Sharing of Knowledge with Neighbours : Alqama ibn Abdul Rahman narrated through his father who narrated through his father that Rasoolullah once gave a special sermon and said:

> *Why is it that some of you do not create religious awareness among their neighbours, they do not give them proper education, warn them of the evils of ignorance and do not forbid them from what is prohibited. And why is it that some of you make no effort to learn* Deen *from their neighbours, acquire religious awareness and know the evils of the ignorance of* Deen. *By Allah! It is the duty of those having knowledge to teach Faith to their neighbours and create a religious awareness among them. They should counsel them, exhort them to do what is good and abstain from what is forbidden. In the same way the less educated people should seek knowledge and understanding of faith from their neighbours and also take advice from them. Otherwise, I will soon have a severe punishment for them.* *(Tibrani)*

The commentators of Hadith say that the Prophet in this Hadith referred to the people of the tribe of Ashari, who had some knowledgeable persons among them, but close to them lived a community which had very little knowledge. When Asharis came to know of this Hadith, they approached the Prophet and promised him to teach their neighbours in one year. It is clear from this Hadith that meeting the material or emotional needs alone does not fulfill our obligations towards neighbours. We are also required to meet their educational and spiritual needs. We should give them proper education and create among them a religious awareness. It is equally important for the less knowledgeable in the community to seek knowledge from their learned neighbours.

Orphans : There are generally a few orphans in every community. Their number often increases manifold due to wars or natural calamities.

Since Islam is a *Deen*, it addresses their needs as well. First, it guarantees their basic rights in society. It then promotes a feeling of love and compassion for them so that each orphan may find a family that takes care of his physical and emotional needs.

COMMANDMENTS IN HOLY QURAN

Basic Rights of Orphans

> *And know that out of all the booty that you may acquire, a fifth share is assigned to Allah, and to the Prophet, and to near relatives, orphans, the needy and the wayfarer.* *(Anfal 8:41)*

The verse of Sura Nisa 4:36 mentioned earlier also states the importance of the rights of orphans.

Kindness to Orphans

> *They ask you concerning orphans; Say: The best thing to do is what is for their good; If you mix their affairs with yours, they are your brethren.* *(Baqara 2:220)*

> *Therefore, treat not the orphans with harshness.* *(Dhuha 93:9)*

> *Have you observed the one, who denies the Day of Judgement; That is he who repulses the orphan, and encourages not the feeding of the indigent.* *(Maun 107:1-2)*

Safeguarding Orphan's Property

> *To orphans restore their property (when they reach their age of maturity); Do not substitute (your) worthless (substance) for (their) good ones, and devour not their substance (by mixing it up) with your own; For this is indeed a great sin.* *(Nisa 4:2)*

Come not near to the orphan's property except to improve it, until he attains the age of full maturity.
(Bani Israel 17:34)

Spending on Orphans

They ask you: What they should spend (in charity); Say: Whatever you spend that is good; It is for parents and kindred and orphans and those in want and for wayfarers; And whatever you do that is good, Allah knows it well. *(Baqara 2:215)*

Punishment for Usurping Orphan's Right

Those who unjustly eat up the property of orphans, eat up a fire into their own bodies, they will soon be enduring (the punishment of) a blazing Fire. *(Nisa 4:10)*

COMMANDMENTS IN TRADITIONS

It is related by Sahl ibn Saad that Rasoolullah said: Whoever supports an orphan belonging to his own or any other family will be as close to me in Paradise as these fingers. *(Bukhari)*

Sahl added that the Prophet then raised his index and middle finger and there was only a little space separating the two at that time. The Prophet, in the world Hereafter, will be at the highest stage of Paradise. This Hadith states that those who will care for the needs of orphans will be at the stage of Paradise very close to that of the Prophet. It should, however, be recalled that one good deed alone will not lead one to Paradise. One has to live a virtuous life and then care for the orphans in order to receive the blessings mentioned in this Hadith. Abdullah ibn Umar reported that Rasoolullah said:

The person who took care of an orphan from among the Muslims and shared his food and drink with him, Allah will allow him to enter Paradise, provided he is not guilty of an unpardonable sin. *(Tirmidhi)*

The Hadith reiterates the importance of living a virtuous life in order to receive the blessings of caring for an orphan. A few of the major unpardonable sins are, associating partners with Allah, murder, backbiting and usurping the rights of fellow human beings. It is narrated by Abu Hurrayrah that Rasoolullah said:

> *The best of Muslim homes is the home in which an orphan lives and is treated in a loving and affectionate manner, and the worst of Muslim homes is the home in which an orphan lives and is treated unkindly or cruelly.* *(Ibn Majah)*

Abu Shuraih Khuwailad ibn Amr Khuzai related that Rasoolullah said:

> *O Allah! I declare sinful any failure to safeguard the rights of two weak ones; orphans and women.* *(Nasai)*

The rights of orphans are like those of neighbours. They are irrespective of their religious beliefs, race or color. Ahadith, however, make it clear that our first obligation is towards the Muslim orphans. Lately, the Muslims are going through numerous persecutions in different parts of world. Innumerable Muslims have either been killed or are still being killed in places like Afghanistan, Chechanya, Bosnia, Palestine and Iraq. The Muslim Ummah is now faced with a vast number of Muslim orphans. We should do our best to help these orphans. We can then justly hope for the blessings mentioned in these Ahadith.

TOWARDS THE POOR

Commandments of the Quran

Commandments Concerning the Rights of the Poor

> *And render to the kindred their due rights, as (also) to those in want, and to the wayfarer.(Bani Israel 17:26)*

> *Alms are for the poor and the needy, and those employed to administer the (funds), for those whose hearts have been (recently) reconciled (to Islam), for those in bondage and in debt, and for the cause of Allah, and for the wayfarer; (Thus is it) ordained by Allah, and Allah is full of knowledge and wisdom.* *(Tauba 9:60)*

> *That which Allah gives as spoils to His Messenger from the people of townships, it is for Allah and His Messenger and for the near of his kin, and the orphans and the needy and the wayfarer, that it becomes not a commodity between the rich among you.* *(Hashr 59:7)*

Feeding the Poor

As to the righteous, they shall drink of a cup mixed with Kafur, a fountain where the devotees do drink, making it gush forth abundantly; They perform (their) vows and they fear a Day whose evil flies far and wide; And they feed, for the love of Allah, the indigent, the orphan, and the captives, (saying) we feed you for the sake of Allah alone, no rewards do we seek from you, nor (even) thanks.

(Insan 76:5-9)

And (ask) of the sinners: What led you into Hell-Fire? They will say: We were not of those who observed Salat, nor were we of those who fed the indigent, but we used to talk vanities with vain talkers, and we used to deny the Day of Judgement. *(Mudassir 74:42-46)*

Allah will not call you to account for what is futile in your oaths, but He will call you to account for your deliberate oaths; For expiation, feed ten indigent persons, on a scale of the average for the food of your families, or cloth them,... *(Maidah 5:92)*

Those who divorce their wives by Zihar, then wish to go back on the words they uttered, (it is ordained that such a one).... should feed sixty indigent ones.

(Mujadalah 58:3-4)

Zihar was a pagan custom of divorce, where the husband said to his wife: "You are to me as the back of my mother". Islam abolished this system of divorce.

COMMANDMENTS IN TRADITIONS

Abu Hurrayrah reported that Rasoolullah said:

A poor one is not he who goes around asking people and who can be turned away with a morsel or two or a date or two. A truly poor one is he who does not find enough to suffice him, does not disclose his poverty so that he might be given alms, and does not stand up to ask.

(Bukhari)

The Hadith asks us to look for those respected ones in the community who do not have sufficient means to support themselves, but do not disclose their needs to others due to their modesty and shyness.

Helping the Poor : Abu Hurrayrah reported that a man complained to Rasoolullah about the hardness of his heart and he said:

Be benevolent to orphans and feed the poor.(Ahmad)

Anas ibn Malik narrated that Rasoolullah said:

O Aishah! Do not turn away the poor without giving them something, though it be just a piece of date. O Aishah! love the poor and let them come to you for help. Allah will then, surely, take you near Him on the Day of Judgement. (Ibn Majah, Tirmidhi)

Abdullah ibn Umar narrated that Rasoolullah said:

There is a key for every thing and (one of the) keys to Paradise is love for the poor. (Daraqutni)

Anas ibn Malik related that Rasoolullah said: The best charity is to satisfy a hungry belly. (Baihaqi)

THE WIDOW

Abu Hurrayrah narrated that Rasoolullah said: He who exerts himself on behalf of a widow is like the one who strives in the cause of Allah.

Abu Hurrayrah added that probably he also said: He is like the one who spends the nights in prayer and fasts during the day permanently. (Bukhari, Muslim)

Striving for the cause of Allah is one of the most virtuous acts in Islam. Similarly spending nights in praying and days in fasting are also deeds of utmost merit. This Hadith states that the same is the reward of a person who takes pain to help a widow.

SLAVES AND SERVANTS

Slavery was a common practice in Arabia and in most parts of world at the time of the advent of Prophet Muhammad The victorious nations took their captives as slaves and treated them most mercilessly for their advantage. Slaves were treated as personal commodity and subjected to the most inhuman treatment. Such practices were continued even in America as late as hundred years ago. Prophet Muhammad is the first person in history who safeguarded the rights of slaves more than fourteen centuries ago.

He gave them basic human rights, upgraded their position in society and exhorted his followers to treat them with utmost love, care, and compassion. The Islamic teachings were directed at a gradual reform of the age-old practice of slavery. Islam did not abolish slavery in one sweep. This would have meant throwing the most underprivileged social class of people out in the cold, without making any reasonable arrangements for their survival as free citizens.

Any abrupt and thoughtless action would surely have created a class of unskilled vagabonds, beggars and thieves. The Islamic approach was instead designed to let these people continue to live with their masters as household members of their families. In the transitory period the masters were required to treat their wards in a fraternal manner, and provide them the same food and clothing that they themselves consumed. At the same time, they were supposed to facilitate the eventual freedom of slaves and to integrate them as free and independent members of society.

It is because of this teaching that slavery is now practically extinct throughout the Muslim world. The Holy Quran and Ahadith give clear injunctions for safeguarding the due rights of slaves and servants.

COMMANDMENTS IN HOLY QURAN

Kind Treatment to Slaves and Servants

> *Serve Allah and join not any partners with Allah, and do Ehsan with parents, kinsfolk, orphans, those in need, neighbours who are near, neighbours who are strangers, the companions by your side, the wayfarer (you meet), and what your right hand possesses.* *(Nisa 4: 36)*

"What your right hand possesses" includes not only slaves and servants but also the animals that a person could have. The Quran commands us to treat all of these with *Ehsan* i.e. the excellence of kind and just treatment.

Freeing of Slaves

And if any of your slaves ask for a deed in writing (to enable them to earn their freedom for a certain sum of money), give them such a deed; if you know any good in them, give them something yourself out of the means which Allah has given to you. (Moor 24: 33)

A slave in a Muslim society has the right to ask his master for a written agreement that may set him free. The master is required not only to honour this agreement, but to help his slave through his own money to earn his freedom. This was a common practice in early Muslim history and a number of free slaves later rose to important positions in the society.

Have We not made for him a pair of eyes, and a tongue, and a pair of lips, and shown him two different highways? But he made no haste on the path that is steep. And what will explain to you the path that is steep? (It is) the freeing of slaves, or the giving of food in a day of hunger to the orphan with claims of relationship, or to the indigent (down) in the dust.

(Balad 90:8-16)

COMMANDMENTS IN TRADITIONS

Forgiving a Servant : Abdullah ibn Umar reported that a man came to the Prophet and asked him: O Messenger of Allah! How many times should we pardon a servant? He remained silent. The man repeated his question and he again remained silent. The man then repeated his question a third time. Rasoolullah then answered:

Pardon him seventy times every day.

(Abu Daud, Tirmidhi)

Rights of Servants and Slaves : Abu Zar reported that Rasoolullah said:

The servants and slaves are your brethren that Allah has put under your hands. So, feed them out of what you eat yourself, clothe them as you clothe yourself, do not give them such work that will overcome them. If you give them what will overcome them, then assist them therein. (Bukhari, Muslim)

Abu Hurrayrah related that Rasoolullah said:

When one of your servants prepares your meal and then brings it to you, let him sit down with you and eat some of the food. If the food consists of only a few morsels, put a morsel or two in his hands therefrom.

(Muslim)

Abu Zar reported that Rasoolullah said:

Whoever from your slaves obeys you, give him food of what you yourself eat, clothe him of what you yourself clothe. And whoever among them does not obey you, hand him over to another person and do not inflict punishment on the creation of Allah. (Abu Daud, Ahmad).

Freeing of a Slave

Abdullah ibn Umar related: I heard Rasoolullah saying: Whoever scourges his slave for an ordained crime which he did not commit or slaps him, then his expiation is to emancipate him. (Muslim)

Punishment for Mistreating the Slave (Servant) : Abu Bakr Siddique reported that Rasoolullah said:

One who mistreats those under his authority shall not enter Paradise. (Ibn Majah, Tirmidhi)

It has been explained earlier that such a person will not go to Paradise with complete forgiveness. He will first go to Hell and stay there until he pays for his sins and then shall enter Paradise.

Respect for the Knowledge of Slave : Ummul Hussain narrated that Rasoolullah said:

If a slave with limbs cut off be put in command over you to guide you by the Book of Allah, hearken him and obey him. (Muslim) No religion or society in the world other than Islam has given such respect and dignity to its slaves and servants. It is because of these noble teachings of Islam that numerous slaves acquired their freedom and rose to very prominent positions in the early history of Muslims. Abu Hurrayrah was formerly a slave who later became one of the greatest scholar of

Hadith. Bilal was also a freed slave who occupied the most dignified position of Muezzin in the Prophet's mosque. Later, when the Prophet conquered Mecca, he asked Bilal to give the first Adaan *at Haram. History has recorded that unbelievers of Mecca were astonished to hear Bilal giving the first* Adaan *at Haram. The Prophet once pointed to four scholars in Medina and said: If you want to learn the Quran, learn it from them. One of these scholars was Salem, a freed slave of Medina. The last expedition that the Prophet sent during his lifetime was commanded by Usamah, the son of a slave. Numerous such examples can be quoted from the entire history of Muslims, e.g. a family of slaves rose to be Emperors of India for many years. This is recorded in Indian history as the dynasty of slaves.*

3

Parents' Rights

COMMANDMENTS IN HOLY QURAN

The Quran gives us very detailed and explicit commandments regarding our duties and obligations towards parents. Though the Quran teaches us to be kind and compassionate to everyone, it uses a very special term to describe our relationship with our parents. It commands us to treat our parents with *Ehsan*. Imam Raghib, who is regarded as an authority on the Arabic language, explains this term as follows: *Ehsan* is that state of a relationship in which a person is pleased even, when he receives less than his due rights and offers more than what his duties call for. It is clear from this definition that the Quran does not merely ask us to treat our parents on the basis of equality and justice. It commands us rather, to be pleased with whatever parents could offer us. Simultaneously, it also commands us to try our best to please them by giving them our greatest love, respect and obedience. Following are a few Quranic verses pertaining to this issue.

> *And remember We took covenant from the children of Bani Israel (to the effect) : Worship none but Allah and treat your parents with Ehsan.* *(Baqara 2:83)*
>
> *Serve Allah, and join not partners with Him and treat your parents with Ehsan.* *(Nisa 4:36)*
>
> *Say : come, I rehearse what Allah has prohibited for you: Join not anything with Him and treat your parents with Ehsan.* *(Anam 6:151)*
>
> *Your Lord has decreed that you worship none but Allah and that you treat your parents with Ehsan.*
> *(Bani Israel 17:23)*

It should be noted that, in all of these verses the Quran first calls for our duties towards Allah and immediately after this calls for our duties to our parents. This in itself speaks for the relative importance of parents position in our *Deen*. Following is another verse reminding us that next to the obligations to Allah, our obligation is to our parents.

Show gratitude to Me and to your parents.

(Luqman 31:14)

In fact, it is the beauty and the blessing of our *Deen* that it gives such a dignified and respected position to parents in the Muslim community. We should also remember, and realize, that it is Allah the Almighty who has given this position to parents. It thus becomes our duty to obey the commandment of Allah and to treat our parents with *Ehsan*. If we fail to do so, we shall be guilty of disobeying Allah. Following are a few other related commandments of the Quran.

Benevolence to Parents

Your Lord has decreed that you worship none but Allah; and that you treat your parents with Ehsan; if one or both of them attain old age in your life, say not to them (even a word of) 'uf', nor repel them, but speak to them in terms of honour; And out of kindness, lower unto them the wings of submission through mercy, and say: My Lord! have mercy on them both, as they did care for me when I was a child. *(Bani Israel 17:23-24)*

As in other verses, here also the Quran first gives us the general commandment of treating our parents with *Ehsan*. It then gives us a few specific commandments. First, it states that when our parents reach old age, we should be so kind and compassionate towards them that we should not even say "*uf*" to them. It should be noted that during their old age, parents are usually dependent on children for their financial and physical needs. Moreover, people during old age usually become more emotional and demanding. The Quran commands us that when our parents reach this stage of life, we should be so kind and understanding that we should not utter even a single word of contempt before them. Imam Hasan ibn Ali said that this is the last level of showing disrespect to parents. If there was something beyond this level, Allah would have mentioned that as well. Second, the Quran simultaneously commands us to speak to them with honour and dignity. Third, it commands us to treat them with utmost respect and humility and lastly we should remember them in our supplications. *Ehsan* even with non-Muslim parents :

> *We have enjoined on man Ehsan with their parents, but if they strive (to force) you to associate with Me (in obedience and worship) anything of what you have no knowledge, obey them not. (Remember!) You have to return to Me, and I will (then) tell you all that you did (in the world).* *(Ankabut 29:8)*

> *But if they strive to make you join in worship with Me things of what you have no knowledge, obey them not; yet consort with them in the world kindly and follow the path of him who turns to Me, then unto Me is your return and I shall (then) tell you all that you did (in the world).* *(Luqman 31:15)*

A person who believes in the unity of Allah will never ask anyone to associate any other person with Allah. Only an unbeliever can do so. The Quran in these verses talks about such unbelieving parents and reminds us that if parents force their children to join partners with Allah, the children should not obey them, but should still treat them with *Ehsan*. It is clear from these verses that if parents invite children to commit a sin, the children should not obey them, but should still love and treat them with kindness and compassion.

Spending on Parents

> *They ask you, what they should spend (in charity); Say: whatever wealth you spend (in charity) is good, it is for the parents and kindred and orphans and those in want and for the wayfarers, and whatever you do that is good, Allah knows it well.* *(Baqara 2:215)*

This verse again reminds us the position of our parents. It states that whatever we want to spend in the cause of Allah, it should begin with the parents rather than any other person in the family or community. Thus, if someone spends money on his family members or donates for a noble cause in the community, but ignores the rights of his parents, he disobeys Allah. Our first duty is to take care of the needs of our parents and to treat them with *Ehsan*, even in spending money.

Leaving Money for Parents

> *It is prescribed that when death approaches any of you, if he leaves any good, he should make a bequest to parents and next of kin according to reasonable usage; this is due for the God fearing.* *(Baqara 2:180)*

Islam is the only *Deen* that establishes a social system where inheritance is given not only in descending, but in ascending order as well. All other systems of the world have laws governing the inheritance for descendants. This verse reminds us that our first duty is towards our parent's even when making a will of inheritance.

Being Thankful to Parents

> *Show gratitude to Me and to your parents; to Me is your (final) goal.* *(Luqman 31:14)*

As one cannot count the blessings of Allah, one cannot count the blessings of parents. The Quran, therefore, commands us to be thankful first to Allah and then to our parents. Being thankful does not mean simply saying "thank you". It calls for having an attitude in life that should reflect our gratitude towards Allah and then to our parents.

Being Thankful on Behalf of Parents : And he (Solomon) said:

> *O my Lord! Arrange things for me so that I may be thankful for Your favours which You have bestowed upon me and my parents, and that I do good deeds that will please You, and admit me by Your Grace to the ranks of Your righteous servants.* *(Namal 27:19)*

At length, when he (man) reaches the age of full strength and attains (an age of) forty years, he says:

> *O Lord! Grant me that I may be grateful to You for Your favours which You have bestowed upon me, and upon both of my parents, and that I may be righteous, such as You may approve and be gracious to Me; truly have I turned to You and truly do I submit (to You) in Islam;*

Such are those from whom We shall accept the best of their deeds and pass by their ill deeds.

(Ahqaf 46:15-16)

These verses describe the attribute of those Believers whose good deeds are accepted and bad deeds are forgiven by Allah. One of their attributes is that they are thankful to Allah for His favours on them and simultaneously thankful to Allah for His favours bestowed upon their parents.

Praying for Parents : And out of kindness, lower to them the wings of humility and say:

My Lord! bestow on them Your Mercy as they cherished me in childhood. *(Bani Israel 17:24)*

No matter how kind and caring we may be towards our parents, we cannot give them everything that they deserve or need. The Quran is, therefore, reminding us that we should also pray for our parents that Allah may bestow His Mercy upon them and bless them with the things that we are unable to provide them.

Reminder for Special Position of Mother

We have enjoined on man (to be good) to his parents; His mother bore him in weakness after weakness.

(Luqman 31:14)

We have enjoined on man Ehsan to his parents; In pain did his mother bear him, and in pain did she give birth.

(Ahqaf 46:15)

These verses are self-explanatory and call for having an extra regard for our mothers.

Prophet Nuh's Prayer for his Parents

My Lord! Forgive me, my parents, all those who enter my home in Faith, and all Believing men and Believing women, and to the wrongdoers grant no increase but in destruction. *(Nuh 71:28)*

Prophet Ibrahim's Prayer for his Parents

O our Lord! Cover (us) with Your forgiveness me and my parents, and (all) Believers on the Day that the reckoning will be established. *(Ibrahim 14:41)*

Prophet Yahya's (John) and his Parents

O Yahya! Take hold of the Book with might, and We gave him wisdom as a youth and compassion (for all) from Our presence and purity, and he was devout, and kind to his parents and he was not arrogant, rebellious.

(Maryam 19:12-14)

Prophet Esa (Jesus) and his Parents : He (Jesus) said (in the cradle):

I am indeed a servant of Allah; He has given me revelation and made me a Prophet; And He made me blessed wherever I may be, and has enjoined on me Salat and Zakat as long as I live, and made me kind towards my mother and not arrogant and rebellious.

(Maryam 19:30-32)

As Muslims, we believe in all the Prophets of Allah. The Quran reminds us that other Prophets have also been kind and compassionate towards their parents and also remembered them in their supplications. Needless to say, we should follow the conduct of Allah's Prophets by honouring the due rights and obligations of our parents.

COMMANDMENTS IN TRADITIONS

Ahadith give us more detailed account of the rights and obligations towards parents. They also describe the blessings for honouring the rights of parents and the punishment for disobeying them. Following are a few related Ahadith:

Importance of Obedience to Parents : Anas ibn Malik related that Rasoolullah was asked about the major sins and he answered:

They are: To associate something or someone with Allah, to disobey one's parents, to wrong them or injure them, to kill someone unlawfully, and to give false evidence.

(Bukhari)

Abudullah ibn Masud reported: I asked Rasoolullah Which action is most acceptable to Allah? He answered:

Performing Salat *at its due time.*

I then asked: What comes next? He answered :

Benevolence towards parents.

I then asked again: What comes next? He answered :

Striving in the cause of Allah. *(Bukhari, Muslim)*

Abdullah ibn Amr ibn As narrated that a man came to Rasoolullah and said: I have come to make a covenant with you to migrate and also to fight in the cause of Allah. He inquired if his parents were living. The man answered: Indeed both of them are living. He then said to him:

Go back to your parents and serve them well.

(Bukhari, Muslim)

Based on this Hadith, the scholars state that if it is not a state of emergency, a person is not allowed to go to Jihad and even leave his town for learning *Deen* without the permission of his parents. The following Hadith also states the same thing:

Abu Saeed Khudri narrated that a man migrated from Yemen to Medina with the intention of engaging in Jihad. Rasoolullah asked him if he had any relatives in Yemen. The man answered that his parents were there. Rasoolullah asked him if he had migrated after taking their permission. The man answered: No. He then told him:

"Go back to your parents and seek their permission to migrate. If they give you permission, then go and engage in Jihad. If they do not give you the permission, then stay with them and serve them well."

(Abu Daud, Ahmad)

Hijrat and Jihad (migration and fighting for the cause of Allah) are two of the dearest things to Allah. However, if someone's parents are old or sick, he is exempted from these acts. Serving his parents well, then, becomes his first duty and this will bring him the same rewards as those for Hijrat and Jihad.

It is clear from these Ahadith that if someone leaves his parents in old age or during their sickness because of some worldly desires and needs, he is guilty of a grave sin.

Respecting Parents of Other People : Abdullah ibn Umar reported that Rasoolullah said:

One of the greatest sin is the man's abusing his own parents. They inquired: Does any man abuse his parents? He answered: A man abuses the father of a person, who then abuses his own father (in return), and he abuses the mother of a person, who then abuses his own mother (in return). *(Bukhari, Muslim)*

This is the beauty and blessing of Islam, that it teaches us not only to love and respect our own parents, but to have similar regards for the parents of others as well.

Significance of Parent's Rights : Abu Umama related that a man asked:

O Rasoolullah What are the rights of parents over their children, and he answered: They are your Paradise or your Hell. *(Ibn Majah)*

The Quran has repeatedly stated that the rights of parents are next to those of Allah. If we honour them, we shall obey Allah and thus hope to enter Paradise. If we disregard them, we then disobey Allah and may thus enter Hell.

Special Care of Parents in Old Age : Abu Hurrayrah reported that Rasoolullah said :

May his nose be rubbed in sand, may his nose be-rubbed in sand, may his nose be rubbed in sand, he who found his parents, one or both of them approaching old age and did not enter Paradise through serving them. *(Muslim)*

"May his nose be rubbed in sand" is a form of rebuke. This Hadith reminds us that when parents reach old age, Paradise comes to our home. If we wish to enter Paradise, we should take utmost care of our parents and serve them well.

Special Status of Mother : Abu Hurrayrah related that a man asked Rasoolullah: Who is most worthy of my good treatment? He answered:

Your mother.

The man asked: Who comes next? and he answered:

Your mother.

The man then asked again: Who comes next? and he answered:

Your mother.

The man then inquired a fourth time, and he answered: Your father. *(Bukhari, Muslim)*

The position of parents in Islam is next to that of Allah and His Prophet. The position of the mother, however, is three times more important than that of the father. The commentators of the Hadith say that this is because of three special hardships which the mothers undergo for their children, namely, pregnancy, delivery and feeding during the early years of their lives. It is stated that once Jareeh's mother called him while he was engaged in *Salat*. Jareeh still continued his *Salat*. When Rasoolullah came to know of this, he said:

If Jareeh had the knowledge, he should have known that responding to a mother's call is more important than praying before the Lord.
(Fatah al Bari, commentary of Bukhari)

The commentators of the Hadith add that this refers only to voluntary (Nail) *Salat*. On the other hand, if parents call their children during an emergency, they should break their *Salat* and respond to their call even if they are engaged in a Fardh (mandatory) *Salat*. It is stated that a man brought his old mother to the Haram. He put her on his back and started circling around the Kaaba. He saw Rasoolullah and asked him: Have I now completed my duty towards my mother? Rasoolullah answered him: You have not fulfilled the right equal to one breath of your mother. (Commentary of the Quran by Ibn Katheer Volume: 3) Muawiyyah ibn Jahema narrated that a person came to Rasoolullah to seek his advice to join the battle for the cause of Islam. He asked if his mother was living. When the man replied, 'yes', Rasoolullah said:

Then go back and stay close to your mother, because Paradise lies at her feet. *(Ahmad, Baihaqi, Nasai)*

This Hadith commands the children to stay close to their parents, especially their mother. It also reminds them to serve their mother as best as they can since Paradise lies under her feet. These basic teachings of Islam give a very respected and dignified position to mothers in a Muslim community. She is the center of love and respect of all family members till her last breath of life. Lately, Western society has also realized the importance of mothers. They express it by earmarking one day of the year as "mother's day". All the children come together on that day and show their love and affection to their mothers. Unfortunately, in most cases these mothers pass their old ages in a nursing home. On the other hand, every single day in the life of a Muslim mother is a "mother's day" and she never ends her life in a nursing home.

Special Regards for Mother's Sister : Abdullah ibn Umar related that a man came to Rasoolullah and said: O the Messenger of Allah! I have committed a sin. Is there any way of repentance for me? He inquired if his mother was living. When the man said, 'no', he inquired if his mother's sister was living. When the man answered, 'yes', he said:

Then serve her well. *(Tirmidhi)*

This Hadith teaches us two basic things. First, if a person has committed a sin and thus displeased Allah, he can gain Allah's pleasure back by serving his mother. Second, if his mother is not alive, he can still gain Allah's pleasure back by serving his mother's sister. Bara ibn Aziz narrated that Rasoolullah said:

A mother's sister has the same status as a mother.
(Tirmidhi)

Kindness even to Non-Muslim Mother : Asma bint Abu Bakr reported that her mother, while she was a polytheist, came to visit her in Medina. She asked Rasoolullah that her mother was still an unbeliever but was expecting something from her; should she gratify her? He said:

Yes, be benevolent towards your mother.
(Bukhari, Muslim)

Asma was the elder sister of the Prophet's noble wife Aishah from a different mother. Abu Bakr had divorced her even before he became a Muslim. She did not accept Islam and came to see her daughter Asma after the treaty of Hudaibiya, when the unbelievers were allowed to visit Medina.

It was at that time that Asma inquired of the Prophet as to how she should treat her mother. He told her to be kind and considerate towards her mother, even though she was an unbeliever.

Position of Father

Abdullah ibn Amr narrated that Rasoolullah said:

The pleasure of the Lord is in the pleasure of the father, and the displeasure of the Lord is in the displeasure of the father. *(Tirmidhi)*

Abdullah ibn Umar reported: I had a wife whom I loved but my father Umar disliked her. He asked me to divorce her, but I refused. Umar went to Rasoolullah and mentioned this to him. Rasoolullah then called me and asked me to divorce her. *(Abu Daud, Tirmidhi)*

(It is stated that ibn Umar then divorced his wife.)

It should be noted that the right to marry and divorce in Islam belongs only to the husband. If the parents do not like someone's wife, they cannot force their son to divorce her. Since Umar was one of the most righteous Sahabi, the Prophet asked Abdullah ibn Umar to honour the wish of his father. Abu Hurrayrah related that Rasoolullah said:

No son can repay his father, unless he should find him a slave and set him free. *(Muslim)*

Abdullah ibn Umar narrated that Rasoolullah said:

One of the highest virtues (in Islam) is that a person should be benevolent towards his father's friends. *(Muslim)*

Abdullah ibn Umar reported that Rasoolullah said:

Three invocations are granted without doubt therein; the invocation of a father (for his children), the invocation of a traveller (for the cause of Allah) and the invocation of an oppressed person.
(Abu Daud, Ibn Majah, Tirmidhi)

Though the position of a mother in Islam is three times more important than that of a father, this in no way lessens the role and position of a father. This Hadith gives a very unique position to a father and states that Allah will not reject the invocation of a father for his children. We should therefore try to seek the pleasure of our father as much as we try to seek the pleasure of our mother.

Parent's Rights after Death : Abu Usaid Sayedi related: We were close to Rasoolullah when a man from the tribe of Banu Salma approached him and asked: O Rasoolullah! Is there any obedience to parents left upon me after their demise that I should honour? He replied:

Yes, pray for them, ask Allah's forgiveness for them, fulfill their promises, exercise benevolence towards those related to you through them, and also honour their friends. (Abu Daud, Ibn Majah)

The rights of parents in Islam are so unique and respected that they do not come to an end even after their death. This Hadith tells us a few of their basic rights after death. Abdullah ibn Umar reported that Rasoolullah said:

The most excellent form of obedience to parents is that a man befriends the friends of his father after he has passed away. (Muslim)

Abdullah ibn Dinar reported that Abdullah ibn Umar met a Bedouin on his way to Mecca. He greeted him and asked him if he was so and so the son of so and so. The man replied, "yes". Abdullah ibn Umar gave him his donkey and asked him to ride it. He also gave him his turban and asked him to cover his head with it. Some of his companions told him: May Allah bless you! He is just a Bedouin and the Bedouins are pleased with only a little thing. You gave him your donkey and turban whereas you needed them yourself. Abdullah ibn Umar answered: His father was my father's friend and I have heard Rasoolullah saying:

One of the most virtuous act is that a person should be benevolent towards his father's friends and their family members. (Muslim)

Though this Hadith only refers to a father, and since the rights of a mother in Islam are three times more than that of a father, it follows that we should give a better treatment to the family members and friends of our mother as well. Abdullah ibn Abbas narrated that Saad ibn As said to Rasoolullah : My mother has died. Before she died, she made a vow, which she had to honour, but she could not do so. He said:

Honour the vow of your mother on her behalf. (Bukhari, Muslim)

Anas ibn Malik reported that Rasoolullah said:

Often it so happens that one or both the parents of a person pass away, while during their lifetime he does not serve them well. He thus deprives himself of their good pleasure. He then remembers them in his supplications and seeks Allah's forgiveness for them. Allah then changes his name from the record of disobedient persons to that of obedient ones.

(Baihaqi)

This Hadith gives a glad tiding to those who have lost one or both of their parents. No one can be sure that he has fulfilled the due rights of his parents. We should therefore try our utmost to serve our parents during their lifetime and remember them in our supplications after their death. This will not only help them, but would also compensate for our shortcomings in serving them during their lifetime.

Blessings for Obeying Parents : Abdullah ibn Abbas reported that Rasoolullah said: Whoever gets up at dawn being obedient to Allah regarding his obligations to parents, two doors of Paradise are open for him in the morning. If he has one of the parents alive, then only one door is open for him. Whoever is disobedient to Allah regarding his obligations to parents, two doors of Hell are open for him. If he has only one of the parents alive, then only one door is open for him. A man inquired: Even if his parents have been cruel to him. Rasoolullah replied:

Even though his parents have been cruel to him, even though his parents have been cruel to him, even though his parents have been cruel to him. *(Baihaqi)*

Jaber related that Rasoolullah said: Whoever has three attributes in him, Allah will make his death easy and also admit him to Paradise. These are: Mercy to the weak, kindness to parents, and doing good to slaves (and servants). *(Baihaqi)*

Thoban narrated that Rasoolullah said:

Nothing but supplication can annul predestination, and nothing but obedience to parents can prolong life. A man is deprived of his provisions for the sins he commits.

(Ibn Majah)

Regarding the prolonging of life, the scholars say that it refers to the amount of virtuous deeds in life and not the increase in the number of years. One who is obedient to parents will get enough time and leisure for doing good deeds in his life. On the other hand, the one who is disobedient to parents will be afflicted with diseases, pains, and worries and be deprived of the opportunities of doing good deeds in his life.

Abdullah ibn Umar related that Rasoolullah said:

Obey your parents and treat them with kindness, for if you do so, then your children will obey you and treat you with kindness. *(Tibrani)*

There is a folk tale that may or may not be true but carries a good message. It is said that there was a man who got tired of serving his old father, so he decided to kill him. One day he wrapped his father in a sheet and took him to a well. As he was ready to throw him in the well, his father told him that he had a last wish and would like him to honour it. His son asked him, what it was. The father replied that his last wish was that he should not throw him in that particular well, but in some other well. The son was amazed and asked him the reason for this wish. His father then told him that he had himself thrown his father in that well. The son got the message and immediately took his father back to his home and served him well all his life. Aishah reported that Rasoolullah once said:

I was sleeping and saw in my dream that I was in Paradise. I heard there someone reciting the Quran and inquired: Who is this slave of Allah reciting the Quran in Paradise? I was told that he was Harith ibn Noman.

Rasoolullah later said that Harith ibn Noman was very obedient to his mother and served her well.(Baihaqi)

Admonition for Disobeying Parents : Abu Barkah Nufai ibn Harith related that Rasoolullah said: Shall I tell you what are the major sins? He repeated this three times and we said: Certainly O Rasoolullah, He then said:

Associating others with Allah, disobedience to parents.

The narrator added that Rasoolullah had been leaning against a pillow, but suddenly he sat up erect and said:

And telling a lie and giving a false evidence.

He then repeated the last sentence so many times that we wished he would stop. *(Bukhari)*

Anas ibn Malik reported that someone asked Rasoolullah about major sins and he replied:

To associate anyone with Allah, to disobey the parents or cause them pain and injury, to kill someone unlawfully, and to give false evidence. *(Bukhari)*

It is important to note in this Hadith the order in which the Prophet described the major sins in Islam. Disobedience to parents is a sin next in gravity to that of polytheism and more serious than murder and false evidence.

Mughira ibn Shuban narrated that Rasoolullah said: Allah has forbidden for you: Disobedience to parents, miserliness, false claims, and burying alive of females, and has disapproved for you: idle talk, too much asking of questions, and waste of provision.

(Bukhari, Muslim)

Punishment for Disobedience to Parents : Abu Baraka reported that Rasoolullah said:

Almighty Allah may forgive all sins He pleases except disobedience to parents; and He hastens punishment in this life before death for one who is disobedient to parents.

(Baihaqi)

Three Unique Incidents : Jaber ibn Abdullah related that a man came to Rasoolullah and reported against his father saying that his father wanted to take away the material things from him. Rasoolullah asked the man to come back to him with his father. Archangel Jibbrail then came to Rasoolullah and told him that when the father would come, he should ask him to narrate those words which he had said about his son, that even his own ears did not hear. Later when the father and son came to Rasoolullah he informed the father about the complaint of his son. The father informed Rasoolullah that he could confirm that he took money from his son only to spend on his maternal and paternal aunt and for his basic needs. Rasoolullah then told them it was enough for the explanation of the dispute. He then asked the father to narrate the words which he said in his heart about his son, the words which even his ears did not hear. The father exclaimed and said: O Messenger of Allah! Allah increases our faith in you in every matter of dealings in our life. In fact, I did compose a few verses of a poem in my heart and my ears have not yet heard these words. He then narrated the following verses:

I nurtured and nourished you in your childhood and was responsible for your needs even when you grew up. If there was a night when you were sick, I kept awake all night for your care and comfort. I passed the night crying as if it was I and not you who was sick. I was always afraid of your death, though I knew that its time was predestined. At last you then reached the age that I desired and prayed for. Alas! you then started paying me back my dues in the form of rude manners and harsh language. Alas! if you could not give me the due rights of a father, you could at least treat me as a good neighbour would treat his neighbour. Oh! If you had given me only the due rights of a neighbour and would have not been miserly towards me in my own belongings.

When Rasoolullah heard this, he grabbed the son with his shirt collar and said:

Go away! You and all that you possess belong to your father. (Commentary of the Quran by Imam Qartabi Vol: 6, P:244) Abdullah ibn Umar reported that Rasoolullah narrated the following incident:

Three men were once overtaken by rain and took shelter in the cave of a mountain. A rock fell down and completely covered the mouth of the cave. The three were completely trapped in the cave. They said to one another: Let each one of us recall one of the virtuous acts that he performed sincerely for the pleasure of Allah, and then supplicate Allah therewith to remove this rock from the cave.

One of them said: O Allah! I had old and weak parents and also young children for whom I used to pasture sheep. Whenever I returned home at night, I gave milk first to my parents and then to my children. One day I returned home late at night and found that both of my parents had fallen asleep. I took milk to them as usual and remained standing near them. I did not want to awaken them and also did not want to give milk first to my children. Though my children cried with hunger, I kept waiting for my parents till it was dawn. O Allah! if You know that I did this act only to seek Your pleasure, then make an opening for us so that we can see the horizon. Accordingly Allah made an opening for them in the cave. The second man narrated this incident. He was in love with one of his cousins and was about to have sex with her when she reminded him of Allah. He then stopped from committing that sin. He then prayed: O Allah! If You know that I did this act only to seek Your pleasure, then make a further opening in the cave. Allah accepted his prayer and the cave had a bigger opening.

> *The third man narrated this incident. He went into a business partnership with a person who disappeared. He then took care of the business alone and kept an account of his partner's share of profit. When his partner returned, he paid him his full share of the profit. He then prayed to Allah: O Allah! if You know that I did this act only to seek Your pleasure, make an opening for us of what still remains. Allah accepted his prayer and the mouth of cave was completely open and they could escape from it.* *(Bukhari, Muslim)*

Abdullah ibn Aufi reported that there was a man named Alqama. He was very punctual in his *Salat* (daily prayers) and *Siyam* (fasting). When the time of his death approached, people instructed him to recite the *Kalima*, but he could not do so. His wife sent someone to inform Rasoolullah of this condition. He asked if his parents were living. He was informed that Alqama's mother was living. Rasoolullah sent for the mother, who immediately came to him. He asked her opinion about Alqama. She replied that he was a pious man, but preferred his wife over her and disobeyed her. She was, therefore, unhappy with him. Rasoolullah asked her to forgive him, but she refused. He then asked Bilal to collect wood, burn it and throw Alqama in the burning fire. The mother became very worried on hearing this and asked Rasoolullah if he really intended to burn Alqama in fire. He then said: Yes! The punishment of Allah is far more than this punishment. By Allah! as long as you are unhappy with your son, neither his *Salat* nor any act of charity is accepted by Allah. Alqama's mother then said: O Messenger of Allah! I want you and all those present to be my witness that I have forgiven Alqama. Rasoolullah then sent someone to ascertain the condition of Alqama. He came back with the good news that Alqama died reciting the *Kalima*. Rasoolullah then himself went to his funeral and said:

> *Whoever from amongst* Muhajir *(immigrants) and* Ansar *(helpers) will be disobedient to his mother or displeases her, he will then have the curse of Allah, His angels and all people. Allah will not accept either his* Fardh *(mandatory) or his* Nafl *(voluntary) prayers until he repents, serves his mother well and pleases her.*
>
> *(Tibrani)*

The Prophet in this Hadith addressed Muhajir and Ansar because they were the only persons present around him at that time. Furthermore, he made mention of only the mother because this incident referred to the pleasure of a mother. It is, however, clear that this commandment is for all the Believers and calls for seeking the pleasure of both parents, especially the mother. We should realize that Alqama was a very pious person and was very punctual of his *Salat* and *Siyam*. He was also a companion of the Prophet. None of these things brought any help to him at the time of his death. He was deprived of the blessings of reciting *Kalima* only because he had displeased his mother. We should also recall the Hadith that states: whoever dies in such a state that his last words are the recitation of *Kalima*, he shall enter Paradise. No one knows when the time of his death will come. We should, therefore, hasten to seek the good pleasure of our parents, especially our mothers, otherwise we may also be deprived of reciting the *Kalima* at the time of our death.

4

Relatives' Rights and Duties

The family institution in Islam is not comprised merely of one's immediate family members. It includes, in addition to parents, husband, wife, children and other close relatives as well. Islam encompasses all relatives by blood or marriage within a broad concept of family and defines their respective rights and obligations. A Muslim is required to honour these rights as a commandment from Allah and His Prophet. If one fails to do so, he is guilty of a sin that will not be forgiven on the Day of Judgement, unless the person concerned forgives him. The Quran has repeatedly stated the importance of family obligations and their rights. Following are a few basic commandments.

COMMANDMENTS IN HOLY QURAN

Importance of Family Ties

> *He causes many to (go) astray and many He leads into the right path; but He causes not to (go) astray except those who transgress; those who break Allah's covenant after it is ratified and sever (the relations) which Allah has ordered to be joined; and so do mischief on the earth; those are the losers.* *(Baqara 2:26-27)*

The right guidance in life comes only through the blessings of Allah. Moreover, Allah gives this guidance to those who seek for it sincerely, and not to those who transgress His set limits. Joining of family ties is a commandment of Allah. The Quran states that those who sever these ties, transgress Allah's limits are deprived of receiving Allah's guidance. Thus maintaining family ties is one of the prerequisites for receiving Allah's guidance in life. Those who are guilty of severing family ties, deprive themselves of receiving Allah's guidance. It is for this reason that the verse states: those are the losers.

Rights of the Relatives

Allah commands justice, Ehsan and giving (their due) to near relatives. *(Nahl 16:90)*

The practice of justice and *Ehsan* in Islam is as important a duty as praying *Salat* or observing *Siyam*. This is because of the fact that Islam is a *Deen* and provides guidance in one's social as well as personal life. It is evident from the above verse that the practice of justice and *Ehsan* should start with the near relatives. The importance of this commandment is evidenced by the fact that this verse has been incorporated as the last part of Friday sermon and is recited in each and every mosque throughout the Muslim Ummah. Every Muslim is thus reminded every Friday to remember his duties towards his relatives and to treat them with kindness and *Ehsan*.

Serve Allah, and join not any partners with Him; and do Ehsan with parents, kinsfolk, orphans, those in need, neighbours who are near, neighbours who are strangers, the companions by your side, the wayfarer (you meet), and what your right hands possess. *(Nisa 4:36)*

The essence of Islam is not only to serve Allah, but also to serve our fellow human beings. It also calls for achieving a level of *Ehsan*, i.e. excellence in our attitude and practice. This is a wider and more comprehensive concept than the Western concept of: "Love God and love your neighbour".

The above verse commands us to do *Ehsan* not only with parents but with all persons whom we come across in our lives. Furthermore, the verse also shows that doing *Ehsan* with relatives is a duty next to that of parents and supersedes the rest of our social obligations. And give to the relatives their due rights, as well as to those in want, and to the wayfarer, but waste not (your wealth) in the manner of a spendthrift.

The verse makes it clear that helping a relative, a needy person or a traveller is not just an act of charity but a commandment of Allah. Each member of a Muslim community has certain rights upon us and we have to honour these rights.

It should be noted that this commandment starts with the rights of relatives.

> *So give what is due to relatives, the needy, and the wayfarer; That is best for those who seek the favour of Allah, and it is they who will prosper.* (Rum 30:38)

The verse states clearly that those who desire the pleasure of Allah should fulfill their social obligations, especially those concerning to the relatives. The verse further states that only those who fulfill these obligations shall prosper in life. It thus follows that no matter how righteous a person is in his personal life, he cannot receive the good pleasure of Allah unless he also fulfills his family and social obligations.

Spending on Relatives

> *They ask you: What they should spend (in charity). Say: Whatever you spend that is good, is for parents and relatives and orphans and those in want and for wayfarers; And whatever you do that is good, Allah knows it well.* (Baqara 2:215)

Islam is the *Deen* of nature. It sets the human rights according to their respective needs and positions. The parents in this hierarchy of rights occupy the first position. Next to them comes the position of the nearest relatives. This is then followed by the other social obligations towards the community.

Admonition to the Rich in the Community

> *Let not those among you who are endowed with grace and amplitude of means resolve by oath against helping their relatives, those in want, and those who have left homes in Allah's cause; Let them forgive and overlook; Do you not wish that Allah should forgive you? For Allah is Oft-Forgiving, Most Merciful.* (Noor 24:22)

Each family has a few persons who bear some personal dislikes or disputes with a few other members. The Quran commands that these differences should not stop a person from meeting his family obligations and that the rich in the family should always help the poor members of family. The Quran then reminds us that each one of us wishes for Allah's forgiveness. Hence, we should also practice forgiveness in our mutual dealings. It is not appropriate to wish forgiveness from Allah unless we forgive others.

Kindness to Relatives

And if you have to avoid them, seeking some mercy which you may expect from your Lord, yet speak to them a word of kindness. *(Bani Israel 17:28)*

One may avoid a poor relative for two reasons. First, one may not have the means to meet his needs. Second, a relative can demand far more than what he can afford. In both these cases, the Quran commands us to be considerate to our relatives and to speak to them with kind words.

The Cardinal Principle of Family Help

Kind words and covering of fault are better than charity followed by injury. *(Baqara 2:263)*

If a person helps another person by charity and then hurts his feelings by reminding him of his favours, this is against the basic spirit of Islam. The Quran states very clearly that speaking kindly and covering others' weaknesses is better than helping a person and then hurting his feelings.

A Criterion of Righteousness

It is not righteousness that you turn your faces towards East or West; but it is righteousness to believe in Allah, and the Last Day, and the Angels, and the Books, and the Messengers; and to spend of your substance, out of love for Allah, for your relatives, for orphans, for the needy, for the wayfarer, for those who ask, and for the ransom of slaves; to be steadfast in prayer, and to practice regular charity; to fulfill the contracts which you have made; and to be firm and patient in pain and adversity, and throughout all periods of panic; Such are the people of truth, the God-fearing. *(Baqara 2:177)*

This verse gives the most comprehensive criterion of righteousness in Islam and also describes them in the sequence of their relative importance. It should be noted that next to having the proper *Eman* (Faith), the most important criterion of righteousness is to spend on family members and other needy persons of society. The criterion of observing *Salat* and other virtues comes next to that of spending on family members.

Will of Inheritance

It is prescribed, when death approaches any of you, if he leaves, any goods, that he makes a bequest to parents and next of kin, in a proper manner, this is due from the God fearing. *(Baqara 2:180)*

Islam has clearly defined the respective share of various family members in the inherited property of a person. This verse reminds us to follow the limits set by Allah and to give the due share of our property to our family members.

Regarding Relatives not Covered under the Will

But if at the time of division, other relatives, or orphans or poor, are present, feed them out of the (property), and speak to them words of kindness and justice.
(Nisa 4:8)

If there be a distribution of property and a few persons do not receive a share from it, they may feel deprived or grieved. This verse commands us to make them happy by feeding them and by speaking to them words of kindness and justice.

COMMANDMENTS IN TRADITIONS

Ahadith give us a more comprehensive account of the importance of family obligations in Islam. Following are a few related Ahadith.

Prophet's First Sermon in Medina : Abdullah ibn Salam reported: When Rasoolullah, came to Medina, I approached him. When I examined his face, I could recognize that he surely did not have the face of a liar. The first thing which he uttered was:

O people! Spread (the greeting of) Assalamu Alaikum, give food (to the poor), maintain the blood ties, pray at night when people are asleep; you will then enter Paradise with ease. Abdullah ibn Salam was the most learned Jewish scholar in Medina. Later he became a Muslim and then narrated this Hadith. It should be noted that the Prophet entered Medina as the head of a well organized Muslim community, which later grew into a very powerful state. The above sermon of the Prophet could thus be regarded as the inaugural speech of a president of a country. One should also note that the sermon was very short, yet carried a comprehensive message. He gave only four commandments; three of which refer to the family and social obligations and only one refers to prayers. The Hadith thus reiterates the importance of family and social obligations in Islam.

Criterion of Upholding Family Ties: Abdullah ibn Umar narrated that Rasoolullah said:

One who reciprocates in doing good is not the one who upholds the ties of kinship. It is the one who upholds them when the other party severs them. (Bukhari)

Importance of Upholding Family Ties: Abu Hurrayrah reported that Rasoolullah said:

The word Rahim *is derived from the word* Rahman *(one of the names of Allah); So Almighty Allah says: Whoever keeps connection with* Rahim, I will *keep connection with him; And whoever cuts it, I will cut his connection with Me. (Bukhari)*

The Arabic term for upholding family ties is *Silat al Rahim,* which means joining of uterus ties. Aishah narrated that Rasoolullah said:

Rahim *(Blood ties) is suspended with the Throne (of Allah) and says: Whoever joins me, Allah will join him; and whoever severs me, Allah will sever connection with him. (Bukhari, Muslim)*

Abdul Rahman ibn Auf reported that Rasoolullah said: The Blessed and Almighty Allah says: I am Allah and I am Merciful; I created blood ties and derived its name from my name; I shall keep connection with him who joins it, and I shall destroy one who cuts it off. (Abu Daud)

Durra bint Abi Lahab related that Rasoolullah was asked: Who among men is the best? He answered:

One who is most dutiful to Allah and most dutiful towards blood connections. (Ahmad, Tibrani)

Abu Hurrayrah narrated that Rasoolullah said:

He who believes in Allah and the Last Day should join the ties of kinship and he who believes in Allah and the Last Day should speak beneficently or keep quiet.

(Muslim)

Abu Sufyan relates that in the course of meeting with Heracles, the latter asked him: What does Rasoolullah teach you? I answered him:

He tells us to worship Allah, the One, and not to associate anything with Him, to discard what our ancestors said, and to perform the daily Salat, *to tell the truth, keep chaste, and exercise benevolence towards kindred.*

(Bukhari, Muslim)

History tells us that the Prophet sent a letter to Heracles, the Roman emperor, inviting him to Islam. The emperor enquired from his companions in the court if there was any Arab who could tell him something about the Prophet. Abu Sufyan at that time was an unbeliever and present at Rome. Heracles called Abu Sufyan to his court and asked him to describe the teachings of the Prophet. The above Hadith was narrated by Abu Sufyan after he accepted Islam. One should note the comprehensiveness of Islamic teachings that involve not only faith and prayers but social obligations as well.

Blessings for Upholding Family Ties : Anas ibn Malik reported that Rasoolullah said:

Whoever desires that provisions (for life) might be extended to him and that his time of life be prolonged, let him keep affinity with his relatives.

(Bukhari, Muslim)

The commentators of Hadith state that this Hadith does not refer to prolonging one's life in terms of physical age. It rather means that such a person will receive Allah's blessings that will enable him to do much good deeds in his life. Furthermore, increase in provision also does not mean increase by weight or number. It refers to increase in Allah's blessings that will save the provisions from waste and make them last longer. Abu Hurrayrah reported that a man said: O Messenger of Allah! I have some relatives, with whom I live in amity, while they treat me badly. I do them good, while they do me evil; I am gentle to them, while they are rough to me. Rasoolullah said:

> *If you are as you say, it is then as though you give them hot ashes, and as long as you continue as you are, you will always have a helper from Allah against them.*
> *(Muslim)*

The Hadith teaches us to be benevolent to our relatives regardless of their attitude towards us and that as long as we shall practice this, Allah's help will be with us. Abu Ayub Khalid ibn Zaid Ansari related that a man asked: O Messenger of Allah! tell me that which will cause me to be admitted to Paradise and will keep me away from the Fire of Hell. Rasoolullah answered:

> *Worship Allah and do not associate anything with Him; observe* Salat, *pay* Zakat *and uphold the ties of kinship.*
> *(Bukhari, Muslim)*

It is clear from this Hadith that prayers alone will not help us enter Paradise. We also have to uphold the ties of kinship and try our best to be benevolent towards them. We can then justly hope to enter Paradise.

Spending on Relatives : Abu Hurrayrah narrated that Rasoolullah was asked: Which charity is the best? He answered:

> *The charity to the needy, and begin it with one who is related to you.* *(Abu Daud)*

Solaiman ibn Amer reported that Rasoolullah said:

> *Charity to a poor man has one merit of reward, and to a relative has two merits of rewards, one for charity and the other for upholding family relations.(Ahmad, Ibn Majah, Nasai, Tirmidhi)*

Jaber ibn Samorah related that Rasoolullah said:

> *When Allah gives wealth to any of you, let him begin spending it with himself and then with the members of his household.* *(Muslim)*

Punishment for Breaking Family Ties

> *Zubayr ibn Mutem reported that Rasoolullah said: One who severs blood ties shall not enter Paradise.*
> *(Bukhari, Muslim)*

The commentators of the Quran and Hadith agree that all the Believers will ultimately enter Paradise. These will be divided into two classes. There will be some who will enter Paradise with complete forgiveness and the Fire of Hell will not even touch them. There will be others who will first go to Hell and suffer for their sins and then enter Paradise. The above Hadith means that Allah will not forgive the sin of breaking family ties. Those who break the family ties will first go to Hell for their sins and then enter Paradise. Abu Barkah reported that Rasoolullah said:

> *There is no other sin for the doer of which Allah hastens punishment in this world along with what is in store for him in the next world than severance of blood ties.*
> *(Abu Daud, Tirmidhi)*

The Right of Elder Brother : Said ibn al As narrated that Rasoolullah said:

> *The right of elder brother upon the younger is (like) the right of the father upon his son.* *(Baihaqi)*

Regard for the Young and Old in the Family : Amr ibn Shoaib relates on the authority of his father, who heard it from his father that Rasoolullah said:

> *He who is not kind to our younger ones and does not respect our older ones, is not one of us.*
> *(Abu Daud, Tirmidhi)*

This Hadith does not mean that one who is guilty of the above acts does not belong to the Muslim community. It means that he does not have the proper attributes of a Muslim. Thus he is not a befitting member of a Muslim community.

5

Children's Rights

Just as treating parents with *Ehsan* has been enjoined upon children, the Quran and Hadith have also enjoined the rights and obligation of children upon parents. Love and care of children is an integral part of human nature, hence the Quran outlines basic principles regarding treatment of children and leaves the details to the good judgement of parents.

COMMANDMENTS IN HOLY QURAN

According to the teachings of the Quran, the material things of this world and our children are two criteria of our *Eman* and good conduct. Allah has given us these things as a test to find out if we can enjoy the material things of this world and our children, and still remember our duties and obligations towards Him. Blind love and extra care for the children often leads parents to ignore their duty towards Allah. This is one of the most common weakness of parents. The Quran has repeatedly warned us to guard ourselves against this weakness.

> *O you who believe let not your wealth or (the love of) your children divert you from the remembrance of Allah; Those who do so, surely they are the losers.*
>
> *(Munafiqoon 63:9)*

> *Your wealth and your children are only a temptation; whereas with Allah is an immense reward.*
>
> *(Taghabun 64:15)*

Another human weakness is parent's fear that children will become a financial burden upon them and that they may not feed them properly Hence they adopt various means to kill them or stop their birth by unnatural means. Lately, this has become a major social problem of the Western society and has resulted in numerous crimes and social disorders. The Quran has warned us against this weakness as well.

Lost are those who slay their children from folly, without knowledge, and forbid food which Allah has provided for them, inventing (lies) against Allah; they have indeed gone astray and heeded no guidance. (Anam 6:140) Kill not your children on the plea of want; We provide sustenance for you and (also) for them.(Anam 6: 153)

Kill not your children for fear of want; We shall provide sustenance for them; as well as for you, verily the killing of them is a great sin. (Bani Israel 17:31)

The birth of female children was looked upon as a bad omen by the pre-Islamic society of Arabs. This practice is still continued in many parts of the world, especially in India. The Quran condemned this practice and restored the respect and dignity of female children.

When the news is brought to them of the birth of a female (child), his face darkens and is filled with inward grief. With shame does he hide himself from his people, because of the bad news he has heard, shall he retain it on (sufferance and) contempt, or bury it in sand? Ah, what art evil choice they decide on. (Nahl 16:58-59)

The unbelievers of Mecca used to claim that Allah had daughters, while they themselves were ashamed of fathering female children The Quran describes this:

What! Has He (Allah) taken daughters (for himself) out of what He eyeates, and granted to you sons for choice ? When news is brought to them (of the birth) of what he sets up as a likeness to (Allah) IV-lost Graciou (i.e., a daughter), his face darkens, and he is filled with inward grief. (Zukhra 43:16-17)

The Quran commands parents to provide the basic needs of the children. It states the duties of the mother and father separately.

Mothers should suckle their children for two whole years; (that is) for those who wish to complete the suckling, the duty of feeding and clothing nursing mothers in a seemly manner is upon the father of the child.

(Baqarah 2:2.33)

The Quran also commands that parents should provide basic Islamic teachings to their children. *Salat* is the second most important pillar of Islam after *Eman*. The Quran commands that parents should enjoin *Salat* on their children and should also be regular in their own practice of *Salat*.

Enjoin Salat on your family, and be constant therein.

(Ta Ha 20:13)

The Quran also commands that parents should give their children the best of education and training that can help them to be good Muslims. If parents fail in their duty, children may be misguided and may thus earn Allah's wrath and punishment. The Quran states:

O you who believe! Save yourself and your family from a Eire whose fuel is man and stone over which are (appointed) angels, stern (and) severe, who flinch not (from executing) the commands they receive from Allah, but do (precisely) what they are commanded.

(Tahreem 66:6)

This is a very comprehensive commandment and cabs for a total commitment from parents for the teaching and training of their children. Parents are supposed to give their children the best of education, guidance, training, love, home, and facilities that may help them to live a righteous life. If the children are misled due to some negligence of their parents, they shall be equally responsible for the sins of their children.

COMMANDMENTS IN TRADITIONS

Ahadith provide us a more detailed and comprehensive description of the rights of children upon parents. Following are a few basic commandments:

Adaan in the Ears of Newborn

Abu Rafai reported that when Fatima gave birth to Hasan, Rasoolullah proclaimed Adaan *in his ears.*

(Abu Daud, Tirmidhi)

The very first right of every child is that as soon as he is born, the parents should proclaim *Adaan* in his ears. The first words the child should hear are the proclamation that Allah is his Lord and that Muhammad is His Messenger. We know that the last right of every Muslim is that when he dies, people should offer a congregational funeral *Salat* for his forgiveness. Furthermore, each congregational *Salat* is preceded by *Adaan*, except the funeral *Salat*. It, therefore, follows that the *Adaan* for funeral prayer is given in the ears of a newborn at the time of his birth. The Hadith teaches us that our life is as short as the interval between the proclamation of *Adaan* and the start of *Salat*. We should therefore make the best use of each and every moment of our life and should devote our time to the deeds that may help us in our eternal life in the Hereafter. The proclamation of *Adaan* in the ears of the newborn also shows us the importance of *Salat* in the life of a Believer. It is also reported in Ahadith that the Prophet instructed to proclaim *Adaan* in the right ear and Iqamah in the left ear of newborns *(Tibrani)*. Furthermore, Ahadith also state that when *Adaan* is proclaimed, Satan runs away as far as the voice of *Adaan* is carried. *(Bukhari, Muslim)*. Thus proclaiming *Adaan* in the ears of newborns is a safeguard against the evils of Satan as well.

Tahneek and Supplication

> *Aishah reported that the people would bring their newborns to Rasoolullah. He would pray for them and perform the act of* "Tahneek". *(Muslim)*

The act of "*Tahneek*" is explained in the following Hadith.

> *Asma bint Abu Bakar narrated that when Abdullah ibn Zubayr was born, she took him to Rasoolullah. He held him in his arms, chewed a date, and put a part of the chewed date in the mouth of Abdullah. He then prayed for him.* *(Bukhari, Muslim)*

The Hadith suggests that parents should take their newborns to an elderly and righteous person in the family. He should then pray for the child and also perform "*Tahneek*" with the newborn. This is one of the Sunnah that is not in practice now. We should make a sincere effort to revive this Sunnah of our beloved Prophet.

Celebration of Aqiqah

Boraidah reported: Our custom during the days of ignorance was that when a son was born, the family would slaughter a goat and cover the head of the newborn with its blood. Since we became Muslims, we slaughter a goat on the seventh day after the birth of a newborn, shave his head and cover it with saffron.(Abu Daud)

Umme Karaz narrated that she heard Rasoolullah saying; Two goats should be slaughtered when the newborn is a male and one, when the newborn is a female. The goats could be male or female.

(Abu Daud Nasai)

The scholars say that the slaughtering of two goats for a male and one for a female is only a recommendation. It is permissible to slaughter only one goat for the newborn. This is based on the following Ahadith.

Abdullah ibn Abbas narrated that Rasoolullah performed Aqiqah *for his grandsons Hasan and Hussain and slaughtered one goat for each of them.*

(Abu Daud)

Ali ibn Talib reported that Rasoolullah slaughtered one goat for the Aqiqah *of his grandson Hasan. He asked his daughter. Fatima to shave her son's head and to give in charity silver equal to the weight of his hair.*

(Tirmidhi)

Aqiqah is not only, the right of a newborn, but also represents an important Islamic custom. The meat obtained is distributed among family members and friends. This brings : feeling of happiness and joy in the community, Moreover, when the father performs *Aqiqah* for his newborn, he declares the acceptance of the newborn to be his own child and shuts all doors of suspicion for his wife and family.

Giving of charity, on the other hand, helps the poor and needy in the community and also serves as a means of bringing Allah's blessings for the newborn and the family.

Tasmiyah: Naming a Child : Abu Dardah reported that Rasoolullah said:

On the Day of Judgement, you will be called by your names and the names of your fathers, hence give good names to your children. (Ahmad, Abu Daud)

Abdullah ibn Abbas narrated that Rasoolullah said: *The right of a child upon the father is that he should give him a good name and decorate him with good manners. (Baihaqi)*

Abdullah ibn Umar reported that Rasoolullah said: Amongst your names, the dearest to Allah are Abdullah and Abdul Rahman. (Muslim)

The Sunnah of the Prophet suggests that the names of other Prophets and names with good meanings are also recommended. The Prophet named his son Ibrahim and his grandsons Hasan and Hussain. It was also his Sunnah that if someone had given a bad or undesirable name to a child, he would change it. Imam Muslim reported that the name of one of Umar's daughter was Asfa and the Prophet changed it to Jameela. Similarly, the name of Abu Salma's daughter was Barra, which means righteous. When the Prophet came to know of this name, he said that it represented a claim for righteousness and changed it to Zainab. Imam Bukhari reported that Rasoolullah said: Name your children after any name, but not after my title. i.e. Abul Qasim.

The First Spoken Words of a Child : Abdullah ibn Abbas related that Rasoolullah said:

Teach your children to speak: La ilaha illallah (There is no god except Allah) as the first spoken words in their lives and instruct men to recite the same at the time of their death. (Baihaqi)

This Hadith reiterates the importance of the *Kalima* (there is no god except Allah). First, the Prophet recommended that parents proclaim it into the ears of newborns. Second, he recommended them to teach their children to speak it as the first words in their lives. Third, he also recommended us to recite it as the last words in our life. The Hadith also suggests that the first words proclaimed in the ear and the first words spoken by the tongue have an effect on human growth and personality.

Teaching of Good Manners : Anas ibn Malik reported that Rasoolullah said:

Give due respect and regard to your children and decorate them with the best of manners. (Abu Daud)

Saeed ibn Al As narrated that Rasoolullah said:
No father can give his child a better gift than teaching him good manners. (Tirmidhi)

Jaber reported that Rasoolullah said:
The teaching of good manners by a person to his children is better than giving a Saa in charity. (Tirmidhi)

Saa is a measure of Arabic weight. Giving of charity is a virtuous deed, but teaching good manners to children in Islam is more virtuous than giving of charity.

Abu Hurrayrah reported that Rasoolullah said: Every child is born on the Fitrah (the religion of Islam). His parents then make him a Jew or a Christian or a Magian. He then recited the following verse of the Quran: Set your face truly to the religion being upright, the nature (Fitrah) in which Allah has made mankind; No change (there is) in the creation of Allah; that is the true religion; but most among mankind do not realize it (30:30). (Bukhari, Muslim)

A Muslim considers the worldly life as a journey towards the eternal life of the Hereafter. He is more concerned with the success of his eternal life than that of this worldly life. It therefore, follows that parents should be more concerned with the success of their children in the life Hereafter rather than success in their worldly life. Parents should give the best of teaching and training to their children and ensure an everlasting success for them in the life Hereafter.

Greetings to Children

Anas ibn Malik passed by some children and offered them the greetings of "Assalamu Alaikum" *and said: Rasoolullah used to do the same. (Bukhari, Muslim)*

The best way of teaching good manners to our children is by setting good examples for them. When we greet our children, we express our respect and regard towards them. We can then expect the same treatment from them.

Anas ibn Malik related that Rasoolullah said:

> *Show respect to your children and adorn them with good manners.* (Ibn Majah)

One of the ways for showing respect to our children is to greet them as we greet our elders. Showing respect also means to acknowledge and honour their rights in the family and their position in the society.

Setting a Good Example : Abdullah ibn Amer narrated that once Rasoolullah was sitting in my home and my mother called me and promised to give me something. Rasoolullah asked her what she wanted to give me. My mother said that she wanted to give me a date. He then said:

> *If you had called your child by a deceptive promise, this would have been recorded in your account as a lie on your part.* (Muslim)

The Hadith teaches us that parents should serve as role models for their children and should not tell a lie even in ordinary day to day dealings.

Admonition for Salat

> *Amr ibn Shoaib reported that Rasoolullah said: Admonish your children to pray* Salat *when they are seven years old, spank them if they do not observe it when they are ten years old and then separate them in their beds.* (Abu Daud)

The Hadith is the explanation of the Quranic commandment: *Save yourselves and your children from the Hell-Fire (66:6).* Most of our habits are formed between the ages of seven and ten. If parents could make their children pray *Salat* regularly during this period, this would hopefully become a permanent habit of their lives. The Quran also states: *Salat restrains from shameful and unjust deeds (29:45). Salat* would thus help our children to stay on the right path and save them from the punishment of Hell-Fire. This Hadith also states that it is the right of every child to have a separate sleeping bed when he is ten years old. At the same time, the Hadith reminds us of the beauty of Islam which gives us guidance in the spiritual as well as the material aspects of our lives.

Teaching of the Quran : Muaz Johainy reported that Rasoolullah said:

> *Whoever learned the Quran and obeyed its commandments, Allah on the Day of Judgement, will crown his parents, the glow of which shall be brighter than that of the sun. He then asked: What reward do you expect for the person himself?(Abu Daud, Ahmad)*

Ali ibn Abi Talib related that Rasoolullah said:

> *Whoever learnt the Quran by heart, regarded its Halal as Halal and its Haram as Haram, Allah will enter him in Paradise. Allah will also accept his intercession for ten other persons who have been destined to enter Hell.*
> *(Ahmad, Darimi, Ibn Majah, Tirmidhi)*

As far as intercession on the Day of Judgement is concerned, Allah will give this right to those whom He wants and these persons will intercede on behalf of others only by Allah's permission. The Quran states: *On the Day, the Spirit and the angels will stand in ranks, none shall be allowed to speak, except (one who is permitted by (the Lord) Most Gracious, and he* will speak (only) what is right (78:38). According to the above Hadith, a *Hafiz* will also be given the right to intercede on the Day of Judgement. It should, however, be noted that the unbelievers and hypocrites are destined to enter Hell and no one can intercede on this behalf.

The intercession mentioned in this Hadith refers to the Believers who had committed sins and died without seeking Allah's forgiveness. If the parents could give their children the proper knowledge of the Quran and could also help them to be a Hafiz, they are sure to receive the intercession of their children. Love and kindness to children.

Love and Kindness to Children : Abdullah ibn Masud related that Rasoolullah said:

> *All children are Allah's children, and dearest to Allah are those who treat His children with kindness.*
> *(Baihaqi)*

The Hadith teaches us to be kind not only to our children but to all children, irrespective of their race, religion or origin. Aishah reported that a desert Arab came to Rasoolullah and was surprised to see him kissing the children. He exclaimed: What! do you kiss children! Rasoolullah replied to him:

> *I cannot help you, if Allah has taken kindness out of your heart.* (Bukhari, Muslim)

Abu Hurrayrah narrated that Rasoolullah kissed his grandson, Hasan, in the presence of Aqra ibn Habith. Aqra said: I have ten children and I have never kissed any of them. Rasoolullah looked towards him and said:

> *He who is not kind to others will not receive Allah's kindness. (Bukhari, Muslim) Practicing the Sunnah of the Prophet is one of the most virtuous deeds that brings Allah's blessings and Thawab. According to these Ahadith, the kissing of children is a Sunnah of our beloved Prophet. We should therefore follow this practice as well.*

Equal Treatment with All Children : Numan ibn Bashir reported that his father once took him to Rasoolullah and informed him that he had given me one of his slaves. Rasoolullah asked my father if he had given a slave to all of his children. My father replied that he had not done so. Rasoolullah then told him:

> *Remember your duty to Allah, and be fair to all your children.* (Bukhari, Muslim)

The Hadith adds that, after hearing this, Numan's father took the slave back from his son. Another version of this Hadith states that Rasoolullah said: I do not want to be a witness to an unjust deed. Based on this version of Hadith, a group of *Fuqaha* regard the unequal or unjust treatment of children as "Haram" (forbidden) in Islam. A few others like Imam Abu Hanifah, Malik and Shafai consider this to be "*Makrooh*" (undesirable). The unequal treatment of children is not only allowed but preferred if there is a genuine need. If, for example, one of the children is permanently sick, disabled or in financial trouble, the parents could give him more love and care than the other children. Abdullah ibn Abbas narrated that Rasoolullah said:

> *In terms of your presents and financial help, treat your children with justice and equality. If I would have*

preferred someone in this respect, I would have preferred the girls over boys. *(Tibrani)*

Based on this Hadith, the Fuqaha say that though the portion of inheritance for girls is half than that of boys, the parents during their lifetime should treat girls as equal to boys in every respect.

Treatment with Girls : Abdullah ibn Abbas related that Rasoolullah said:

Whoever becomes the father of a girl, he should neither hurt her nor treat her with contempt nor prefer his sons over her. Allah will grant him Paradise in return for the kind treatment of his daughter.

(Ahmad, Hakim)

Abdullah ibn Abbas also reported that Rasoolullah said:

If anyone is blessed with a daughter, and does not bury her alive, nor prefers his sons over her, Allah will make him enter Paradise. *(Abu Daud)*

We should recall that during the Pre-Islamic period, Arabs disliked girls so much that if someone was blessed with a newborn daughter, he would bury her alive. Islam not only eradicated this practice, but gave the girls a position equal to that of boys.

The glad tiding in this Hadith: "Allah will make him enter Paradise," means that treating girls with respect and honour is one of the means for receiving Allah's Mercy and Rewards. It should, however, be added that in order to receive the blessings of this Hadith and similar ones narrated earlier, one has first to obey Allah in all aspects of his life and then practice this Hadith. If someone disobeys Allah in his life and then treats girls with respect and honour, this act alone may not help him enter Paradise.

Aishah reported: A woman once came to me begging for food with her two daughters. All I could find in my home was a single date, that I gave to her. She divided it between her two daughters and ate nothing of it. She then left my home. When Rasoolullah came, I told him about this woman. He then said:

Anyone who has daughters and is kind to them will find that on the Day of Judgement, they will serve as a shield for him against Hell. (Bukhari, Muslim)

Anas ibn Malik related that Rasoolullah said:

One who raises two daughters with love until they become mature, he and I, on the Day of Judgement will be like this. Anas added that while saying this, he raised two of his fingers and kept them close together. (Muslim)

Abu Saeed Khudri reported that Rasoolullah said:

One who took the responsibility of raising three daughters or sisters, treated them well, gave them good training, and also arranged their marriage, his reward with Allah is Paradise. (Abu Daud, Tirmidhi)

Taking Care of a Divorced or Widowed Daughter : Soraiqah ibn Malik reported that Rasoolullah said:

Shall I not tell you the best form of charity? It is supporting your daughter, who has been returned to you, and who has no earning partner except you. (Ibn Majah)

In the western society, parents often do not feel responsible for their grown-up children. Islam, on the contrary, considers this as one of the basic responsibilities of the parents. Islam also promises special rewards for the care of grown-up daughters, and considers this act as the best form of charity. Thus, Islam gives girls, not only a respected and dignified position, but also safeguards their basic rights and needs. It is because of such noble teachings of Islam that the problem of single mother does not even exist in a Muslim community.

Such women always become a part of someone's household where their material and emotional needs are met either by a father or a brother. The problem of single mothers is a growing issue of the Western society where the number of single women living without any material or emotional protection is increasing everyday. Western society has yet to find a respectable solution for these women.

Glad Tiding to Divorced or Widowed Mothers : Auf ibn Malek Ashjai reported that Rasoolullah said:

I and the woman with worn-out cheeks shall be like these two fingers on the Day of Judgement. The worn-out woman is one who has been deprived of her husband, possesses beauty and respect in society, but confines herself to the care of her children, until they mature or die.

The narrator added that while saying this, Rasoolullah raised his middle and forefinger. (Abu Daud)

Though Islam encourages the second marriage for the divorced and widowed, the judgement for marriage is left with the women. If a woman chooses not to marry for the love and care of her children, her reward is the good company of the Prophet on the Day of Judgement. It is, however, clear that a single act in life will not bring any rewards on the Day of Judgement. In order to receive this reward a woman has to live a righteous life and also take care of her children.

Spending on Children : Abu Masud Badri narrated that Rasoolullah said:

When a person spends on his wife and children hoping for a reward from Allah, this is regarded as an act of charity on his part. (Bukhari, Muslim)

Umme Salma reported: I asked: O Messenger of Allah! shall I have any reward if I spend on my children from my first husband? Rasoolullah replied:

Spend on them, for you shall have the reward for whatever you spend on them. (Bukhari, Muslim)

Abu Hurrayrah related that Rasoolullah said:

Out of the Dinar you spend in the cause of Allah, the Dinar you spend in procuring the freedom of a slave, the Dinar you give way in charity to the poor and the Dinar you spend on your wife and children, the highest in respect of reward is the one you spend on your wife and children. (Muslim)

Abdullah ibn Amr ibn As reported that Rasoolullah said: It is a significant sin for a person to deny the due rights of persons, whose living He controls.

(Abu Daud)

Regarding Children's Marriage

> *Abu Saeed Khudri reported that Rasoolullah said: Whoever is blessed with children, should teach them good manners and when they reach the age of puberty, arrange for their marriage. If parents ignore or postpone this, and the children get involved into forbidden acts, the father will be held responsible for their sins. (Baihaqi)*

This does not mean that children will not be responsible for their sins. The Hadith states that it is a duty of parents, especially the father, to arrange for the marriage of their children and if they fail in their duty and the children get involved in sins, the father will be equally responsible for their sins.

6

Mutual Responsibilities

The entire Muslim Ummah is one big family cemented together by the common bonds of belief in one Allah and His Last Prophet. It is one homogenous body with no distinctions in colour, race or nationality. Islam recognizes that all Believers, men and women, are equal in the sight of Allah. The only distinction recognized by Islam relates to one's piety and righteousness.

The Quran states:

The most respected of you in the sight of Allah is the most righteous amongst you. *(Hijrat 49:13)*

The Prophet in his Farewell address also declared: Neither is a white superior to a black nor an Arab superior to a non-Arab, and all Muslims are brothers to one another.

This brotherhood is so cohesive and strong that the entire Muslim Ummah is like one body. Whenever a certain individual or a part of the community is in distress, the whole community reacts and responds to its needs.

Islam gives clear injunctions that safeguard the due rights of each Believer. It also provides a comprehensive code of moral values and ethics that promote a feeling of love and unity among all Believers. At the same time, it gives stern warning to those who break these codes and offers glad tidings to those who honour these codes.

This raises the position of Islamic moral teachings from the level of mere religious guidance to that of legal injunctions. Islam thus ensures the individual and the collective rights of all members of its community.

COMMANDMENTS IN HOLY QURAN

Unity of Muslim Ummah

Verily, this Brotherhood of yours is a single Brotherhood, and I am your Lord and Cherisher; therefore serve Me (and no other). *(Anbia 21:92)*

All Believers are Brothers

The Believers are but a single brotherhood. *(Hijrat 49:10)*

Believers are Compassionate to One Another

Muhammad is the Messenger of Allah, and those who are with him are strong against unbelievers, (but) compassionate towards one another. *(Fatah 48:29)*

Believers are Protectors to One Another

The Believers, men and women, are protectors, one of another. *(Tauba 9:71)*

Believers' social obligations :

O you who believe! Let not some men among you laugh at others; It may be that the (latter) are better than the (former); Nor let some women laugh at others; It may be that the (latter) are better than the (former); Nor defame, nor be sarcastic to one another, nor call each other by (offending) nicknames; seeming is a name connoting wickedness (to be used for one) after he has believed; And those who do not desist are (indeed) doing wrong. *(Hijrat 49:11)*

Making Peace between Believers

The Believers are but a single brotherhood, so make peace and reconciliation between your two (contending) brothers; And fear Allah, that you may receive (His) Mercy. *(Hijrat 49:10)*

Greeting a Believer

When a (courteous) greeting is offered to you, meet it with a greeting still more courteous, or (at least) of equal courtesy; Allah takes careful account of all things. *(Nisa 4:86)*

Taking Revenge from a Believer

The recompense for an injury is an injury equal thereto (in degree); but if a person forgives and makes reconciliation, his reward is due from Allah; For Allah loves not those who do wrong. *(Shura 42:40)*

Killing a Believer

If a man kills a Believer intentionally, his recompense is Hell, to abide therein (for ever), and the wrath and the curse of Allah are upon him, and a dreadful penalty is (also) prepared for him. *(Nisa 4:93)*

COMMANDMENTS IN TRADITIONS

The Nature of Islamic Brotherhood

Numan ibn Bashir reported that Rasoolullah said: You will see the Believers in their mutual kindness, love and sympathy just like one body. When a limb complains, the whole body responds to it with wakefulness.

(Bukhari, Muslim)

Abu Musa narrated that Rasoolullah said:

The Believer is for another Believer like a building, some of which strengthens the other. Saying this Rasoolullah interlaced his flingers.(Bukhari, Muslim)

Admonition for bringing division amongst the Believers Usamah ibn Sharik reported that Rasoolullah said: Whoever comes out to make division among my followers, smite his neck. *(Nasai)*

Islam does not allow a person to take the life of another person under any condition. This Hadith refers to the responsibility of the state. If a person revolts against the state and thus brings about disunity amongst the Believers, the state then has the right to kill him.

Abdullah ibn Abbas related that Rasoolullah said: Whoever sees anything in his leader that he dislikes, he should be patient, as I find that there is none who secedes himself from the united body even to a hand's span and dies, then he dies as one during the days of ignorance. *(Bukhari, Muslim)*

One has to obey a Muslim leader as long as he does not cross the limits set by Allah. If a person or a group of people find something that they do not like in their leader, they should correct it by constitutional means. Islam does not allow one to revolt against a leader and thus create a disunity among the Muslims. If one goes out of the Muslim community and dies, then according to this Hadith, he will die as an unbeliever during days of ignorance. Abdullah ibn Umar reported that Rasoolullah said:

> *Follow the biggest party, because whoever becomes separate will be separated in Hell.* *(Ibn Majah)*
>
> *Abdullah ibn Umar narrated that Rasoolullah said: Allah will not gather together my followers over misguidance, and the Hand of Allah is upon the united body, and whoever becomes separate, will be separated in Hell.* *(Tirmidhi)*

This Hadith gives us the glad tidings that the majority of the Muslim Ummah will always be on the right path. We should therefore stay with the majority and dissociate ourselves from those who bring disunity to the Muslim community. The Hadith also states that one who separates himself from the Muslim community will first go to Hell and suffer for his sin for causing disunity and then be allowed to enter Paradise.

Mutual Obligations of Believers: Abu Hurrayrah related that Rasoolullah said:

> *The rights of a Muslim upon a Muslim are six: When you meet him, salute him; When he calls you, respond to him; When he seeks your advice, give him advice; When he sneezes, and praises Allah (by saying Al Humdu Lillah), respond to him (by saying Yarhamu kum Allah); When he falls ill, visit him;*
>
> *And when he dies, follow his bier.* *(Muslim)*

Aishah reported that Rasoolullah said:

> *It is not befitting for a Muslim to keep apart from another Muslim beyond three days; then when he meets him, he shall salute him. He shall salute him three times if he does not receive any return for his salutation.* *(Abu Daud)*

The Hadith refers to two Muslims who have been separated from each other due to some dispute between them. It calls for having a reconciliation within three days. Another version of this Hadith reported by Bukhari and Muslim adds: The better of them is he who is the first to give a salutation to his brother. Abdullah ibn Umar reported that Rasoolullah once ascended the pulpit and proclaimed with a loud voice:

> *O Congregation! Whoever has accepted Islam with his tongue while* Eman *(faith) is not (yet) firmly rooted in his heart! Oppress not the Believers, nor scold them, nor follow their secrets, for whoever follows the secrets of his Muslim brother, Allah will follow his secrets, and whosoever's secrets are followed by Allah, Allah will disgrace him even though he may be in the interior most of his home.* *(Tirmidhi)*

This Hadith teaches us that no man is free of faults and that the individual members of Muslim Brotherhood should cover the faults of their fellow brothers. It also calls for respecting the privacy of their fellow brothers and not for investigating their secrets. The Hadith also makes it clear that these are amongst the essential attributes of *Eman*. Abdullah ibn Umar reported that Rasoolullah said:

> *A Muslim is a brother to a Muslim. He neither wrongs him, nor hands him over (to another). Whoever helps his brother in need, Allah will help him in his need. Whoever removes a calamity from his brother, Allah will remove a calamity from him from the calamities of the Day of Judgement; and whoever conceals the faults of his brother, Allah will conceal his sins on the Day of Judgement.* *(Bukhari, Muslim)*

Abu Hurrayrah narrated that Rasoolullah said:

> *The Believer is a mirror to a Believer, and the Believer is a brother to a Believer. He removes his injuries from him and protects him (even) in his absence.* *(Abu Daud, Tirmidhi)*

Abu Hurrayrah reported that Rasoolullah said:

> *A Muslim is a brother to another Muslim. He should not cheat him, nor tell him a lie, nor humiliate him.*

Everything owned by a Muslim is forbidden for another Muslim. Righteousness is an attribute of the heart. It is sufficient evil for a man even to look down on his Muslim brother with disdain. *(Tirmidhi)*

Reward for Loving a Believer

Abu Hurrayrah related that Rasoolullah said: You shall not enter Paradise until you Believe, and you will not Believe until you love one another. Shall I not guide you to this thing? When you will do it, you will love one another. Spread the greetings of Salam. *(Muslim)*

The Hadith states that loving our fellow Believers is one of the criterion as well as a means for increasing our faith. The more.we love our brothers, the more we shall have faith and this will help us enter Paradise. Abu Hurrayrah reported that Rasoolullah said:

Surely there are pillars made of emeralds with engravings of fine silk therein. They have open doors shining like bright stars.

They inquired: O the Prophet of Allah! Who will live therein? He answered:

The mutual lovers for the cause of Allah, those who assemble together for the cause of Allah, and those who meet one another for the cause of Allah. *(Baihaqi)*

Warning for having Malice Against a Believer

Abu Hurrayrah narrated that Rasoolullah said: The actions of men are submitted to Allah, twice a week, on Monday and Thursday. Then Allah forgives every Believing man except the two persons between whom is malice. It is said: Leave these two until they come to terms. *(Muslim)*

The Hadith makes it very clear that if there be malice between two Believers, both are deprived of Allah's Mercy. It' is the duty of both to bring reconciliation no matter who happens to be at fault.

Having Good will Towards Believers : Tamim Dari related that Rasoolullah said: Faith is good will. He was asked:

Towards whom? He answered: Towards Allah, His Prophet, leading Muslims and the general public. (Muslim) Anas ibn Malik related that Rasoolullah said:

A person is not a true Believer unless he desires for his brother that which he desires for himself. (Bukhari, Muslim)

Giving of Proper Counsel : Jarir reported: I took allegiance to Rasoolullah on conditions of observing *Salat*, paying *Zakat*, and advising every Muslim. (Bukhari, Muslim) This Hadith reminds us that social obligations in Islam are as important as the religious obligations.

A Muslim is not supposed to be indifferent to the needs of his fellow brothers. If he sees one of his brothers committing a mistake or making a wrong decision, it then becomes his duty to give him proper advice and to save him from making a mistake.

Safeguarding the honour of a Believer Jaber narrated that Rasoolullah said: There is no Muslim who dishonours another Muslim in a place where his honour is at stake or injured except that Allah Almighty will dishonour him in a place where Allah's help is needed; And there is no Muslim who helps another Muslim in a place where his honour is at stake or injured except that Almighty Allah will help him in a place where Allah's help is needed. (Abu Daud)

Anas ibn Malik reported that Rasoolullah said:

Whoever hears backbiting of his brother and he, being capable of helping him, helps him, Allah will help him in this world and also in the Hereafter. If he does not help, being capable of helping him, Allah will overtake him in this world and in the Hereafter.

(Sharah al Sunnah)

Islam calls for taking an active role in safeguarding the due rights of every Muslim in the community. A Muslim is supposed to care for the good name of his brothers and sisters even in their absence.

Helping a Needy Believer : Abu Saeed reported that Rasoolullah said:

> *If a Muslim clothes a naked Muslim, Allah will clothe him in the green robes of Paradise; if a Muslim feeds a hungry Muslim, Allah will feed him from the fruits of Paradise, and if a Muslim gives a drink to a thirsty Muslim, Allah will give him the drink from the closed up Fountain.* (Abu Daud, Tirmidhi)

It appears that the word "closed up fountain" refers to the Fountain of Kauthar. Everyone on the Day of Judgement will be extremely thirsty. The Believers will gather on the Fountain of Kauther and shall receive the most refreshing drink from the hands of the Prophet. The Hadith gives this glad tiding to those who quench the thirst of their Muslim brothers in this world. Anas ibn Malik reported that Rasoolullah said:

> *If anyone provides help to one of my needy people out of a wish to please me, he has pleased me. He who has pleased me has pleased Allah, and he who has pleased Allah will be brought by Him into Paradise.*
> (Baihaqi)

This Hadith is another reminder to those who claim to love the Prophet. The true love of the Prophet calls for a few commitments in life and one of them is to help the needy Muslims in the community. Anas ibn Malik related that Rasoolullah said:

> *Help your brother whether he is doing wrong or is being wronged. A man said: O Messenger of Allah! I can help him when he is being wronged, but how can I help him when he is doing wrong? and he replied:*
>
> *By preventing him from doing wrong. That is your help to him.* (Bukhari, Muslim)

Abu Hurrayrah reported that Rasoolullah said:

> *Allah, the Lord of Honour and Glory, will say on the Day of Judgement: Son of Adam! I asked you food and you did not feed Me. The man will exclaim: Lord! how could I have fed You, while You are the Lord of the Worlds! Allah will say: Did you not realize that My servant so and so asked you for food and you did not feed him? Did you not realize that if you had fed him, you would have found your reward with Me? Son of*

Adam! I asked you for a drink and you did not give Me a drink. The man will exclaim: Lord! How could I have given You a drink while you are the Lord of the Worlds! Allah will say: My servant so and so asked you for a drink and you did not give him the drink. Did you not realize that if you had given him the drink, you would have found its reward with Me. (Muslim)

The Hadith shows the importance of social obligations in Islam. Helping the poor and needy is as virtuous in Islam as serving the Almighty Allah. The Hadith also warns us that if we do not help the poor and needy in our community, Allah will be displeased with us on the Day of Judgement.

Visiting the Sick : Abu Hurrayrah narrated that Rasoolullah said:

When a Muslim visits his Muslim brother in sickness, he certainly continues to pluck fruits of Paradise, till he returns. (Muslim) Abu Hurrayrah reported that Rasoolullah said:

Allah, the Lord of Honour and glory, will say on the Day of Judgement: Son of Adam! I was sick and you did not visit me. The man will exclaim: Lord! how could I have visited you while you are the Lord of the Worlds. Allah will say: Did you not realize that My servant so and so was sick and you did not visit him. Did you not realize that if you had visited him, you would have found Me with him? (Muslim)

A part of this Hadith has been presented earlier. It reiterates the importance of our social obligations in Muslim community.

Covering up of Faults : Abu Hurrayrah related that Rasoolullah said:

Allah will cover the faults, on the Day of Judgement, of the person who covered up the faults of another person in this world. (Muslim)

Making Peace between Believers : Abu Hurrayrah reported that Rasoolullah said:

To bring out just reconciliation between two contestants is an act of charity. (Bukhari, Muslim)

Abu Dardah narrated that Rasoolullah said:

Shall I not inform you about what is better than fasting and praying? It is to restore peace between two contending persons, since a dispute between the two is harmful to both of them. *(Abu Daud, Tirmidhi)*

The Hadith speaks of the beauty of the teachings of Islam. The word Islam means peace. Hence bringing peace between two Believers in Islam is more virtuous than the offering of ritual prayers.

Umme Kulthum relates that she heard Rasoolullah saying: One, who tries to bring about peace between people, and has to say something which is not true is not a liar. *(Bukhari, Muslim)*

Telling a lie is a sin in Islam. Based on this and a few similar Ahadith, the *Fuqaha* (Islamic Jurists) say that telling a lie is permissible to bring peace between two Believers and also between a husband and his wife.

Making Intercession for a Believer

Abu Musa Ashari narrated that whenever a needy person came to Rasoolullah he would turn to those present and say: Intercede for him, you will have your reward and Allah causes that which He likes to issue from the tongue of His Prophet. *(Bukhari, Muslim)*

This Hadith teaches us two basic things. First, whatever the Prophet said was not out of his desire but was inspired by Almighty Allah. This is what the Quran has also stated very clearly: *He does not speak of his own desire. It is no less than inspiration sent down to him (53:3-4).* Second, it was the noble practice of the Prophet that when a needy person approached him and he was not in a position to help him, he asked his companions to help him. Needless to say we should follow this practice in our lives.

Respecting an Aged Believer : Abu Musa related that Rasoolullah said:

It is part of glorification of Allah to respect an aged Muslim, and one who has learned the Quran by heart, provided he makes no interpolations in it and does not contradict it by his conduct, and also a just ruler. *(Abu Daud)*

This Hadith equates the act of respecting an aged Believer to that of glorification of Allah. It is because of this basic teaching of Islam that old age persons occupy a very respected and dignified position in the Muslim community. Anas ibn Malik reported that Rasoolullah said:

If a youth respects a person on account of his old age, Allah appoints someone who will respect him in his old age. *(Tirmidhi)*

This Hadith gives an indirect glad tiding to those who honour old persons, that Allah will give them long lives and that they also shall reach old ages.

Punishment for Killing a Believer : Abu Saeed reported that Rasoolullah said:

If all the inmates of the heavens and earth join together to take the life of a Believer, Allah will surely throw all of them to the Fire (of Hell). *(Tirmidhi)*

Abdullah ibn Umar narrated that Rasoolullah said:

The passing away of the world is surely easier to Allah than the murder of a Muslim. *(Nasai, Tirmidhi)*

Islam gives utmost importance to the sanctity of human life especially the life of a Believer. According to this Hadith, the life of a Believer is dearer to Allah than the whole world. It is because of this basic teaching of Islam that street crimes and murders are almost non-existent in a Muslim community. Jorair reported that Rasoolullah said:

You must not become un-believers after me, some of you smiting the necks of others. *(Bukhari, Muslim)*

This Hadith suggests that killing each other is an act that does not befit the Believers. One who does this act commits a sin as great as going out of the folds of Islam. The Hadith also suggests that killing each other is an act that befits the unbelievers. The statistics of murder in the Western society confirm this point beyond any shadow of doubt.

7

Ideal Family

"Worship Allah and be obedient to Him: and do not associate any partner with Him. And be benevolent to:

> *Your parents, near kindred, and the orphans, and needy persons, the neighbour who is related to you, and the neighbour who may not be related to you, and the companion of the journey, and the traveller, and slaves your right-hand possess."* *(4 : 36)*

SERVING THE PARENTS

Parents are to be treated well, and Allah's blessings in having enabled you to do this virtuous act, be considered as a great asset in this world as well as in the Hereafter. After Allah and the Holy Prophet (S.A.W.) you have the greatest duty towards your parents. The respect we ought to pay to our parents has been time and again emphasised in the Quran wherein duties towards parents have been enumerated alongwith the duties towards Allah, and the Muslims have been commanded to render thanks to Allah and also to their parents. Allah has decreed:

> *"Your Allah has decreed that you worship none save Allah, and (that you should) be kind to your parents."* *(17 : 2 3)*

Hadrat Abdullah Ibn Masud (R.A.A.) narrates: "I asked the Prophet of Allah (S.A.W.) as to which act Allah likes best. The Holy Prophet (S.A.W.) said: "the prayer offered in time." I asked "What, is it that Allah likes next best. "The Holy Prophet (S.A.W.) said, "Good treatment of your mother and father." When I asked him about the third most excellent act, he (S.A.W.) said, "Fighting in the way of Allah." *(Bukhari - Muslim)*

Hadrat Abdullah Ibn Masud (R.A.A.) further says: "A man once presented himself before the Holy Prophet (S.A.W.) and said, "I affirm solemnly before you for Hijrat and Jihad and wish for recompense from Allah." The Holy Prophet (S.A.W.) thereupon enquired: "Is anyone of your parents alive?" He said: 'Yes, O Prophet of Allah, and by the grace of Allah both are living." The Holy Prophet (S.A.W.) then asked "Do you really wish for recompense from Allah for your Hijrat and Jihad?" When he said he did want it, the Holy Prophet (S.A.W.) commanded: "Go and stay with your parents and serve them well." *(Muslim)*

Hadrat Abu Umamah says that once a person asked the Holy Prophet (S.A.W.) about the rights of the Parents upon their children. The Holy Prophet (S.A.W.) said, "Your parents are your Paradise and they are your Hell," *(Ibn — Majah)*

That is by doing good to them you will earn Paradise and if you ignore their rights you will go to Hell.

Be Grateful to Your Parents : It is among the cardinal principles of good manners and acknowledgment of debt that one should be grateful for all the acts of kindness one has received. It is a fact that the main reason for our physical existence are our parents. We grow up under their tender care and reach adulthood. They suffer great hardships and show extraordinary love and suffer unparalleled sacrifices in bringing us up and it is, therefore, befitting that we should be grateful to them from the core of our hearts. This is why Allah has decreed that when we render thanks to Him, we should express gratitude to our parents as well.

"(We have decreed) that you should render thanks unto Me and unto your parents." *(31 : 14)*

You should always try to please your parents and not do anything that may hurt their feelings, particularly when they get old, and become somewhat peevish and short tempered. In old age, parents very often make such claim., and demand which may seem to be unusual. This be tolerated cheerfully, and do not retort in anger which may cause annoyance to them. Allah has specifically commanded:

"If one or both of them (your parents) attain old age with thee, say not "Fie" unto them nor repulse them."
(17 : 23)

In fact, in old age a person becomes weak in nerves, and consequently touchy and somewhat irascible; and on slightest excuse start feeling as if they are being ignored. As such, they should not be given any chance for being annoyed. According to Hadrat Abdullah bin Umar (R.A.A.), the Holy Prophet (S.A.W.) has said:

"The pleasure of Allah is in the pleasure of the father and His displeasure in father's displeasure."
(Tirmidhi, Ibn Habban, Mustadrak Hakim)

Hadrat Abdullah bin Umar (R.A.A.) also narrates an incident in which a man left his parents crying, and presented himself before the Holy Prophet (S.A.W.) seeking permission for Hijrat (migration). The Holy Prophet (S.A.W.) thereupon commanded him to go back to his parents and to return after making them happy as he had made them sad earlier. *(Abu Daud)*

Parents should be Served Earnestly and with Sincerity : Even if they appear to be a bit hard and inflexible, you should be kind to them. Keeping in view the unparalleled kindness and affection shown by them, you should fulfil even such demands which may be contrary to your taste and liking, but not against religion. It is our service to the parents that would lead to our redemption and earn for us Allah's blessings making us immune from calamities in both the worlds.

According to Hadrat Anas (R.A.A.), the Holy Prophet (S.A.W.) has said that he, who wishes for long life and greater prosperity, should be good to his parents and be) fine towards his kith and kin.
(At-Targhib wat Tarhib)

The Holy Prophet (S.A.W.) has also said that:
"That man may be disgraced; again disgraced and again disgraced." The companions asked: "O Prophet of Allah

(S.A.W.), who is that man?" The Holy Prophet (S.A.W.) said: "He who found his parents in old age, both or one, but could not enter the Paradise due to his failure to serve them." *(Muslim)*

Entry into Paradise : Fully respect your parents, and do not say a word or commit an act which may be derogatory to them. Be humble and modest before them. The Holy Quran says:

"Speak to them (parents) with grace and respect." *(17 : 23)*

And again the Holy Quran enjoins:

"And lower unto them the wing of submission through mercy!" *(7 . 24)*

This means that you should always be mindful of your parent's position and dignity, and never talk boastfully in presence nor in any way belittle them.

Once Hadrat Abdullah Ibn Umar (R.A.A.) asked Hadrat Ibn Abbas (R.A.A.): "Do you wish that you should be immune from the Hell and enter Paradise,?" Hadrat Ibn Abbas said: "Why not? By Allah I wish to enter Paradise." Hadrat Ibn Umar asked; "Are your parents alive"? Hadrat Ibn Abbas said: "Yes, my mother is living." Hadrat Ibn Umar said: "If you talk with her graciously and look after her comforts, boarding and lodging you shall certainly enter Paradise, provided you avoid major (serious) sins." *(Al-Adab-Al-Mufrad)*

Once Hadrat Abu Hurrayrah (R.A.A.) came across two persons. He asked one of them. "What is the other person to you?" He said, "He is my father." Hadrat Abu Hurrayrah said; "Be careful, never call him by name, nor walk ahead of him and do not take a seat before he is seated." *(Al-Adab Al-Mu frad)*

Love your parents and this love should be regarded as an honour and means of recompense and redemption in the Hereafter. Hadrat Ibn Abbas narrates the following Hadith of the Holy Prophet (S.A.W.):

"Dutiful and good natured children who cast one loving and affectionate look at their parents, receive from Allah

a blessing equivalent to one approved pilgrimage (Hajj). When the companions asked: "O Prophet of Allah (S.A.W.), what happens if a person looks like that a hundred times a day?" The holy Prophet (S.A.W.) said: "Yes, even if he does so a hundred times: Allah is far greater (benevolent) than your imagination and is not narrow-minded (i.e. He will bestow upon him so much recompense)." (Muslim)

Hadrat Ibn Abbas Narrates the following Hadith of the Holy Prophet (S.A.W.) in this Connection

"If a man has passed the night having fulfilled the commands of Allah concerning his parents, he will find in the morning two doors of Paradise opened to receive him. If either of his parents is living, one door of Paradise shall receive him. And, if on the contrary he has disobeyed the commands of Allah in this connection, he will find two gates of Hell gaping at him, and, if he has one of his parents living, he will have one gate of the Hell opened for him." The man whom the holy Prophet (S.A.W.) had thus addressed asked: "And if the parents are being unfair to him?" The Holy Prophet (S.A.W.) said, "Yes, even then, even then, even then."(Mishkat)

Parents are to be regarded as the owners of your assets, and you should spend your money generously upon them. Holy Quran tells us:

"People ask you as to what they should spend: tell them whatever you spend for good (must go) to parents." (2 : 215)

Once a man presented himself before the Holy Prophet (S.A.W.) and complained that his father takes away everything from his assets whenever he wanted something. The Holy Prophet (S.A.W.) thereupon sent for his father. There appeared an old man, physically weak walking with the help of a stick. When the Holy Prophet (S.A.W.) asked him, he said: "O Prophet of Allah (S.A.W.), there was a time when this son of mine was weak and helpless, and I was powerful. I had money and he was empty-handed. I never checked him from taking anything from me. Today I am weak and he is strong; I am empty handed and he is rich. Now he hides his money from me. The Mercy of the Prophet (S.A.W.) could not resist his tears on hearing this poignant story and told the son: "You and your wealth belong to your father." Even if the parents happen to be non-Muslims, they are to be treated well and all courtesy to be shown to them. But obedience in matters of religion should be refused and they are not to be followed if they ask you to do a sin or an act associating somebody with Allah.

> *"And if your (non-Muslim) parents press you to associate somebody with Me about whom you have no knowledge, obey them not, and (but) treat them well in the world."*
> *(3 : 15)*

> *Hadrat Asma (R.A.A.) says that her mother came to see her during the lifetime of the Holy Prophet (S.A.W.). She was an infidel at the time. Hadrat Asma (R.A.A.) said to the Holy Prophet (S.A.W.): "My mother had come to see me but she abhors Islam. How she should be treated?" The Holy Prophet (S.A.W.) asked her to continue to treat her mother affectionately as a kindred."*
> *(Bukhari)*

Continue to pray for your parents, recalling their kindness; beg for their weal from Allah and His mercies for them. Allah has said:

> *"Always say my Lord! have mercy on both of them, just as they both nourished me when I was a little child."*
> *(17 : 27)*

That is to say, "O Allah! When I was helpless in my childhood, they nourished me with full attention and devotion, affection and mercy, and for my sake sacrificed their comforts. Now in their old age, in helplessness and infirmity, they are more deserving of kindness and mercy, O Allah! I cannot return their kindness. You alone can sustain and patronise them and have mercy upon them." You should have special regard for the mother who is generally weaker and more sensitive. As such, she needs looking after all the more. Moreover, her kindness and sacrifices (towards the offspring) are greater than the father. Therefore, Islam has laid down greater rights for the mother and has exhorted special treatment for her. The Holy Quran says:

"And We have commanded unto man to treat his parents kindly. His mother carried him (in her womb) with difficulty and delivered him with a pang. The period of carrying him in her womb and sustaining him on her milk is 30 months." *(46 : 15)*

While the Quran has prescribed love and kindness towards the parents, it has described that of the mother in bearing and bringing up a child, very graphically and effectively, and points to the act that in view of her sacrifices and services, the mother is entitled to your service and kindness more than your father.

This fact has been elucidated very clearly by the Holy Prophet (S.A.W.).

Hadrat Abu Hurrayrah (R.A.A.) reports that a man presented himself before the Holy Prophet (S.A.W.) and asked him: "O Prophet of Allah, who is the most deserving of my courteous and kind treatment." The Holy Prophet (S.A.W.) said, "Your mother . "He asked, "Who next ?" The Messenger of Allah (S.A.W.) said: "Your mother," He again asked: "Who next ?" The Holy Prophet (S.A.W.) repeated: "Your mother." The man asked the Holy Prophet (S.A.W.) for the fourth time, "Then who next?" The Holy Prophet (S.A.W.) said "Your father."
(Al-Adab-Al-Mufrad)

The foster-mother also is to be treated and served with love and courtesy. Hadrat Abu Tufail (R.A.A.) narrates the following Hadis:

"I saw the Holy Prophet (S.A.W.) distributing meat at a place called Jaranah. In the meantime a lady came and reached very near the Holy Prophet (S.A.W.). He immediately spread his sheet for her and she sat upon it. I enquired from those present, as to who she was. I was told that she was the foster mother of the Holy Prophet (S.A.W.)." *(Abu Daud)*

Even after their death, the parents should be remembered and repaid their kindness follow this schedule:

(a) Constantly pray for their redemption. The Quran has taught us the following prayer for this purpose:

"Allah! Pardon me and my parents; and (also) forgive all who have accepted the faith, on the Day of Reckoning."

(14 : 41)

(b) Hadrat Abu Hurrayrah (R.A.A.) says that when the position of the dead is exalted after death, he is taken by surprise and asks as to how this could happen. He is told on behalf of Allah that his offsprings (in the world) have been praying for him, and Allah has graced the prayer with acceptance.

Hadrat Abu Hurrayrah (R.A.A.) has also said:

The Holy Prophet (S.A.W.) said: "When a man dies, the period of his activities in the world ends, but there are three things, which benefit him even after his death; these are firstly a continuing Sadaqah or charity, secondly, the knowledge disseminated by him for the benefit of others; and thirdly, the noble offspring whom he had left behind and who continue to pray for his salvation."

(c) The offspring should fulfil the contracts and Undertakings made by the parents and execute their will. The parents, while alive, would have made promises to individuals, entered into covenant (Nazar) with Allah, promised payment of money to some persons. They might be having some debt, which remains to be repaid, or made some will to be executed. All these are to be fulfilled to the best of one's ability.

Hadrat Abdullah Ibn Abbas (R.A.A.) says that Hadrat Sad bin 'Ibadah asked the Holy Prophet (S.A.W.) "O Prophet of Allah (S.A.W.), my mother had made a vow, but she died before fulfilling it; can I do it for her?" The Holy Prophet (S.A.W.) said: "Why not? You should do it for her."

(d) The friends of your father and the female colleagues of your mother should also be well treated. They should be associated and consulted in your matters and their advices be respected. Once the Holy Prophet (S.A.W.) remarked: "The best act of courtesy consists in kindness towards the friends of one's father.

It so happened that once Hadrat Abu Darda (R.A.A.) fell sick and his condition worsened to the extent that there was no hope left for his recovery. Hadrat Yusuf bin 'Abdullah (R.A.A.) undertook a long journey and came to enquire after his health. Hadrat Abu Darda (R.A.A.) felt surprised and asked him as to how he was there. Hadrat Yusuf Ibn Abdullah (R.A.A.) said: "I have come here to see you, as you had very close relations with my father."

Hadrat Abu Dardah (R.A.A.) says that when he went to Medina, Hadrat Abdullah Ibn 'Umar (R.A.A.) visited him and said: "Do you know, O Abu Dardah, why I have come to see you?" Hadrat Abu Dardah expressed his ignorance, whereupon Hadrat Abdullah Ibn Umar said: "I have heard the Holy Prophet (S.A.W.) saying that he who wants his parents to be treated well in the grave, should observe courtesy towards their friends after they are no more." And then he said; "O Brother your father and my father were very good friends and I wish to sustain that friendship and concede their rights." (Ibn Habban)

(e) Kindred relations of the parents should also be treated well and helped by all means. Indifference towards them is indifference towards parents. The Holy Prophet (S.A.W.) has said: "Never be indifferent to your ancestors. Indifference towards parents is like ingratitude to Allah."

Make up for Omission in Treatment of Parents : If by chance you have failed to treat well your parents in their life time, you should not feel disappointed from the mercies of Allah. After their death, pray constantly for them. It is possible Allah will forgive your lapses and accept you as one of the pious persons. Hadrat Anas has reported the following Hadis of the Holy Prophet (S.A.W.).

> *"If a servant of Allah has failed to treat his parents well during their life time, and if either one or both of them has died in this state the son should continuously pray for the salvation of his parents and for their redemption, till Allah writes his name among his good servants."*

DOMESTIC LIFE

The exalted and magnificent civilization and way of life which Islam represents, is only possible when we are able to establish a noble and clean society and for this it is necessary that the family life which is the basic unit of the social order is stable, well-knit and organised. The foundation of family rests on the happy relations between the husband and wife. But this is only possible when the husband and wife themselves are aware of their duties and rights as partners for life; these are reciprocal in nature, which they should discharge with all sincerity, trust and affection. We shall first describe the rights and duties of a wife and later on that of the husband.

The Rights of the Wife **:** A wife has the right to be treated with affection and due consideration. The husband, if necessary, should be ready to make sacrifices for her sake. Allah has decreed:

"And live with them in a proper manner." *(4 : 19)*

The Holy Prophet (S.A.W.) on the occasion of the Hajjatul-wida (the last Hajj) addressing a very large gathering, said:

"Listen to me; O People! Treat your women nicely as they are under your control. You have no authority to maltreat them except when and if they misbehave. If they do so then you ought to separate yourself from them in your bedroom. If you deem it necessary to punish them, then see that they are not severely beaten. And, when they obey you, do not seek excuses thereafter to tease them. Bear in mind! You have certain rights upon your wives and they have certain rights upon you. They owe an obligation that they should not allow people you dislike, to pollute your beds and should not allow persons you do not like to enter your house. And listen it is their right upon you that you should feed and clothe them well." *(Riyaz-us-Salehin)*

That is to say, the wives should be clothed and fed in such a manner as may be appropriate for a unique and intimate conjugal relationship. As far as possible, you should always entertain a good opinion about your wife. She should be treated with consideration, patience, justice, and high-mindedness; even if the wife suffers from lack of manners, domestic skills, and has bad features, you should put up with her patiently. Her virtues should be considered and her weak points ignored. Allah has said:

"And harmony is better." *(4 : 128)*

And the Muslims have been directed:

"......... For, if you dislike her (for some reasons) it may happen you hate a thing wherein Allah has placed much good (for you.). *(4 : 19)*

The Holy Prophet (S.A.W.) has explained this point in this *Hadis*:

"A Muslim should not hate his Muslim wife. If he dislikes some habit of his wife, it is just possible that he may like some other traits in her."'

In fact, every woman is likely to have some shortcomings. If the husband starts disliking her on this account, it would be impossible for a household to have any domestic peace or happiness. The right course is that the husband should display broad-mindedness and tolerance and reposing his trust in Allah, adjust himself with the situation and live with her. It is quite possible that the husband may be rewarded by Allah with some blessings, which his short sight had failed to visualize, e.g., the wife may be possessing excellent qualities of faith and nobility, character and manners, which may prove a blessing for the whole household, or she may give birth to a noble child who may benefit mankind, and be a source of beneficence to the father. Or it may be that the wife serves as a means for the reformation of the husband, and bring him closer to Heaven, or that the husband may be blessed through his wife by Allah with increased prosperity and subsistence. In short, one should not go after the outward shortcomings of the wife, and cause disharmony in his domestic life, but should try to make the same as pleasant as possible. In marital life, adopt an attitude of give and take and forgiveness. The shortcomings, ignorant acts and other faults of the wife should be ignored. The woman is the weaker sex and more emotional, and therefore, she should be dealt with patience, affection, and kindness.

Allah has said : "O who believe! some of your wives and children are your enemies, therefore beware of them. And if you efface and overlook and forgive, then Allah is Forgiving and Merciful" (64 : 14)

The Holy Prophet (S.A.W.) has said:

"Treat the womankind well. She has been created out of the (man's) rib and the uppermost part of the rib is crooked. If you try to straighten, it will break, while, if you leave it as it is, it would remain crooked. Therefore treat the womankind well." (Bukhari-Muslim)

Extend all courtesy and affection to your wife. The Holy Prophet (S.A.W.) has said:

" The most perfect in faith are those Muslims who are the best in their deportment; and the best among you are those who are most conscious of the rights of their wives." (Tirmidhi)

The field where the noble disposition and good nature of an individual can be tested is his home. It is the members of the family who come into most intimate contact with him and it is here that his temperament and deportment are exposed to the full. And It is a fact that it is that Muslim who is perfect in his faith, who would treat the members of his household with love, affection and kindness.

Hadrat Aishah (R.A.A.) narrates that she used to play with dolls and her female companions also joined her. They all used to hide at the approach of the Holy Prophet (S.A.W.), who used to search and gather them up and send them to her to resume their game.

(Bukhari-Muslim)

Once on the occasion of Hajj the camel of Hadrat Safiyah (R.A.A.) sat down, and she was left behind. The Holy Prophet (S.A.W.) saw her crying. He had to stop, and wiped her tears with the corner of his sheet.

Be generous in meeting expenses in connection with the needs and necessities of your life-partners. You should feel happy in having spent your hard-earned money on your family members. Maintenance is the right of the wife and by discharging this responsibility with an open heart, the husband is not only assured of a happy life in this world but he becomes entitled to reward in the Hereafter. The Holy Prophet (S.A.W.) has said, " There is a Dinar which you have spent in the cause of Allah; another is one which you have spent in helping the liberation of a slave; there is another Dinar which you have given as Sadaqah to a beggar; and yet there is a Dinar which you have spent upon your family. The greatest reward is carried by the Dinar which you have spent upon the members of your household."(Muslim)

The wife should be taught the principles of Islam and good manners. She should be inducted into the basic principles of Islamic culture so that she may become a good wife, and affectionate mother, and a pious servant of Allah so that she may be able to lead a successful and happy domestic life. The Quran says:

"O ye who believe! Protect, yourself and your household from the fire of Hell."

The Holy Prophet (S.A.W.) carried on missionary work among his people as well as among his family members. Addressing the wives of the Holy Prophet (S.A.W.), Allah has said:

"And remember the verse of Allah (Quran) and wise talks which are recited in your homes." (33 : 34)

And the Muslims have been commanded through the Holy Prophet (S.A.W.):

"And instruct your household people to offer prayers and be constant therein." (20 : 132)

Holy Prophet (S.A.W.) said :

"When a man wakes his wife and both husband and wife offer two rakats of prayers together, the name of the husband is recorded in the register of those males who remember Allah and that of the wife in the register of females who remember Allah. (Abu Daud)

Hadrat Umar, the second Caliph, prayed at night and in the morning woke his wife asking her to offer prayers, and recited the ayat:

"And direct your family members to offer prayers and be constant therein." (20 : 132)

If there be more than one wife, all the wives are to be treated equally. The Holy Prophet (S.A.W.) was very particular in treating his wives equally. When he proceeded upon journey, he used to draw lots, and the wife winning the toss would accompany him. According to Hadrat Abu Hurrayrah (R.A.A.), the Holy Prophet (S.A.W.) has said:

"If a man having two wives does not treat them equally and justly, he shall have his half body paralysed on the Day of Judgment. *(Tirmidhi)*

By justice and fairplay we mean equal treatment in day-to-day matters and dealings. However, if a man (through natural urge) feels more inclined towards a particular wife, this is beyond the control of human beings and he shall not be made to account for this by Allah.

The Rights of Husband **:** The wife should obey her husband sincerely. The wife should feel pleasure in obeying her husband as this is the command of Allah. The wife who obeys His command pleases Him. The Quran says:

"So good women are obedient (to their husbands)." *(4 : 34)*

The Holy Prophet (S.A.W.) has said:

"No wife should fast without taking permission from her husband." *(Abu Daud)*

Further, highlighting the importance of obedience and devotion to the husband, the Holy Prophet (S.A.W.) has said:

"There are two kinds of persons whose prayers do not rise above their heads that is, their prayers are not accepted; one is the slave who has fled from his master, till he returns; the other is the wife who has disobeyed her husband's command, till she regresses." *(Targhib-o-Tarhib)*

The Wife should Guard her Chastity **:** She should avoid all that might bring a stigma on her chastity. This is the intention of the directives of Allah to the women, and also in order to keep the domestic life happy and successful. If the slightest of suspicion in this connection creeps into the husband's mind, then no amount of service and obedience by the wife would succeed in clearing that doubt. The slightest negligence in this regard helps the Devil to create doubts in the husband's mind. Keeping in view the human weakness in this regard, the wife should be extra cautious, The Holy Prophet (S.A.W.) has said:

The woman who offers prayers five times a day, protects her honour and is obedient to her husband, can enter Paradise from whichever gate she likes."

(Targhib-o-Tarhib)

The wife should not leave the house without prior permission of the husband. Nor should she visit house where her husband would not like her to go, nor allow such persons to enter her house whom her husband does not like.

Hadrat Miaz bin Jabal (R.A.A.) says:

"The Holy Prophet (S.A.W.) has said: 'It is not lawful for a woman, who believes in Allah, to allow a person whom her husband does not like, to enter the house of her husband, nor that she should go out of the house when her husband does not want her to go out, and also a woman should not obey anyone else in her husband's affairs." (Targhib-o-Tarhib)

The wife should only obey her husband and should not follow suggestions of others in contravention of the husband's wishes.

The Wife should try to please the Husband : This is the secret of a successful married life as well as the means of pleasing Allah and attaining Paradise.

The Holy Prophet (S.A.W.) says: "A woman who died while her husband was pleased and happy with her, shall enter Paradise." (Bukhari—Muslim)

There is another Hadis stating that, "If the husband sends for the wife for marital functions and she refuses, causing resentment to the former, the angels send curses upon such a wife whole night." (Muslim -Bukhari)

Love your husband and appreciate his companionship. The love between the couple is the mainstay of life; it is the flower of life, and the beacon-light for a successful living. Be grateful to Allah for a successful living. Be grateful to Allah for this great favour, and appreciate this bounty from the core of your heart. The Holy Prophet (S.A.W.) once said: "There is nothing better than marriage between two persons who love each other." Hadrat Safiyah (R.A.A.) had great love for the Holy Prophet (S.A.W.). When he fell ill, she spoke with great pathos: "I wish 1 would have been sick in your place." The other wives of the Holy Prophet (S.A.W.) looked with surprise at her, but the holy Prophet (S.A.W.) said: "This is not a showing off; what she speaks is true." The wife should be grateful to the husband: it is the husband who is her greatest benefactor, who plods the whole day to please the wife and satisfy her wants, and then he feels pleasure in having provided her comfort. Hadrat Asma narrates:

> *"Once the Holy Prophet (S.A.W.) passed by me, I was then with my neighbour girl-friends. He greeted us and said: Be not ungrateful to your benefactors. You remained unmarried at your parents house till Allah granted you a husband; then He favours you with a baby. And yet, despite all these kindnesses, the wife if she even happens to fly at husband in a fit of temper, says: "I have never seen any kind act from you."* *(Al-Adab-al-Mufrad)*

The Holy Prophet (S.A.W.) cautioning an ungrateful wife has said:

> *"On the Day of Judgment, Allah shall not look upon the woman who has been ungrateful to her husband; although a wife cannot do without the husband."*
>
> *(Nasai)*

A wife should feel happy by serving her husband, even at the cost of her own comfort. She should try to win his heart and good-will through service. Hadrat Aishah (R.A.A.) used to wash the Holy Prophet's clothes, oil and comb his hair, and apply perfume on his persona. This was the routine of the wives of the companions as well.

> *The Holy Prophet (S.A.W.) has once said : "A man is not permitted to prostrate himself before another. Were it permitted, the wife would have been commanded to prostrate herself before her husband. The husband has great rights over the wife, so great that even if the whole body of the husband is full of wounds and the wife licks them, the husband's rights will not be repaid.*
>
> *(Musnad Ahmad)*

The wife should look after the husband's house and household effects. After your marriage his home should be regarded as yours. Spend your husband's money judiciously and wisely, in order to improve the condition of his house. The improvement and prosperity of the husband should be regarded as your own improvement and prosperity. The Holy Prophet (S.A.W.) praising the womenfolk of the Quraish, said "How nice are the Quraish women! they are very affectionate to the children and guard the household of their husbands so well." (Bukhari)

The Holy Prophet (S.A.W.) describing the virtues of a good wife, has said:

"The most useful and full of blessing bounty for the faithful, after the fear of Allah, is a good wife who would carry out his orders cheerfully, and when the husband looks at her, she pleases him. When the husband swears by the trust he has placed in her, she would fulfil it. When he goes out on a journey, she would guard her chastity and look after his property. (Ibn Majah)

Everything in the House should be Arranged Properly **:** Household effects should be arranged decently and should be used in a decent manner. A neat and tidy house well-arranged rooms, good taste in domestic chores; a well-mannered and well-dressed pious wife's smiling looks, is not only rich in love and affection, prosperity and welfare for others, but is also a means to achieve salvation and Allah's pleasure for herself.

Once the wife of Hadrat Uthman bin Mazun (R.A.A.) met Hadrat Aishah (R.A.A.), who found the former clothed in very rough clothes and without any decoration or make up. Hadrat Aishah felt surprised, and asked: "Has Uthman gone out on a journey?" This note of surprise shows how pleasing is the act of personal make up by the wife for the sake of her husband.

A female companion once presented herself before the Holy Prophet (S.A.W.). She had gold bracelets on her hands. The Holy Prophet (S.A.W.) advised her not to wear them, whereupon she said: "O Prophet of Allah, if the wife does not properly adorn herself, she would lose her importance in the eyes of the husband." (Nasai)

CARING FOR CHILDREN

Children ought to be regarded as a blessing from Allah and their birth should be celebrated with zest and exchange of greetings. The arrival of the baby should be welcome with prayers for his or her welfare. Allah may he thanked for having blessed you with an opportunity to bring up one of His creatures and that you will be able to leave behind a successor in this world and the Hereafter.

Pray for Pious Children : If you have no issues, pray for the grant of pious children just as Prophet Zachariah (Zakriya) prayed for a noble offspring. The Prophet prayed:

"Allah give me from your bounty a pious issue; undoubtedly you are the Hearer of the supplication."
(2 : 38)

Do not feel unhappy on the birth of child on account of straitened circumstances, ill health or other reasons, and do not consider the birth of a child as a sign of misfortune for you. Abortion should never be practised. The destruction of a child either before or after birth is rank heartlessness, a heinous crime and extreme cowardice. It brings disaster both in this world and in the Hereafter. Allah has said:

"They are losers who have slain their children foolishly and in ignorance" ***(6 : 140)***

And again we are told that:

"Slay not your children, fearing a fall to poverty. We shall provide for them and indeed it is We who provide for you. Lo! the slaying of the offspring is a great sin".
(17 : 131)

During the pre-Islamic (Jahilliya period) the Arabs disliked the birth of a female baby which was considered very humiliating and, therefore, the pagan Arabs used to bury girl babies alive or hurl them from the top of a mountain. Once a companion asked the Holy Prophet (S.A.W.) "O Prophet of Allah, which sin is the greatest? The Holy Prophet (S.A.W.) said: "Associating a partner with Allah." The Companion asked, "And the next?" The Holy Prophet (S.A.W.) replied: "Insubordination of parents." He asked once again. The Holy Prophet (S.A.W.) replied: "Killing the offspring through the fear that it shall share your food".

Prayers at the Time of Childbirth : The *ayatul-kursi* (verse of the Throne, chapter 2 : 255) and the two ayats from Surah Al-Aaraf 17 : 54,55) are to be recited near the woman in labour pain. Surah. The translation of Ayat ul Kursi is as follows :

> *"Allah: There is no Allah save Him, the Alive, the Eternal. Neither slumber nor sleep ovetaketh Him, Unto Him belongeth whatsoever is in the heavens and whatsoever is in the earth. Who is he that intercedeth with Him save by His leave? He knoweth that which is in front of them and that which is behind them, while they encompass nothing of His knowledge save that what He will. His throne includeth the heavens and the earth and He is never weary of preserving them. He is the Sublime, the Tremendous".*

And the two translations of two ayats from Surah Al-araf are as follows:

> *"Lo! Your Lord (Sustainer) is Allah Who crated the heavens and the earth in six Days, then mounted His throne of Power. He covers the day with the night, which is in haste to follow it; and has created the sun, and the moon and the stars and made them subservient to His command. Listen: Creation is His job and command is His right. Blessed is the Allah, the Master and Sustainer of the worlds. Beseech your Sustaniner humbly and meekly and secretly. Indeed He does not like aggressors". (7 : 54,55)*

> *The newly-born baby should first of all be given a wash and the Adaan should be recited in the right ear and the Iqamat in the left ear. When Hadrat Hussain, the maternal grandson of the Holy Prophet (S.A.W.) was born, the Holy Prophet (S.A.W.) recited the Azan and Iqamat in his ears. (Tibrani)*

The Holy Prophet (S.A.W.) also said that the child in whose ears these two prayers are recited would be safe from the incidence of epilepsy. Tahnik means chewing the date and rubbing its paste on the skull of the baby. After the Azan and Iqamat, a pious man or woman should be asked to chew a date and the paste of the fruit applied to the skull of the newly born child and that pious person should pray for the welfare of the baby. Hadrat Asma narrates that, when Hadrat Abdullah bin Zubayr was born, I placed him in the lap of the Holy Prophet (S.A.W.). He sent for a date, chewed it and applied the saliva to the mouth of Hadrat Abdullah bin Zubayr, and its paste on the skull and prayed for the well-being of the baby. According to Hadrat Aishah, the Holy Prophet (S.A.W.) performed Tahnik upon the children brought to him and prayed for them.

Name the child with a decent and appropriate name, like that of the Prophets, or Allah's names with the prefix of Abd e.g., Abdur Rahman, Abdullah, Abdur-Rahim, Yusuf, Ibrahim. The Holy Prophet (S.A.W.) has said: "On the Day of reckoning, you will be called by your names; therefore have better names.(Abu Daud)

The Holy Prophet (S.A.W.) has further said, "Of your names, Allah likes Abdullah and Abdur Rahman the most, and that the children should be named after the names of the Prophets". The Holy Prophet (S.A.W.) said that the child should be named after him, and not after his patronyms or filionyms.

Name wrongly given should be changed into a good or auspicious one. The Holy Prophet (S.A.W.) used to change bad names. One of the daughters of Hadrat Umar (R.A.A.) was named Aishah. Her name was changed to Jamilah by the Holy Prophet (S.A.W.)

(Muslim)

Hadrat Zainab was the daughter of Hadrat Abu Salma (R.A.A.). Her name was Barrah which means chaste. When the Holy Prophet (S.A.W.) heard this name, remarked: "You parade your piety yourself". When asked about the other name, he suggested the name, Zainab.

(Abu Daud)

Aqiqah or the ceremony of shaving off the hair of the infant, should be celebrated preferably on the seventh day after the birth. Two goats are to be sacrificed for the male and one goat for the female. But even one goat could be sacrificed for the boy. Gold or silver equivalent to the weight of the hair should be distributed as alms. The Holy Prophet's *Sunnah* is that the *Aqiqah* should be performed on the seventh day. The name of the child is to be chosen on this very day, and the head shaved. The prayer to be offered at the time of the Aqiqah is as follows:

> *"O Allah: This is the Aqiqah of (Name of the child to be recited). Accept this as Thou hast accepted on behalf of Thine loved one, Muhammad (S.A.W.), and Thine friend, Ibrahim (A.S.). This offering of blood is the ransom for the blood of the child; flesh is the ransom for the flesh of the child; the hair are the ransom for the hair of the child; and these bones are the ransom for the bones of the child. O Allah, accept".*

Circumcision of the Male Child : Circumcision of the boys may preferably be performed on the seventh day. If on account of some circumstances this may not be possible, it should be done before the boy attains the age of seven years. The circumcision is an Islamic ritual.

Kalima the First Utterance : When the child begins to speak, he should be taught to speak the Kalima Tayyabah, that is:

La-Ilaha Il-lal-lahu Muhammad-ur-Rasool-ullah : (There is no god but Allah. Muhammad is Messenger of Allah). The Holy Prophet (S.A.W.) has said:

> *When your baby begins to talk, teach it'* La-Ilaha-il-lal-lah. *Then do not worry about its consummation. When the milk teeth of the child have been shed off, command your child to offer prayers.* *(Ibn e Sani)*

The Hadis has it that, when any member of the Holy Prophet's family started talking, he used to teach it the second ayat from Surah Furqan (Chapter 25 : 21, wherein the basic Islamic principle of Oneness of Allah has been succinctly narrated. It is as follows:

> *"He unto Whom belongs the sovereignty of the heavens and the earth; He has chosen no son nor has He any partner in the sovereignty. He created everyone and has meted out for it a role."*

Suckling the Child : The child has a right to be fed on mother's milk. It is this bounty of the mother which the Quran reminds the child and exhorts him to treat his mother with exceptional love and kindness, in return for this service. It is the duty of the mother to inculcate into the child with each drop of her milk, the concept of oneness of Allah, love for the Holy Prophet (S.A.W.), and devotion for Islam. She should try that this love for Islam should seep into the heart and soul of the child. Responsibility for bringing up the child ought not to be thrown upon the nurse to lighten your burden.

The parents should bring up the child themselves and feel spiritual pleasure and happiness in having performed this pleasant religious duty. Do not frighten the children. Once thrown into a fright it is likely that this fear may persist in them even after their attaining adulthood. Such children are usually rendered incapable of achieving a big success in life. Note that children should not be chided on trifles. In the first place, too much rebuking loses its effectiveness. In the second, it makes the child feel he is not loved. Therefore, instead of chiding and reproving the child on trivial matters and showing annoyance at their faults, one should try to be affectionate and tactful in handling them. They should be allowed to follow their aptitudes, but on one thing you should be firm that, at no cost, an act, contrary to the Shariat, would be tolerated.

The children should always be treated with sympathy and consideration, and their requirements should be satisfied as far as possible, This will not only make them happy, but would also develop sentiments of obedience and service in them. Once Hadrat Muawiyyah asked Hadrat Ahnaf bin Qais as to how the offsprings should be treated. This companion of the Holy Prophet (S.A.W.) replied:

> *"Leader of the Faithfuls: Our offsprings are the fruits of our desires. They are props for our backs. We ate for them like the earth which is soft and harmless; our existence for them is like the sky which provides them with shade (protection); and through them we are able to perform marvelous tasks. Thus if they ask you for something, give them generously and if they feel sad try to enliven then. As a result of this they would develop love for you and appreciate your paternal affection. Never become an unbearable burden upon them lest they should become disgusted with you and even desire your demise and dislike your association"*

Don't be always a dour-faced, stern-looking, hard task master. Be affectionate towards the children, run your hand lovingly on their heads; take them in your lap and fondle with them. An irate and grim attitude does not generate sincere love in the hearts of the children for their parents and retards their natural growth and development and destroys their self-confidence.

Once Hadrat Aqra bin Habith (R.A.A.) presented himself before the Holy Prophet (S.A.W.) who was kissing Hadrat Hasan. Hadrat Aqra was astonished to see this and said: "O Prophet of Allah: you also cuddle children. I have ten children, yet I have never shown any affection to them". The Holy Prophet (S.A.W.) looked at Hadrat Aqra, and said: "What can I do if Allah has deprived you of love and compassion."

Hadrat 'Amair (R.A.A.) held an important appointment during the caliphate of Hadrat Umar (R.A.A.). He once went to see the Caliph. He saw that Hadrat Umar was lying and some children were riding on his chest and playing with him. Hadrat ' Aamir was somewhat displeased to see this.

Hadrat Umar guessed this from the wrinkles on his forehead and asked Hadrat 'Aamir as to how he treated his own children. 'Aamir explaining his views said: "Leader of the Faithfuls: Whenever I enter the house, the inmates get stunned and every body is put to silence". Hadrat Umar spoke with great regret: "Aamir! how unfortunate it is that, even being a Muslim, you do not know that you should treat your kith and kin with affection and kindness." You should try your level best to impart your children with a decent and befitting education and a dedicated discipline. No sacrifice should be spared in this regard. This is your religious duty and great favour to the children is also good for you. *The Holy Quran says :*

> *"O ye who believe: Protect yourselves and your family members from Hell's fire."* *(66 : 6)*

Safety from the fire of Hell lies only in knowing the basic principles of Islam, and in living according to the commandments of Allah and obedience to the Holy Prophet's Hadis.

> *And the Holy Prophet (S.A.W.) has said that the best legacy a father can leave for his offspring comprises proper training and good education.* *(Mishkat)*

In reality a virtuous and well behaved progeny can only advance your cultural traditions and religious principles after you and it is for this reason, the Muslim aspire and pray for well mannered and virtuous children.

Inducing Children to Prayers: When the children attain the age of 7 years, they should be induced to prayers and taught how to pray. For this purpose they should be taken to the mosque with a view to creating a liking for prayers. And when they attain the age of ten, they should be forced to pray, and even punished, if they neglect to do so. It should be impressed upon them that this negligence will not be tolerated.

Segregation of Children: When the children have attained the age of ten, they should be made to sleep on separate cots. The Holy Prophet (S.A.W.) has commanded:

> *"Ask your children to offer prayers by the time they are seven years of age. Punish them for (missing) prayers when they are ten and, allot separate beds to them at this age."*

Keep the children always neat and clean. Pay special attention towards their personal hygiene, cleanliness, bathing, ablution etc. They should wear neat and clean clothes, but avoid pomposity and ostentation. The dress for girls should be specially plain and unornamented. Expensive and gaudy clothes are likely to spoil the habits of children. Never express disappointment on reforming and correcting your children on their face. On the contrary, applaud even minor good deeds done by them and be generous in appreciation of any virtue in them. They should he encouraged so as to build up self confidence and courage in them, so that they may achieve a high place in their life.

You must tell your children stories of Prophets and pious persons and heroic deeds and sacrifices of the venerable companions of the Holy Prophet (S.A.W.). This is essential for their education and training, character building and inculcating a love for Islam. This has to be done at all costs. Occasionally recite Holy Quran rhythmically before them; and relate incidents, anecdotes teachings and tradition from the life of the Holy Prophet (S.A.W.). This would instil into them an intense love for the Holy Prophet (S.A.W.).

Cultivate the Habit of giving and Respecting other's Rights : On some occasions distribute some food, money, etc., to the poor through the children so that they may cultivate the habit of charity and sympathy for the poor. Similarly, occasions should also be furnished to the children for distributing eatables among themselves, so that they get accustomed to the distribution of things equitably among themselves and do justice to each other by recognising each other's rights and develop mutual cooperation. Do not concede each and every demand of the children. Tactfully try to dissuade them from this practice. If necessary use force in this behalf and see that they do not become obstinate and self willed by unnecessary cajoling.

How to Talk with Children : Do not shout at your children, nor talk to them harshly. Likewise, tell them not to talk in this way even among themselves. They should be told to talk in a sweet and mild tone. Train your children to do their work themselves. They should not look to the servants to do their small chores. Dependence upon servants is likely to make them lazy and even to take up most difficult jobs.

Do not side your Children Unjustly : If there is fighting amongst children, you should not side your children unfairly. It should be remembered that every father loves his children. You should watch whether your children are to be blamed; if so, then taking into consideration future mishaps, you should try to adopt preventive measures by finding out if it is the misbehaviour of your children which has caused the trouble and take appropriate measures to correct them. You should treat all your children equally and avoid injustice and unfair attitude in this connection. However, if due to some natural causes you feel more inclined towards a particular child it may be an exception. But in matters of treatment, bestowal of gifts and social matters, strict equality and fair play should be maintained. Never be partial towards a particular child, as which may be noted and felt by other children. This may create inferiority complex, hatred, frustration, and at last, it may develop rebellious attitude in your children. And such sentiments constitute a great hindrance in the growth of the natural capabilities of the children and act as a deadly poison to the evolution of spiritual and ethical progress.

Once Hadrat Bashir, the father of Hadrat Noman, presented himself alongwith Hadrat Noman, before the Holy Prophet (S.A.W.) and said: "O Prophet of Allah: I had a slave whom I have gifted to this son." The Holy Prophet (S.A.W.) asked: "Have you gifted each of your son a slave?" "No, O Messenger of Allah," said Hadrat Bashir. The Holy Prophet (S.A.W.) said, "Then take back the slave. Fear Allah, and treat all your sons equitably." Hadrat Bashir on his return home, took back the slave. According to another version, the Holy Prophet (S.A.W.) said: "Do not make me a witness to a sin: I shall not be witness to an injustice." Still another version has it that the Holy Prophet (S.A.W.) said: "Do you desire that all your children should treat you well?" The Holy Prophet (S.A.W.) then said: "Then do not do such a thing." (Bukhari—Muslim)

Your life is a permanent and silent teacher for your children. They constantly learn and adopt from your life. Never speak a lie before them even as a joke or as a matter of expediency.

Hadrat Abdullah bin 'Aamir narrates that one day the Holy Prophet (S.A.W.) had graced the house of his father in his presence. His mother called Aamir and said: "Come here; I shall give you something." The Holy Prophet (S.A.W.) saw her calling her son, and asked her what she would give to him. His mother said: "I wish to give him dates." The Holy Prophet (S.A.W.) said: "Had you pretended to give him anything, it would have gone as a lie in your account." (Abu Daud)

Do not be Downcast on the Birth of a Daughter : The birth of a daughter should be celebrated in the same way as that of a son. Whether it is a son or a daughter, both are gifts from Allah, and He alone knows what is good for you. To frown at the birth of a daughter is not befitting a Muslim. This is sheer ingratitude and disrespect to Allah.

The Hadis *has it that "When a daughter is born in a house, Allah sends angels to that house who say: O Ye who reside in the house ! peace be upon you. Having said this, they take the daughter under the protection of their wings, and, moving their hands softly upon her head, say: Here is a frail life, born to another frail being. Allah shall extend His succour to him who will look after her and bring her up.* *(Tibrani)*

Girls should be brought up with immense pleasure, spiritual satisfaction and sense of religious devotion pervading our minds and expecting entry into Paradise. The Holy Prophet (S.A.W.) has said; "If a person brings up three daughters or three sisters, educates and teaches good manners to them, and treats them with compassion till they become independent, Allah will certainly admit him to the Paradise." One companion asked: "And if there are only two." The Holy Prophet (S.A.W.) said: "They too will carry the same recompense." Hadrat Ibn Abbas says that the Holy Prophet (S.A.W.) would have given the same Basharat (happy news) for the upbringing of even one girl." *(Mishkat)*

Hadrat Aishah (R.A.A.) says that once a woman called upon her with her two daughters and asked for something. Hadrat Aishah had only one date with her, which she gave to the woman. She divided the date into two pieces and gave one each to her daughters, without eating herself anything. Then she stood up and left. When the Holy Prophet (S.A.W.) came Hadrat Aishah narrated the incident to him (S.A.W.). He said: "Anybody who is tested through the birth of daughters and negotiates that test successfully by treating them well, these daughters will serve as a shield against the fire of Hell." *(Mishkat)*

The daughter is not to be regarded as inferior to the son, nor he should be given preference over her in any matter. Both should be loved and treated equally. The Holy Prophet (S.A.W.) has said: "If a man has a daughter born to him, he does not bury her alive, as the pagans did and he has neither treated her with contempt nor preferred his son over her, he would be granted entry into Paradise by Allah." *(Abu Daud)*

Be very careful and pleased to give the fixed share of the girl from your property. This is the share which has been prescribed by Allah, and no one has the right to increase or decrease her share. It is not befitting a devout Muslim to deprive a girl of her share on some excuse, or to give her something less than her due, according to his own calculations, and feel satisfied. This amounts to misappropriation and an insult to the religion of Allah.

Pray for Your Children : Parents should follow these practical guidelines and pray for their children with the depth of their heart. The most Merciful and Benevolent Allah will certainly grant these heart touching supplication of the parents.

INSTITUTION OF MARRIAGE

Marriage is an important social institution which perfects the human personality. Every young man able to support a wife and family should marry, for marriage preserves one from immorality. Living in celibacy is an act abhorred in Islam. Moreover, there is nothing like marriage for increasing the love of two people. Those who cannot marry for financial reasons are advised to fast from time to time, for fasting is a means of suppressing sexual desire. If a Muslim has no desire for marriage, or does not need it, even though he is financially able to support a family, then he should not marry.

SELECTION OF LIFE PARTNER

- A man cannot marry a woman who is mahram according to the Islamic law. Seven classes of women are prohibited by reason of consanguinity and seven by reason of relationship by marriage.
- The woman who most adheres to Islam is the ideal wife. A woman may be married for her property, her rank, or her beauty. These foundations of marriage, however, never last and can unbalance the relationship between the couple. Therefore, there must be common ground to enable understanding and to overcome misunderstanding, and that ground is adherence to Islam.
- A decorous shyness and sensitivity are other attributes required in a wife.
- Satisfaction with moderate material demands, with life at a moderate and not lavish standard, is a good quality in a wife. Waste of money is an indication of an irresponsible wife.

- Marriage with a non-relative enlarges the circle of relatives by adding new ones.
- One should avoid marriage with an infertile woman, and marry a woman who is fertile, for children are an important element in a successful marriage.
- There is nothing at all wrong in marrying a divorced woman provided that she does not wish to return to her first husband.
- Marriage to a virgin is preferred to marriage to a woman who has been married previously, though there is nothing wrong in marrying the latter.
- A man should not ask a woman to marry him unless he has enough knowledge about the degree of her adherence to Islam, her background represented by the life of her parents, and other necessary information.
- It is necessary for a man to see the woman he intends to marry, and for a woman to see the man she intends to marry.
- Meeting the woman a man plans to marry is allowed only in the presence of a mahram, with whom marriage is forbidden.
- The parts of the woman's body allowed to be seen by the man are her face and hands. The face can give an idea of her beauty and the hands can give some idea of the size of her figure.
- The Woman's Right and Responsibility in Choosing a Husband:

A woman should exercise her right to approve or disapprove of marriage to a particular man, but should be farsighted and wise in making such a decision. Wealth, rank, good position and job, or any other material privilege, do not alone add up to proper attributes for a future husband.

Engagement Ceremony

- Marriage and having a family are responsibilities which must be taken seriously.
- Asking for a woman's hand in marriage while she is in her 'iddah' is un-Islamic conduct.

- Asking for a woman's hand in marriage when another man has done so already is impolite, and must be avoided. One is allowed to do so only if the other has relinquished her.
- The woman's guardian has no right at all to make the marriage decision. The only one who has the full right to accept marriage is the woman herself, free from any kind of pressure.
- The woman, therefore, should be consulted in matters concerning herself. If she is an orphan or a virgin and says nothing, out of modesty, that indicates her consent, but if she is divorced or widowed then silence is not considered an answer. In either case, if the woman refuses, the authority of the guardian cannot be exercised against her will.
- It is not appropriate to ask a woman directly for her hand; this should be done through the guardian.

CONTRACT OF MARRIAGE

- The best and most worthy conditions ever fulfilled are those included in the marriage contract.
- The marriage contract cannot be written without the presence of the woman's guardian and two Muslim witnesses.
- It is necessary that the couple intend to have a lasting marriage and not a temporary one, which is forbidden in Islam.
- The ideal and most blessed marriage is that which involves the least burden upon the bridegroom.
- The dowry is an important element in marriage. The man should have something to give his bride as a dowry, whatever its value may be. However, he should not be extravagant and go beyond his means in fixing the amount of dowry.
- Going to the extreme in giving a woman her dowry is bad behaviour which could lead to a woman attaching too much importance to the size of the dowry.
- It is prohibited for a man to give his daughter or sister in marriage on the condition that the other man gives

his daughter or sister to him in marriage, without any dowry being paid by either. In other words, every marriage contract must be independent of every other marriage contract.

- The wife's guardian must be male and a Muslim. A woman may not give a woman in marriage, nor can she give herself in marriage without a guardian.
- The Muslim judge or imam is the guardian of a woman who has no guardian at all, or has a guardian who is not a Muslim, i.e. he may have been recognized by non-Islamic jurisprudence, but not by Islamic jurisprudence.
- Agreement by both the man and the woman is an essential condition of Islamic marriage.

Wedding Party

- It is not an Islamic tradition to marry secretly without celebrating the marriage. Making the marriage publicly known is recommended in Islam.
- Amusements are allowed at the wedding occasion. Although normally forbidden in Islam, singing is allowed on the occasion of marriage. It would be correct to send someone along with the bride to sing, when she is being escorted to her husband. But the content of the songs must not be obscene nor the singing disturb the neighbours.
- Asking the bridegroom for unnecessary expenses at the wedding party might cause financial difficulty for the new couple and is considered as non-Islamic behaviour.
- Those participating in hajj (pilgrimage) or 'Umrah' are not allowed to marry or to arrange marriages for others.

Conjugal Relations

- The honeymoon does not exist in Islam and is therefore an alien tradition.
- It is recommended that friends and relatives refrain from frequent visits to the couple during the first few days of marriage.
- Subtlety, gentleness and kindness are the most essential elements in the love-making process.

- To have a pleasant odour and clean bodies at the time of love-making is necessary for both husband and wife.
- The husband should approach his wife in a gentle manner and so avoid creating any barriers between the two.
- The husband should place his hand on his wife's forehead and ask God's blessing on her by saying: 'O God, I ask You for the good in her and in the disposition You have given her, and I seek refuge in You from the evil in her and in the disposition You have given her.'
- It is recommended that husband and wife pray two rakats together before making love.
- Making love in any position is permitted provided that intercourse is done through the vagina; the anus must be avoided.
- If the husband has intercourse with his wife and wishes to repeat it, he would do well to perform 'wudu' between the two acts.
- To sleep after love-making, without bathing, is allowed, though it is better to perform 'wudu' or bathe.
- Having intercourse with a wife while she is menstruating is forbidden. If such a violation is committed, then it is required to give half a golden dinar in alms. A husband can, however, do everything with his menstruating wife except have sexual intercourse.
- Love-making can be resumed only when a wife's monthly period comes to its end and she has thoroughly cleaned and perfumed herself or taken a bath.

Advice for Men

- A wife has the right to have sexual intercourse with her husband from time to time, so a husband should not neglect this duty toward her.
- For a husband to be rude and rough toward his wife during the day hours does not create an atmosphere for love making in the evening or at night; in this case he should avoid love-making.

- The husband should avoid taking medicines or preparations which might weaken or artificially incite his sexual desire.
- Too much love-making can sometimes be harmful. Moderation is recommended.
- A man should keep his body clean and pleasant smelling.

Advice for Women

- A woman should never refuse her husband's request to go to bed, whether this request is expressed directly or indirectly, unless she is either fasting in Ramadan, menstruating, in child-bed or physically unfit.
- If a wife intends to fast voluntarily, then it is her duty to get permission from her husband to do so. If he refuses permission, she may not fast. The reason for this is that her husband may want to make love.
- For a wife to leave the initiative in playing and flattering to her husband, and take a negative attitude toward the act of love can result in disappointing her husband and have serious repercussions for the marriage.
- A wife should keep herself tidy, clean, perfumed and as beautiful as she can before her husband at home.

Wedding Feast : On the day following the marriage day, the husband should visit his relatives who visited him previously, thank them, ask God's blessings for them, and invite them to a wedding feast, known as walimah.

- Holding a wedding feast, even if only with simple refreshments, is an important Islamic tradition. Rejection of the invitation is not allowed, unless the feast is of an un-Islamic nature. Those invited should accept and attend.
- It is sunnah to have a wedding feast after and not before consummation of the marriage. It may be held within the three days following that event.
- Pious and good Muslims irrespective of being rich or poor should be invited to the wedding feast. In fact, the worst wedding feast is that to which the rich are invited and the poor not.

- The wedding feast may include one sheep or more if possible. It can also be celebrated by serving other things such as sweets and simple refreshments.
- Invited guests and relatives who are financially able, may contribute money or food to help alleviate the cost of the feast for the husband.
- Guests and relatives must be invited officially and by name.
- The bride is allowed to serve the guests, as long as this is unlikely to arouse men's interest.
- Since the wedding feast is an occasion for asking God's blessing, un-Islamic elements, such as mixing of the sexes, serving alcoholic beverages, etc. are forbidden.

Polygamy

- It is required in Islam that when a man who already has one wife marries a virgin he should stay with her for seven nights, and then divide the time equally between her and his first wife, but if he marries a woman who has been previously married, he should stay with her three nights and then divide his time between his wives.
- Treating and visiting wives equally must be strictly adhered to under all circumstances.
- If the husband becomes ill, then the question of which of his wives he will stay with is to be decided by them.
- Making love to his wives equally is not required. What is required of the husband is to divide the time between his wives and stay a night with each of them.
- Whenever the husband intends to travel, he must draw lots to decide which wife will accompany him.
- The same procedure must be followed if the husband intends to perform pilgrimage or 'Umrah'.
- The husband may sleep with a wife whose day has not yet come if she has been given the day by the wife whose turn it was.
- If a man cannot establish equality and justice among his wives, in those matters over which he has full control

(i.e. excluding impulses and instincts of the heart), then he should not marry more than one wife.

CONDUCT WITHIN THE FAMILY

In Islam, the family is recognized and dignified as the basis of society. Great value is thus attached to keeping family relationships healthy and harmonious: the rules of conduct governing these relationships are of the highest importance.

Husband-Wife Relationship

- In the view of Islam, the best man is he who is best and kindest to his wife. Acting kindly towards one's wife is an Islamic conduct.
- A man's work life should not be pursued with such all-consuming single mindedness that he runs the risk of destroying his marriage. Regardless of how much he must work to provide for his family, the wife nevertheless has a right to part of her husband's time. This may be spent in entertainments, enjoying each other's company, playing sports or any other pastime permitted by Islam.
- It is part of a husband's kindness toward his wife to fulfil her needs, as long as they do not contradict Islam. In fact, the best way to spend money, in the view of Islam, is to support one's family.
- Though the house is better than the mosque for women to pray in, a wife should not be prevented from attending the mosque when she wishes to do so.
- To talk to others about private affairs, namely sexual matters, is something completely forbidden in Islam.
- A husband's jealousy of his wife is of two kinds: baseless suspicion or jealousy without reason, which is to be avoided, and jealousy where there is a good reason, which is recommended.
- A husband should not hate his wife, for if he dislikes one of her characteristics, he may be pleased with another. It is, incidentally, forbidden in Islam to try to change those characteristics of a wife which a husband does not like, as long as these characteristics do not contradict Islam. A wife has her own personality,

different from a husband's, and he has no right to try to destroy it and make it conform to his own. The husband should note that just as certain elements of his wife's character may be displeasing to him, likewise certain aspects of his own may be displeasing to her.

- A husband should never revile his wife or her relatives.
- The husband-wife relationship is of a special nature. It cannot be fruitful unless the couple try to overcome artificial barriers caused by shyness and social inhibitions.
- The right given to the husband to lead the family should not result in the misuse and abuse of his authority. Therefore, he should not ask his wife for things that are beyond her capacity or give her too many orders.
- For a husband to honour and respect his wife's close relatives will result in strengthening the relationship with his wife.
- To honour, respect and be hospitable to his wife's friends and relations is in fact a mark of respect for her.
- The most necessary conditions to be fulfilled in the marriage are those contained in the marriage contract, so after marriage care must be taken not to neglect or forget them; providing that they are in accordance with Islamic law.
- To dwell on and count a wife's mistakes, to disapprove of her deeds, and to blame her frequently will endanger a marriage. Husbands are advised to ignore their wife's mistakes in many cases.
- A husband's and father's indifference to his wife or children violating the orders of Islam is a grave mistake that a Muslim should not dare to make.
- For a husband to blame his wife or disapprove of her acts in the presence of others, such as their children, relatives, etc., is rude conduct.
- A husband is not allowed to ask his wife to work to earn money. To support her is the responsibility of the husband alone.

- On returning home, a husband should not enter the house without first telling his family of his arrival by ringing the bell or knocking on the door. He should signal his arrival by mentioning God's name in praise, greet them, pray two rakats and then ask them how they are.
- A husband should try to keep the odour of his mouth pleasant, so that his wife may not be offended or displeased.
- A husband's relationship with his wife should be characterized by a balance between resoluteness without harshness and flexibility without weakness.

Correct Conduct of a Muslim Wife

- To be a good wife is so important that from the viewpoint of Islam, a good wife is considered to be the best thing in the world.
- The role of the wife in the marriage is extremely important, indeed it is the decisive factor.
- Wives must do their best to keep their husbands pleased with them.
- The ideal wife combines three merits: she pleases her husband when he sees her, by taking care to appear beautiful before him; she obeys him when he gives a command; she does not go against his wishes regarding her person or property by doing anything of which he disapproves.
- To refuse to go with her husband when he calls her to bed is a grave mistake that a wife must avoid.
- When a wife intends to fast voluntarily, she may do so only with her husband's permission. If she does not receive his permission, then he has the right to make her break her fast when she is observing it. The reason for this is that he might wish to have sex with her, which he cannot do if she is fasting with his permission.
- It is a wife's duty not to allow anyone, that her husband does not want, to enter the house without his permission.

- A wife may not give anything away of her husband's property without his permission.
- A wife should avoid asking a husband for extra money, or for that which he does not possess and cannot provide, and she should show gratitude for whatever is given.
- A wife should acknowledge any assistance given in the house by her husband.
- A good wife is one who is true to her husband's word if he adjures her to do something.
- On a husband's return home, a wife should receive him kindly and meet him with a good and beautiful appearance.
- A wife should try not to neglect her husband's needs or ignore his demands. The more a wife takes care of her husband, the more she will be loved. Most husbands, in fact, consider their wives' care for them as an expression of their love.
- A wife should be careful not to offer to her husband, on his coming home, the family problems, or to complain to him about the children, etc. Instead, she should try to create the peaceful atmosphere that her husband needs after a long and tiring day.
- A wife should discuss family problems with her husband at appropriate times.
- For a wife to hold her husband's close relatives in respect and treat them kindly is, in fact, a mark of respect and honour for the husband.
- Leaving the house excessively is a bad habit for a woman. She should also not leave the house if her husband objects to her doing so.
- A wife must not converse with strange men against her husband's objections.
- A wife should be attentive to her husband when he speaks.
- A wife does not have the right to lend anything of her husband's property against his wishes. However, she can lend from her own property.

- Asking a husband for a divorce without a strong reason is forbidden.
- If a husband's friends inquire about him, a wife should answer them but without indulging in lengthy conversation.
- Too many arguments and disputes with a husband, heaping abuse on him, leads, in fact, to hatred and a deterioration of the relationship.
- Taking care of the house and running the household are the wife's responsibility. Therefore, she should carry out duties in keeping the house, furniture, etc., and be frugal.
- A wife may not give alms from her husband's property without his permission.
- Speaking to or telling others about sexual matters between a husband and wife is a grave sin in Islam.
- A wife should not be afraid to express her love and affection for her husband. It will please him and bind him closer to the family; moreover, if he does not find an attractive, loving woman at home, he may be driven for solace elsewhere, outside the home.
- Leadership in the family is given to the husband. For the wife to demand complete and full equality with her husband will result in having two masters in the family and this does not exist in Islam. However, the husband should not behave in an autocratic manner and misuse his position. He should display love and affection and treat his wife as a partner in life.

Parents' Conduct toward their Children

- Children are usually the joy of one's life as well as a source of pride. Therefore, parents should avoid indulging in overconfidence, false pride, and be on guard against misdeeds which might arise out of love for their children.
- The child's dependence on the parents makes their role in the formation of the child's personality a decisive one.

- The three most inalienable rights of the child in Islam are: the right to life and equal chances in life, the right of legitimacy which holds that every child shall have a legal father, a good upbringing and general care.
- Interest in and the responsibility for the child's welfare are questions of first priority to the parents.
- By the time the child is seven days old, it is recommended that (a) the child be given a good, pleasant name; (b) its head be shaved; (c) a sheep be sacrificed for a baby girl and two for a baby boy and the meat shared with relatives, friends and the poor. The whole ceremony is known as 'aqiqah.
- A father can give his children nothing better than a good education. The most necessary education that he should provide his children with is Islamic education, especially in the Quran and the Sunnah.
- The best of mothers, in the view of Islam, are those who are the most affectionate to their small children.
- Male children should never be preferred over female or vice versa. However, Islam stresses the importance of taking special care of daughters, treating them nicely, and showing them kindness.
- Fathers, if able, should help their sons and daughters to marry when they reach puberty.
- To be fond of children and kind to them is a good quality. In fact, the Muslim society should be noted among other communities for its kindness to children.
- Whether the parents are alive or deceased, present or absent, known or unknown, the child must be provided for with the best care, either by relatives or the state.
- For parents, establishing full justice in all aspects of dealing with their children is of great importance.
- For parents to show affection for their children by embracing and kissing them is good conduct.
- Parents must avoid over protectiveness as well as negligence in bringing up their children.
- Parents must ask their children only to do things according to their capability and must not put heavy

burdens upon them. Abuse of parental authority is a bad thing.

- Parents should accept their children's gifts with appreciation, even though the gifts may be small.
- Bringing up children according to the teachings of Islam is extremely important. Training them in religious life from a very early age is necessary. When they reach the age of seven, parents should make sure that they begin praying.
- Educating children concerning Islamic conduct and the various aspects of Islam is the parents' responsibility.
- Children's obedience to parents depends to a certain extent upon the parents. Being over-demanding and asking too much of them might lead to disobedience.
- From the age of ten, girls and boys should sleep apart.
- It is not permissible for a mother, sister or daughter to expose her body to a grown-up son, brother or father, except: (a) head and face; (b) neck and collar area; (c) from the mid-upper arm to the fingertips; and (d) lower part of the feet.

Children's Conduct toward their Parents: The following directions should govern a child's, even a grown-up child's, relationship with his parents:

- The special relationship between children and parents imposes a heavy responsibility on children towards their parents. There are none who better deserve a child's kindness, patience and good manners than his parents.
- Parents are much more sensitive to any act of discourtesy toward them from their own children than from any others, thus children are advised to be especially considerate when dealing with their parents.
- Parents usually believe that they are more experienced, wise and right, even though they might be wrong. This belief sustains their feeling that they are a child's guardians even after the child has grown up. This attitude must be met with great understanding and patience.

- Though both parents deserve a child's kindness, the most deserving of friendly care from a child is his mother, and then his father. According to the Prophet: 'Paradise is at your mother's feet.'
- It is impolite conduct for a child to call his parents by their first name.
- One of the finest acts of kindness is to respect a father's friends and to treat them in a kind way even after he has died.
- Children are responsible for the support and maintenance of their parents. It is an absolute religious duty to provide for parents in case of need and to help make their lives as comfortable as possible.
- A child should try to avoid anything that might irritate his parents. One of a child's duties toward his parents entails patience and compassion. Even if parents ask a child for something that is beyond his capacity, it is his duty to apologize in a polite manner for not being able to fulfill their wish.
- A man's relationship with his parents and his wife should not be at the expense of each other, nor should one be sacrificed for the other. Both should be characterized by harmony and reconciliation.
- When a child speaks to his parents, he should speak politely and gently.
- If obedience and loyalty to his parents is likely to alienate the individual from God, he must side with God. It is true that parents should expect obedience from their children, but if their actions intrude upon the rights of God, a demarcation line must be drawn and maintained. In this case, to refuse to carry out their orders is obligatory provided that it is done in a polite and proper way.
- Being patient, grateful, compassionate, respectful and affectionate toward parents is a necessity even if they are idolaters and ill-disposed toward Islam.
- Providing parents with sincere counsel is required of a child.

- It is a child's duty to listen well to his parents when they speak to him. He should never interrupt his parents while they are speaking and never argue with them.
- When accompanying one parent outdoors a child should not walk in front of him/her while walking, and not take a seat before he/she has.
- No child may become the cause of harm to his parents.
- Asking a father for extra money, for what he does not possess or for what he cannot give easily, must be avoided.
- For a child to draw attention to his own generosity toward or support of his parents is forbidden.
- To be humble to his parents and to be of service to them in the house and outside is a great honour, whatever a child's position is.
- It is a child's duty to take care of his parents when they get old by having them live with him in his house. To get rid of them by sending them to a home for the aged is considered not only discourteous but also obnoxious.
- If meeting others with a smiling face is considered an act of kindness by someone, it is considered, in the case of a child meeting his parents, a necessity.
- A child should take the initiative and greet his parents when he meets them. He should not expect that his father or mother would greet him first.
- A child is supposed to respect and treat his parents kindly even if they disregard and treat him wrongfully.
- To revile parents is one of the most serious sins. A child should also avoid reviling someone else's parents, lest they should revile his.
- However much a child is in disagreement with one of his parents, he should not say a cross word or make a gesture that would hurt him or her.
- A foster mother is one of his relatives, so a child must not neglect his duties toward her.
- Still other types of kindness are due to parents after their death, such as prayers for them, asking forgiveness

for them, honouring their legitimate commitments and honouring their friends.

- Getting old causes parents to grow physically weak and mentally feeble. This is often accompanied by impatience, degeneration of energy, heightened sensitivity and, perhaps, misjudgement. Therefore, it is a child's duty to take cognizance of that fact when it occurs and increase his patience and kindness to his elderly parents.
- It is the duty of children to help their parents with the household work without having to be asked to do so.
- Disobedience, neglect, unkindness toward parents are considered as sins. All mistakes in life can perhaps be understood and explained away but not those committed against parents.

8

Valuable Practices

The tongue and the language are great gifts of Allah. These gifts that Allah has given him makes him superior to all other creatures

"The Most Gracious Allah has taught the Quran; He has created man; He has taught him speech."

(Ar-Rahman : I-4)

The greater the gift, the higher would be its repayment. Being grateful for it is as necessary as being ungrateful is reprehensible. Islam has explained how people can derive benefit from this unparalleled blessing, and how the speech that flows from their tongues throughout the day be used for goodness and truth. People who are never tired of talking are not few in number. If you examine their talks you will find that most of these consist of senseless, absurd and trash things, whereas Allah has not given men their tongues for this purpose, nor these capabilities were given for such a purpose:

"In most of their secret talks there is no good; but if one exhorts to a deed of charity or justice or conciliation between men, (secrecy is permissible): to him who does this, seeking the good pleasure of Allah, We shall soon give a reward of the highest (value)."(An-Nissa : 114)

Islam has given special attention to speech, its style, its etiquette and rules, because the talk that comes out from a man's mouth discloses his intellectual level and moral nature, because the etiquette of speech in a group reveals its general standard, and shows the standard of decency in their environment.

Take an Account of Yourself : Before addressing others take a glance at yourself, and ask yourself whether this is an occasion which demands speaking. If the answer is in the affirmative, then speak, otherwise silence is much better. To avoid talking unnecessarily on appropriate occasions is a worship of great rewards.

Abdullah bin Masood says:

"By the Being other than whom there is no God, on this earth there is none more deserving of long imprisonment than the tongue." *(Tibrani)*

Abdullah Ibn Abbas says : "Five things are more valuable than the horses with the black-striped legs

1. Do not indulge in senseless talk, because it is useless and absurd, and I am uncomfortable from the fear of your committing a sin.
2. Talk purposefully when there is an occasion for it, for there are many people who talk without an occasion. This is a drawback.
3. Do not indulge in hot discussion with an intelligent man or with a fool. If he is intelligent, he will be angry with you and will hate you, and if he is a fool and uneducated, he will try to harm you.
4. In the absence of your brother speak of him in the same words in which you would like him to speak of you in your absence, and consider him innocent of 'the thing which you would like him to consider you innocent of.
5. Act like a man who thinks that he will be rewarded for a good deed and will be punished on committing a crime." (Ibn Abi-al-duniya)

A Muslim can develop these attributes in himself only when he keeps his tongue in control, and is able to keep silent wherever necessary.

He should be able to hold the reins of his tongue in his hand; wherever necessary he should speak, and wherever it is not necessary he should keep quiet. Those who are ruled by their tongue, they are pushed back, and in the fields of life they receive insults and disrepute.

ART OF CONVERSATION

One loses sense in talking absurdities and aimlessly. Those who want to impress others in meetings by their talk, they speak so glibly and endlessly that the words come out from their mouth like rainwater. Although they try to convince others that they are very wise, intelligent and farsighted, but sometimes the impression created by their long-winding speeches is quite the contrary, and from their talks people feel that there is no relation between what they want the people to believe about them and what actually they are. When a man wants to contemplate over his position and wants to organize his religious thoughts, he runs away from the atmosphere of noise and uproar and takes shelter in a quiet place. And therefore if Islam recommends silence and considers it a means of civilized training, then it is not at all surprising. The Prophet had, among other things, advised Hadrat Abuzar in this way:

> *"Adopt silence. This is a way of causing Satan to run away, it is a support to you in the matter of your religion."*
> *(Ahmad)*

Undoubtedly the tongue is a rope in the hands of Satan. He turns it anywhere he likes. When a man is unable to control his affairs, his mouth becomes a passage for all the negative talk which contaminates the heart and covers it with the sheet of negligence.

> *The Prophet has said: "The faith of a man cannot be straight unless his heart is straight, and his heart cannot be straight unless his tongue becomes straight."*
> *(Ahmad)*

The first stage of this straightens and correctness is that man should wash his hands off all the irrelevant matters and he should not interfere in those things about which he is not answerable.

> *"It is the excellence of a man's faith that he gives up meaningless work."* *(Tirmidhi)*

Avoidance of Nonsense : To avoid irrelevant and nonsensical things is a condition for success and is a proof of perfection. Quran has mentioned it in between two essential duties (Faraiz) of Muslims, which give an idea of its importance:

"Successful indeed are the believers who are humble in their prayers, and who shun vain conversation, and who are payers of zakat." *(Al-Mominoon : I-4)*

If all the men of the world count their efforts which they make in indulging in vain conversation and acts, they will come to realize that a very large part of the long-winding tales and stories, widely circulated news, narratives, speeches and broadcasts comprises of vain, meaningless and useless things, which are eagerly watched, and heard, but no benefit is derived from them. Islam has expressed its disapproval of the meaningless talks and things, because the superficial and useless things have no value in its eyes. It dislikes that man should not busy himself in matters for which he has not been created and instead he should waste his life in involving himself in other irrelevant matters. The more distant a Muslim will be from an absurd and irrelevant thing, the more high will be his rank before Allah. Anas bin Malik says that when a man died another man passed a remark about him in the presence of the Prophet that he would go to Paradise. The Prophet stopped him and said:

"Do not you know? It is likely that he might have indulged in meaningless conversation or might have been miserly in spending his wealth, although this does not effect any reduction." *(Tirmidhi)*

A vain talker, on account of the weak coordination between his thought and his tongue, blurts out whatever comes on his tongue. Sometimes he says something which places him in danger, and he ruins his future. It is said that the more one talks, the more one commits mistakes. An Arabic poet has said:

"The youth dies by the fault of his tongue whereas from the faltering of the feet death does not occur."

In the tradition it is stated: "A man says something so that those present may laugh, although on account of it he is thrown to the most distant region between the earth and the sky. The faltering of the feet cause much less harm than the faltering of the tongue."

(Baihaqui)

Heart-warming Speech : When a man has to speak, he should say something good and worthwhile. He should accustom his tongue to indulge in good, decent and respectable conversation, because the best manifestation of the thoughts and feelings demeanours and mind is the classical literature, with which Allah has blessed the followers of all the religions. Quran has clearly mentioned that the covenant which Hadrat Moosa had taken from Bani Israil also included the condition that they should indulge in good and worthwhile conversation:

"And (recall) when We took a covenant from the Children of Israil, (saying): "Worship none save Allah, be good to parents and kindred and orphans and those in need; and speak a right and kindly to people, and establish salat and pay Zakat." (Baqarah: 82)

Clean and decent conversation impresses both friends and foes, and its sweet fruits can be readily enjoyed. It guards love between friends. It strengthens their friendship and makes it durable and defeats all the tricks of the devil for weakening their relations and for sowing the seeds of discord between them:

"Say (O Prophet !) to my slaves to speak which is kindlier. Verily, the devil sows discord among them. Verily, the devil is for man an open enemy." (Bani Israil: 53)

The devil is hiding in ambush against man. He tries to sow the seeds of discord, enmity and jealousy among them. He wants that the ordinary disputes be converted into big bloody battles, and that no spanner should be thrown in his works by means of good, decent and kindly talk. It you would talk gracefully with your enemies, their enmity would disappear, and their tempers will be cooled, or at least a distinct difference can be witnessed in their hostile attitude.

"The good deed and the evil deed are not alike. Repel the evil deed with one which is better, then surely, he, between whom and you there was enmity (will become) as though he was a bosom friend."

(Ha-Meem-Sajda : 34)

To make Muslims in all conditions well-behaved and of good manners, the Prophet has said : "You will not be able to rule over the people through your wealth, but through good appearance and good manners you can win their hearts." (Al-Bazzar).

In the eyes of Islam not to give a gift to somebody while behaving in a decent way and with good manners is better than giving it in an indecent manner, and by giving him pain.

> *"A kind word with forgiveness is better than charity followed by injury. Allah is Free of All Wants and Most Forbearing."* *(Baqarah: 263)*

Decent conversation is such a habit that it is counted among the virtues and good attributes, and one who, adopts this habit becomes worthy of pleasing Allah and for him is written eternal bliss. Anas narrates that one man asked the Prophet to teach him such an act as would enable him to enter the Paradise.

> *The Prophet replied : "Feed the poor, practise salutation (salaam) in the night when people are enjoying sleep, offer prayers, you will enter Paradise with peace."* *(Al-Bazzar)*

Allah has commanded us to adopt decent and serious manners of speaking when we may discuss matters with the followers of other religions. It should not have intensity nor heat and anger. However those who are aggressive against us, it is necessary to put a stop to their aggression

> *"And argue not with the People of the Book unless it be in (a way) that is better, save with such of them as do wrong."* *(Ankabut : 46)*

Great men always take care in all conditions that no extra and useless word comes out of their mouth, and they do not adopt an attitude of pride and foolishness with every specie of creatures. Malik has reported that Yahya bin Saeed has told him that Hadrat Isa (Christ) one day passed by a pig, and he addressed it: "Pass on peacefully." He was asked : "You talk to a pig in this manner !" He replied: "I am afraid my tongue may not be habituated to rude talk."

Answer to the Uneducated : Some people remain ill-mannered, hot-tempered and lewd talkers for the whole of their lives. Their faith and belief are not at all disturbed by these evils, nor does their morality admonish them on their attitude. They have no hesitation in telling others things which are disagreeable to them. Whenever they find a suitable field to let on their steam, their tongues run away with vulgar and obscene talks like relines steeds. No cries stop them nor does any voice inhibit them. The attitude of a gentleman with such people should be that he should not engage himself in any discussion with them, because any provocation would lead to great disturbance, and it is necessary to seal this source of trouble. For this reason Islam has commanded to ignore the foolish and unwise people.

Once one of these illiterate persons stood at the door of the Prophet's house with a view to entering it. The kind Prophet treated him very decently and managed to persuade him to go away. There was no other go besides this, for tolerance and forbearance is the cloth by which the uneducated and the fool can be gagged. Had the Prophet allowed him to do whatever he intended to do, then he would have had to hear all the trivial and the rubbish talk from which his ears thus remained safe. Hadrat Aishah says that one man sought the Prophet's permission to enter the house, and the Prophet remarked: "What a bad man is he of his family!" When he came in, the Prophet talked to him pleasantly and softly. After he went away, she asked him 'O Messenger of Allah! You heard this man talking in this way, yet there was no sign of perturbation on your face, on the contrary you talked to him pleasantly ?' The Prophet replied:

> *"O Aishah! when did you hear me talking vulgarly ? On the Day of Judgment before Allah the worst man would be the one for avoiding whose vulgar talk people stopped meeting him."* *(Bukhari)*

This policy is such that its truth is borne out by our daily experiences, for how can a man like that could tarnish his good manners by hobnobbing with a bad mannered person ? If he starts teaching manners to every uneducated and foolish person, then his life will become a bundle of troubles. Man swallows his anger once, twice, but later on he bursts. But a well-behaved Muslim is expected by Islam to tolerate more troubles and adversities, so that consequently the evil should not be able to stand firmly on its ground.

> *Saeed bin Musayyab says : "When the Prophet was sitting with his companions one person used insulting words against Hadrat Abu Bakr, causing him pain, but*

Abu Bakr was silent. For the second time also he used the bitter words against him, and still Abu Bakr was silent. When for the third time he hurt him with his tongue, Abu Bakr tried to answer him. The Messenger of Allah got up. Abu Bakr asked him : 'Are you displeased with me, O Messenger of Allah! The Prophet replied : 'No, but from the heaven an angel had come down and he was denying that man's talk, and when you started to answer that man, the angel went away and the devil sat down. And I cannot sit where the devil is sitting'."

(Abu Daud)

To pay respect to the foolish and unintelligent people does not mean that their low and superficial acts should also be accepted. In these two conditions there is a very great difference. The first thing means that man should have control over his self in the presence of folly and unintelligence, and he should not give them a chance to show their true nature which is the bearer of anger and wrath, and be provoked to take revenge. While the second aspect has quite the contrary sense. In that condition it amounts to allow the self to submit to folly, meanness and disrepute, and to accept those low things which no wise and decent man would be ready to accept. The holy Quran has treated the subject of respect to the unintelligent people and the hatred of their low and mean acts in this manner:

"Allah does not like that evil should be noised abroad in public speech, except where injustice has been done; for Allah is He Who hears and knows all things. Whether you express a good deed or conceal it or cover evil with pardon, verily Allah does blot out (sins) and has power (in the judgment of values)" *(An-Nissa : 148-149)*

Avoiding Polemic : The commands that Islam issued to keep the tongue safe from baseless and absurd things is to declare polemical discussion and controversial debating and to shut its doors upon Muslims, irrespective of whether the polemical debating is correct or otherwise. It is so because here such conditions arise that a man tries to score a point and to overcome his opponent. As he wants to defeat his adversary by his talk, he takes the support of even dubious and unreliable things which can strengthen his argument, and he quotes such statements unhesitatingly which help him in his task. In such a gathering people give more importance to winning than on expressing truth. This is likely to result in rancour and disturbances, in which clarification and satisfaction have no place. Islam hates all these conditions and considers them a danger for the religion and morality.

The Prophet has said: "He who has given up controversial discussion in senseless and false matters, for him there will be built a house in the lower section of the Paradise; and he who has corrected his morals, for him there will be built a house in the upper section of the Paradise." (Abu Daud)

There are some people whom Allah has gifted the power of tongue and has made them expert in that line. This prompts them to exercise their expertise over all people, educated or uneducated. It becomes a burning desire in their hearts, and they do not rest content with out satisfying this desire. When this group makes others a victim of their power of speech and shows their expertise, they hurt their feelings, and when this quality is required to be employed in expressing the religious realities then all the beauty and grandeur of their speech vanishes. Islam is extremely displeased with nonsensical talkers who shout at the top of their voices, and admonish them very severely.

The Prophet has said : "Before Allah the most hated are the quarrelsome debaters." (Bukhari)

In another tradition it is stated : "After receiving guidance no community went astray and did not deviate from the path it was following, except when debaters turned them away from it." (Tirmidhi)

On account of the speed of its tongue, this group does not stay within the limits. It goes on talking, feels conceited and struts along. For this group the position of words is of first importance, their meaning takes the second place. As regards the great and clean purpose, many times it is demoted to the last place, and sometimes in this hullabaloo it does not get any place at all.

It is narrated that once a deceitful man, wearing beautiful clothes, went in the presence of the Prophet and during conversation raised his voice higher than the voice of the Prophet. When he went away, the Prophet said : "Allah does not like people of this type. They work their tongue in the way a cow does when it chews the cud. In the same way Allah will twist their faces and mouths on the Doomsday in the fire of hell."

(Tibrani)

When in the fields of religion, politics and other branches of learning the so-called orators and expert writers come forward for indulging in polemics and debates, then the spirit of religion receives a setback. The face of politics, learning and sciences is disfigured. And possibly this helped in hastening the decline of our civilization and culture, in the formation of groupism of the schools of Fiqh, division of the Ummah on the sectarian basis and other diseases of disruption. In other matters of religion and worldly affairs also this controversial debating spread its poison.

Controversial debating is words away from pure, clean discussion, and sober and pleasant argumentation. A number of companions of the Prophet have reported that once they were discussing and debating some religious point, when the Prophet arrived; he was terribly angry. He was never seen so angry before. He admonished them and said:

"Stay put, O Ummah of Muhammad! Nations before you were destroyed by this only. Give up this debating. The portion of good is very little in it. Give up this discussion and argumentation, for this is not a quality of a Momin. Avoid this polemic and disputation, for the loss sustained by one who indulges in it becomes complete. For your being a sinner it is sufficient that you are a debater. Give up this debating, because on the Day of Resurrection there will be none to intercede for the debater. Wash off your hands of this wicked habit, for in Paradise I will lead only to three kinds of houses, its lower floor, middle floor and the upper floor, which will be for that man who has given up debating truthfully and with good intention. Keep away from this bad habit because after idolatry, the first thing that my Lord has forbidden is this very debating." *(Tibrani)*

Such gatherings of men are arranged where novel and attractive talks drive men towards them. Islam dislikes such gatherings, where people sit and waste their time, and where people always lap up news and defects of others. They have wealth in excess under whose shadow they try to have good time. They have no other work besides this that they seek pleasure in the affairs of other people.

> *"Woe to every (kind of) scandalmonger and backbiter, who piles up wealth and lays it by, thinking that his wealth would make him last forever! By no means ! He will be sure to be thrown into that which breaks to pieces."* *(Humaza : 1-4)*

In modern times such gathering in mehfils and clubs are the order of the day. This is a calamity that has caused the society to be infected with a number of diseases. This calamity is found in abundance in big towns and small cities, even though there is no religious necessity for this thing. It is mentioned in the Hadith : "Avoid sitting on the roads." The people said: "O Messenger of Allah! What would happen to our those gatherings without which there would be no life for us." He said : "If you insist on having gathering, then do due justice to them." People asked : "What is their due, O Messenger of Allah ?"

> *He answered : "To keep your eyes down, to remove harmful things, to give answer to salutation, to command performance of good things and to prevent commitment of evil things."* *(Muslim)*

Etiquettes of Talking : Always speak the truth, and never hesitate to do so, whatever the consequences. Open your mouth when it is necessary, and, whenever you talk, speak something useful. Incessant and unnecessary talk is against the norms of seriousness and decency. We have to answer for every word we utter and the angel appointed by Allah notes our conversation.

> *"No sooner a word is uttered by the tongue the angel remains ready to note it."* *(60 :18)*

Whenever you talk, talk softly and with a smile. Speak in a voice neither too low that the listener may not be able to hear, nor so loud that the listener may feel you are trying to overawe him. The Quran has:

"Lo! the harshest of all voices is the voice of the ass."
(41 : 19)

Do not pollute your tongue with vulgar words; don't abuse, backbite or complain against any person; don't imitate or ape others, or ridicule anybody or indulge in self praise or tall talks; do not make false promises. Avoid arguing unnecessarily and playing to the gallery. Do not pass sarcastic remarks nor call anybody with a bad name. Nor you should swear frequently. Always speak what is just, even though you or your friends, or kinsfolk may have to suffer. The Holy Quran says:

"And when you say a thing with your tongue, say what is just, even though the person might be your relation."

If women have to talk with men, they should not talk coquettishly but in a straight-forward and rough manner, lest the man should indulge into harbouring lustful thoughts.

Don't Enter into Argument with Illiterate Persons : When illiterate persons try to entangle you in unnecessary talk, take your leave from such people and quit the place. Such people are among the worst lot of the people. If you are explaining something to a man, bear in mind his mental capacity and intelligence, and then explain the matter to him accordingly. If he does not follow, explain to him again without getting irritated. Always talk to the point and with brevity. It is not wise to prolong conversation.

Explain religious points in simple and appealing style. If you have to explain some theological point to some religious edict, do so in a manner that is both simple and appealing. Seeking a name through oratory, or to impress people with the flow of the words and to deliver speeches just for fun and enjoyment or as an expression of pride, is a despicable habit that blackens the heart. Never flatter or talk in a way smacking of sycophancy. Always keep your self-respect upper most in your mind and do not degrade yourself. Never interrupt conversation between two persons. If you have to speak out at all, do so with their permission.

Talk deliberately and with dignity in an appropriate manner. Do not talk rapidly nor indulge in loose talk or cut jokes too often. This will belittle you. Reply to a question after due consideration. If you are asked a question, listen to it attentively and then reply after due consideration. It is extremely undesirable that a random and unthoughtful reply should be given. And if someone else is being asked a question, do not take upon yourself to reply. Never anticipate what other is saying. If you are being told a thing, do not show by expression or words that you already know what he is saying. It is quite possible that he may come out with something new or may he be able to move you by some particular fact or style of narration. The earnestness and grace of the conversationalist also has its effect on the listener.

While talking, do not point towards third person lest he becomes suspicious. Similarly never try to overhear or eavesdrop other people's conversation. Try to listen to other persons more, and talk as little as possible. Do not reveal anything that is secret. Confiding your secret in others and expecting that it would be kept secret is a foolish expectation.

THE CORRESPONDENCE

Always begin your letter with *Bismillah-ir Rahman-ir Rahim* i.e., in the name of Allah, the Most Beneficent, the Most Merciful. The Holy Prophet (S. A.W.) has said that a work which does not commence with Bismillah remains incomplete and without blessing. Some people write 786 in place of Bismillah. This should be avoided, as only wards approved by Allah are blessed.

Invariably write your address in each letter. Don't neglect it thinking that the addressee already knows your address. It is not necessary that, if the addressee has been communicated your address earlier, he would still remember it or have it in his record. Either below your address or on the top of the right side write the date of the letter.

Write appropriate appellation. Having put down the date, address the addressee in a simple and direct manner with proper appellation. He should be addressed in a manner that reflects sincerity and affection, avoiding appellation indicating artificiality and adulation. In the next line greetings should be offered in the form of "As-Salam-o-Alaikum." End your letter with proper subscription. After having written the heading and the address, write down the object of writing the letter. Once the text of the letter is over, it should he ended with a proper subscription, e.g. "Yours Sincerely," "Yours Truly," "Faithfully," "Affectionately," etc.

The letter should he legible, simple in style and neatly written which may he appreciated by the addressee. Some hints for writing letters. The following guidelines will help you in writing a good letter.

(a) It should be precise and to the point it may not be lengthy but must contain necessary details.

(b) The status of the addressee should he kept in mind throughout.

(c) The tone of the letter should be suave and dignified throughout. Non-serious topics should be avoided.

(d) Never write a letter when you are heated or extremely angry. Ensure that no improper words are written. Write when you are cool and in proper mood.

(e) A general letter should not contain any secret matter.

Reading another person's letter without his permission is ethical misappropriation. Be regular and prompt in writing letters of your welfare to your relatives and friends. Write letter of sympathy when necessary. If somebody falls sick or meets with an accident or gets involved in some difficulty, do write a letter expressing your concern and sympathy.

Similarly when there be a happy event; you must congratulate the person concerned. Post letter before mail leaves. If a letter has been given to you for posting, be particular in posting it well in time. Send stamps for reply. While writing to unfamiliar person within the country and from whom a reply is solicited, it is desirable to enclose stamps or a stamped reply envelope or post-card.

Do not confine your letter to the matters of interest to you alone; but keep in view the sentiments and interests of the addressee as well; while you write about your family members' welfare, do ask him about the health and well being of his relatives also. And mind that you do not pester the addressee with numerous demands. Too many demands degrade a person.

CELEBRATING HAPPY OCCASIONS

It is good to celebrate festive occasions which is a human urge and in commensurate with natural requirement. Islam being the religion of Nature realises the desirability of the celebration of joyous occasions with certain conditions. Islam does not desire that we should impose upon ourselves artificial reserve and seriousness not warranted by the occasion, and wear a pensive aspect all the time, killing all the attractiveness of our personality. Islam gives us full permission to celebrate all legitimate festive occasion so as to enable us to remain fresh with ambitious desires, new and fresh hopes, and ever newer and fresher paths to tread. It is the ignorance of knowledge of Islam to assume that the celebration of festive occasions runs counter to the tenets of Islam.

If you have been privileged to fulfil some religious mission, i.e., Hajj; you or some of your close relation has achieved a high position in learning; you have been blessed with success in business or achieved' some monetary gains; you have a distinguished guest visiting your home; you have a marriage or birth in your house; you have heard the news of the recovery of a relation from long illness; have heard the happy news of the triumph of the Muslims, and, if there may be a feast in any ease, it is your natural right to celebrate such occasions, and Islam not only permits merrymaking, but it considers it quite in conformity with it.

Hadrat Kaab Bin Malik says, when Allah accented his atonement and he heard the good news, he immediately presented himself before the Holy Prophet (S.A.W.) greeting him. The countenance of the Holy Prophet (S.A.W.) was at the time glowing with cheer, and whenever he used to be happy, his face glowed like a part of the moon, and the companions would then understand from the glow of his countenance, that he was in an extremely happy mood. (Riyaz-us-Salihin)

Celebration of Eids : Muslim festivals should be celebrated with an abundance and free play. The Holy Prophet (S.A.W.) when he arrived at Medina said: "You used to celebrate two feasts in a year. Now Allah has granted you two better days that is, the Eid- and Eid-ul-Adha." Therefore, celebrate these two Islamic festivals to your heart's content and mingle with others to join on these festive occasions in a natural way. It is forbidden to fast during these festivals. The Holy Prophet (S.A.W.) has further said:

> *"These days are meant for feasts, mutual enjoyment and remembrance of Allah."* *(Sharh Mani Al Asar)*

On the day of Eid take care for personal and environmental cleaning and washing. Don the best dress which your means may permit, apply perfume on your person and clothes, arrange for good and wholesome food. The children should be given every opportunity to please themselves with legitimate games and sports, and celebrate these occasions as they please. Hadrat Aishah (R.A.A.) narrates that, one day on the occasion of Eid slave girls were singing couplets which the Ansars had composed during the Battle of Buas. (This battle was fought during the pre-Islamic era, between two Ansar tribes Aus and Khazraj). While the singing was going on, Hadrat Abu Bakr came and said: "Why this singing and sportiveness in the house of the Holy Prophet (S.A.W.)." The Holy Prophet (S.A.W.) thereupon said: "Let them, O Abu Bakr, celebrate. Each people have a day marked for their merry making and today we have the day of our Eid."

> *Once on an Eid day few Negro jugglers were performing physical exercise. The Holy Prophet (S.A.W.) himself saw this performance and showed the same to Hadrat Aishah (R.A.A.) who witnessed the show from behind a cover. He was applauding the jugglers all the while. When Hadrat Aishah (R.A.A.) got, tired; he told her; "All right, you may go"* *(Bukhari)*

Rejoicing in Keeping with the Spirit of Islam : *While celebrating festive occasions, we should bear in mind the Islamic spirit and celebrate the event decorously. We must thank Allah for the same who has been the source of that pleasure and offer obeisance and submission to Him. Do not adopt an attitude that is at variance with the Islamic tenets. While celebrating such events, moderation ought never be lost sight of, and under no circumstances show pride and haughtiness to the exclusion of humility and submissiveness. The Holy*

Quran says "And do not strut upon having received those gifts from Allah. He does not like those who show themselves off and boast." *(57 :23)*

One should not get so much intoxicated by pleasure that he may become indifferent towards remembering Allah. The happiness of a Muslim lies in offering thanks to the Benefactor or Giver of happiness all the more, and to express his gratitude to Allah through his acts. When you sight the Eid moon, after having fasted for the whole month of Ramadan, read the Quran and offered Tarawih prayers, you are immensely pleased. On realising the fact that you have carried out the command of Allah and through His Will have given a good account of yourself, you distribute a part of your wealth among the poor, so that if you have failed to carry out any of His commands with regard to prayers, or if you have tripped short of fulfilling your obligations or obedience to Him, this might make up for the same, and the poor and the indigent might also be able to partake in this collective merrymaking. We then thank Allah for munificence on the morning of the Eid by offering two rakats of Eid prayers.

Similarly on the occasion of Eid-ul-Adha we offer prayers and alms to the poor to commemorate Prophet Ibrahim's and Prophet Ismail's (A.S.) unparalleled sacrifice and total submission to Allah's Will. We celebrate this occasion in remembrance of that event unsurpassable in its content of faith, and find our hearts overflowing with sentiments of thanksgiving. Our cities and localities resound with Takbirs and recitations of prayers. When we eat good food and put on our best clothes, our activities, which are based on Shariah, become part of prayers to Allah.

Greeting Friends : When the expiation of Hadrat Kaab Bin Malik was graciously accepted, Muslims in large number went to him to offer their congratulation, and expressed their pleasure; Hadrat Talha's greetings moved him so much that he remembered them for the rest of his life. When Hadrat Kaab described the incident of this ordeal and repentance to his son, Abdullah, he especially mentioned Hadrat Talha with great pleasure, and said he could never forget the spontaneous joy that overflowed from him, and that it was an unforgetable experience. When the Holy Prophet (S.A.W.) himself conveyed to Hadrat Kaab the tidings of the approval of his expiation, the former was very pleased and said:

Kaab! This is the happiest occasion of your life."
(Riyaz-us-Salihin)

Greetings at a Wedding. Hadrat Abu Hurrayrah says that, whenever the Holy Prophet (S.A.W.) greeted anyone on the occasion of his marriage, he used to say:

"May Allah keep you prosperous and bless both of you, and you may gather happiness between you."

Greeting the Birth of a Child : Hadrat Hussain-Ibn-Ali (R.A.A.) once told someone that the birth of a child should be greeted in the following words:

"May Allah bless you with prosperity in this gift and grace you with the ability to thank Him. Allah may enable your child to grow and enjoy youth, and he may be obedient to you."

Greetings on Return from a Journey : A relation or a friend on return from a long journey should be greeted, and pleasure expressed on his safe home coming and success in his mission. If he celebrates his return, one should participate in it. If you come back safely from a journey and celebrate it then invite all those near and dear to you, but do not spend beyond your means.

The Holy Prophet (S.A.W.) on his return from the Battle of Tabuk, was received by the Muslim men and children at Sanniyat Al Wada. *(Abu Daud)*

When the Holy Prophet (S.A.W.) migrated to Medina and was entering the city from the south, the entire Muslim population came out to welcome him. The Ansar girls were singing the following verses in jubilation:

"Tala-al-bdro alaina min Sanniyatil wadai Waja-bash shukro alaina Madaa lillahe dae. Ayyuhal mabuso fina Jaita bit amril mutai."

(Today we have seen the full moon appear before us from the southern hill of Sanniyat Al Wada. It is incumbent upon us to offer thanks for the invitation towards Allah and enlightenment shown to us. O Prophet (S.A.W.) who has been sent to us, you have brought to us such a creed that we shall follow.)

Sanniyat Al Wada was a hillock on the south of Medina. The people of this city used to come to this place to see off their guests. Hence it got this name which means the Hillock of Farewell.

Once when the Holy Prophet (S.A.W.) reached Medina from a journey, he celebrated his return with a feast, sacrificing a cow or camel. (Abu Daud)

Celebrate Weddings with Jubilation: Associate your relations and friends in these festivities. The Holy Prophet (S.A.W.) has permitted singing of some good songs and the bearing of cymbals, on such occasions. This helps expression of happy sentiments and also publicises the marriage.

Hadrat Aishah (R.A.A.) married a lady of her family to an Ansar. When she was being sent to her husband's house, the holy Prophet (S.A.W.) remarked "Why not a slave girl was sent to accompany her to beat the cymbals and sing some songs." (Bukhari)

When Hadrat Rabi bint Moawwiz was being married, some girls sitting around her were playing the cymbals. They were singing verses praising their relatives who had laid down their lives in the Battle of Badr. A girl sang the following verse.

"We have among us a Prophet (S.A.W.) who knows what is going to take place tomorrow."

The Holy Prophet (S.A.W.) having heard this, said: "Leave this. Sing what you were singing earlier". (Bukhari)

Entertaining the People at Weddings : In order to celebrate a wedding, arrangements should also be made to entertain relations amid friends with a dinner or some eatables. The Holy Prophet (S.A.W.) himself invited people to Walima (a feast arranged by bridegroom after wedding) dinners and has strongly recommended it to others. He has said:

"If you have nothing, then at least slaughter a goat and feed (your guests)."

"If one cannot participate in a wedding, he should at least send a message or greetings. Presents and gifts offered on such occasions, revive and revitalize relations and put friendship on more cordial footing. However, the gift should be in keeping with one's financial position, and within limits, avoiding extravagance and show.

Greeting and Blessings : When you come across a Muslim brother express your intimacy and happiness by saying Assalam-o-Alaikum (Peace be upon you). The Holy Quran says:

> *"O Prophet of Allah! And when those who believe in Our revelations come unto thee, say: Peace be unto you!"*
>
> *(6 : 54)*

This verse is addressed to the Holy Prophet (S.A.W.) and the Ummah has been instructed indirectly to follow this principle. When a Muslim meets another, they should exchange these sentiments of love and pleasure for each other. And the best way in which this can be done, is that they should solicit Allah's mercy for each other. One of them should say As-Salam-o-Alaikum (Peace be upon you) and the other should reply by saying Wa-alaikum as—Salam (Peace be upon you too). This greeting is a step for increasing mutual love and sympathy. The Holy Prophet (S.A.W.) has said:

> *"You people cannot enter Paradise unless you become Momin (True Believer) and you cannot become a Momin as long as you do not love each other. Why should I not tell you the way in which you can love each other? You can do this by making salutation a common practice among you."*

Style of Salutation : Whether meeting each other or in correspondence, greetings should be offered in the Islamic way, as laid down by the Holy Quran and not the expressions current in the contemporary society. The mode of greeting prescribed in Islam is both simple, meaningful, effective and a comprehensive prayer invoking good wishes. When we say *As-Salamo-alaikum* to a brother, it means that Allah may protect him and bless him. When we say *As-Salam-o-alaikum,* we condense all the prayers for the welfare and peace for the good of the person addressed. And, if we express these words consciously, what better words can there be for expressing sentiments of affection sincerity and good wishes? When you receive your Muslim brother with *As-Salam-o-alaikum,* you, in reality invoke Allah's blessings and mercies. The source of all mercies and peace, that peace which is *As-Salam,* And only he can achieve peace and tranquillity whom Allah may grant this, and he, whom He deprives of Peace, is deprived of it in both the worlds. The Holy Prophet (S.A.W.) has said:

> *"As-Salam is one of the names of Allah which He has bestowed upon (the inhabitants of the earth) for their benefit. Therefore widely publicise* As-Salam *amidst yourselves,"* *(Al-Adab Al-Mufrad)*

Every Muslim should be greeted, whether known or stranger. Indeed it is enough that he is your brother in faith, and a Muslim must cherish sentiments of love, sincerity and well being for another Muslim . . . .

> *A man asked the Holy Prophet (S.A.W.) "What is the best act in Islam?" The Holy Prophet (S.A.W.) replied "To feed the poor and to greet every Muslim, whether you know him or not."* *(Bukhari - Muslim)*

When one enters his own house, he should greet the people in the house. The Holy Quran says:

> *"But when ye enter houses, salute one another with a greeting from Allah, blessed and sweet."* *(24 :61)*

> *Hadrat Anas states that he was instructed by the Holy Prophet (S.A.W.) "My dear son. Whenever you enter your house, greet the inmates of the house first. The prayer for welfare is a prayer full of blessings and purity which has been taught by Allah."* *(Tirmidhi)*

Likewise when you enter another person's house, greet the inmates before entering the house. The Quran says:

> *"O ye who believe: Enter not houses other than your own, without first announcing your presence and invoking peace upon the folk thereof."* *(24 : 27)*

> *Even children be saluted. This is an excellent way of teaching them the practice of salutation, and it is also* Sunnah *of the Holy Prophet (S.A.W.). Hadrat Anas once passed by children, greeting them and said this was the practice of the Holy Prophet (S.A.W.)*
>
> *(Bukhari - Muslim)*

Hadrat Abdullah bin 'Umar was so much particular in this respect that he used to write "Salam' even to children in his letters.

Women can greet men and vice versa. Hadrat Asma Ansariya says that once she was sitting in the company of her female companions when the Holy Prophet (S.A.W.) passed by and greeted them. (Al-Adab Al-Mufrad)

You should cultivate the habit of generously and lavishly offering greetings. Exchange lavish and generous greetings among yourself. This increases mutual love and affection, and Allah protects against harm and loss. The Holy Prophet (S.A.W.) says:

"I may tell you a thing which may help to increase mutual love and affection among you. You greet each other as much as you can." (Muslim)

He (S.A.W.) also said "Exchange salam all over. Allah will keep you safe and sound,"

Greeting is to be regarded as the right of your Muslim brother. One should be generous in the discharge of this right, as the Holy Prophet (S.A.W.) has said: "It is the right of a Muslim that when his Muslim brother meets him, he should greet him." (Muslim)

Hadrat Abu Hurrayrah says:

"The most miserly person is one who is niggardly in greeting. (Al-Adab Al-Mufrad)

Always take initiative in greeting. Even if there may be differences of opinion. You should be the first person in greeting and making peace. The Holy Prophet (S.A.W.) has said:

"The person who takes lead in greeting is closer to Allah." (Abu Daud)

And further :

"It is not proper for a Muslim to remain estranged with his Muslim brother and avoid meeting him for more than three days. He, who greets first, has precedence." (Al-Adab Al-Mufrad)

Someone asked the Holy Prophet (S.A.W.) who, of the two people who meet, should greet earlier. He said the

one who is better in the eyes of Allah, would greet first.
(Tirmidhi)

Hadrat Abdullah bin 'Umar was so much meticulous in this respect that nobody could ever succeed in saluting him first. Greet loudly. Greetings should be offered orally in a loud voice, so that the person greeted should be able to hear and respond. Sign of greetings may be made with the hands also if necessary. As for example if the person greeted, is deaf or is at such a distance that the greeting would not be heard by him.

Hadrat Abdullah bin 'Umar says: "When a person is greeted he should be made to hear the greeting as it is prayer pure and full of blessings from Allah."
(Al-Adab Al-Mufrad)

Hadrat Asma bint Yazid says that the Holy Prophet (S.A.W.) passed by a mosque where some women were sitting. He greeted them with the signs of his hand.
(Tirmidhi)

This means that the Holy Prophet (S.A.W.) not only greeted with words but with the movement of his hands as wall. This is Confirmed by the tradition in Abu Land. Hadrat Asma says that when the Holy Prophet (S.A.W.) passed by us, he (S.A.W.) greeted us. However it is better to greet verbally, and only where necessary, with the movement of hands. Be careful to offer greetings to your elders. When you ate walking, greet those who are sitting; and when in small group, greet the larger group. The Holy Prophet (S.A.W.) has said:

"The younger should greet the elder, the pedestrian should greet the seated one, and the smaller group should greet the larger one." *(Al-Adab Al-Maufrad)*

Greetings by riders, pedestrians and smaller groups. If you are riding, salute those on foot, and those on foot should greet those who are sitting: and the party of smaller numbers may greet the one with larger numbers. Greet on arrival and departure.

When you go to meet somebody, or reach his sitting room, or pass by a gathering, or arrive at a meeting, salute on arrival at a meeting, salute on arrival as well as when taking leave. The Holy Prophet (S.A.W.) has said:

"When you join a meeting, greet them and when leaving them, greet them again; and remember that the first salam (on arrival) is not worthy of more recompense than the second one. This means that you may be equally particular about your first and second greetings."

(Tirmidhi)

Don't greet a person by name in a gathering. When you go to a meeting, greet the gathering as a whole and you should not greet any body in particular. Once Hadrat Abdullah was in a mosque when a beggar came and greeted him by name. Hadrat Abdullah said:

"What Allah has said is true, and His Prophet (S.A.W.) has fulfilled his mission." He then went home; while those who heard this could not follow the real meaning of what he had said. However when he came back, Hadrat Tariq asked him to elucidate what he had said. He replied; "The Holy Prophet (S.A.W.) has said that towards the advent of Doomsday, people would start greeting particular persons individually by naming them in a meeting." *(Al-A dab Al-Mufrad)*

Send greetings through post. If you get an opportunity to send greetings to your friend, relative or senior through a third party, do send your greetings.

Hadrat Aishah says: "The Holy Prophet (S.A.W.) said to me; "Aishah! Jibbrail is greeting you. I replied: Wa Alaikum us-Salam wa Rahmatullah wa Barakatuhu."

(Bukhari - Muslim)

Greeting mixed gathering of wakefuls and asleep. If you go to a place where some people are sleeping and some are awake, you should greet wakeful ones in such a tone that those who are asleep may not get disturbed, while only those who are awake may hear you.

Hadrat Miqdad says:

"We used to keep a little milk for the Holy Prophet (S.A.W.). When he came late at night, he greeted in such a way that those awake heard him and those sleeping did not feel disturbed. The Holy Prophet (S.A.W.) came and greeted (us) in his customary way." *(Muslim)*

Start talking only after salutation. When you meet somebody, do not start talking with him spontaneously; but greet him first with *As salam-o-Alaikum* and then start talking. The Holy Prophet (S.A.W.) has directed: "Do not reply to a person who starts talking before saluting."

No Greetings are to be Offered when:

(i) People are busy reading or teaching or listenting to Holy Quran or the Hadis,

(ii) When a person is engaged in delivering or listening to a Khutbah (sermon),

(iii) When someone is calling for the prayers or announcing Takbir,

(iv) When an assembly is discussing religious matters or when somebody is explaining some theological matters to someone,

(v) When a teacher is busy in teaching; and

(vi) When someone is in the bathroom (lavatory).

And under the following situations you should not only avoid greeting a person but also show your indifference abhorrence and dislike with tact:

(i) When someone is busy in acts amounting to licentiousness, blasphemy and anti-religious games and amusements and thus is insulting the faith.

(ii) When a person is uttering abuses and having filthy nonsensical and false dialogue and cutting indecent and vulgar jokes, thus ridiculing Islam.

(iii) When a man is busy propagating views against Islam and Sunnah and exhorting the people to abandon Islam and take up atheism.

(iv) When somebody is abusing Islam, its tenets principles and exhibiting his inner vile nature and hypocrisy.

The Holy Prophet (S.A.W.) has said that: "Do not take initiative in greeting the Jews and Christians. A believer should avoid all such acts that may reflect even an iota of adoration or respect for the Jews. In fact he should always adopt an attitude which would make the Jew understand that the ultimate result of hostility to the truth results in disgrace and ignominy.

> *"The Holy Prophet (S.A.W.) has said: Never take a lead in offering salutation to the Jews and Christians. When you come across them on the road, see that they give way and move to one side."* *(Al-Adab Al-Mufrad)*

> *Salute a mixed gathering. When an assembly has both Muslims and non-Muslims, they be greeted with "Salam". The Holy Prophet (S.A.W.) once passed a gathering of Muslims and non-believers and he thus saluted them.*
> *(Al-Adab Al-Mufrad)*

When you have to greet a non-Muslim, do not salute him in the conventional Islamic manner. Instead, words like Adab Arz, Taslimat, etc (Respects to you) should be used or you can use western style of salutation like 'Good Morning,' Good Evening or simply how do you do, hello etc. No signs with your hands or head should be shown in a way that may be contrary to Islam. When the Holy Prophet (S.A.W.) sent his message to Heraclius (Hiraql) the emperor of the Eastern Roman Empire, he greeted him as follows:

> *"Greetings be upon him who follows the guidance (of Allah)."*

> *After greeting, clasp the hands of your friend or relative to express your happiness and affection. The Holy Prophet (S.A.W.) and his companions used to do this. When a group of persons from Yemen came to the Holy Prophet (S.A.W.) he told his companions that among all the visitors they (the visitors from Yemen) were more deserving of a cordial hand shake than others."*
> *(Abu Daud)*

Hadrat Hudhaifa bin Yaman reports the Holy Prophet (S.A.W.) as having said:

> *"When two believers meet each other and shake hands after salutation, their sins are shed like dry leaves from a tree."* *(Tibrani)*

According to Hadrat Abdullah bin Masud, the Holy Prophet (S.A.W.) said: "A complete greeting is that in which hands are also shaken after salutation."

On the return of a friend, relative, or an elder from a journey, embrace him as well. When Hadrat Laid bin Harith returned to Medina from a journey, he knocked at the door of the Holy Prophet (S.A.W.). He (S.A.W.) came out with the sheet trailing behind and embraced him, and kissed him on the forehead. (Tirmidhi)

Hadrat Anas narrates that when the august companions met each outer, they used to shake hands with each other followed by an embrace, if they returned from a journey. (Tibrani)

CUSTOMARY BEHAVIOUR

Always try to sit in the company of well behaved and virtuous people. Take lively part in the deliberations of the gathering. To sit tongue-tied with a gloomy face is a sign of diffidence, while sitting quiet with wrinkles on the forehead reflects pride. When the companions of the Holy Prophet (S.A.W.) held discussions in company, the Holy Prophet (S.A.W.) used to join them in those parleys. Therefore, never wear a dour face in an assembly. Sit with a smiling face. Sit wherever you find a place. Do not rush or push others in order to reach the front line, This is an obnoxious practice and causes inconvenience to those who are already sitting there, and makes the person doing this, look haughty.

Do not try to snatch a seat from a person already seated from his seat in a meeting. This will not be tolerated by any body and will send a wave of resentment and hatred for you among those present there. It will, by the way, indicate as if you are somebody big and important. Don't behave ridiculously while sitting in a meeting. If people are sitting in a circle, do not sit in the empty space, in the centre. This is extremely rude and absurd. The Holy Prophet (S.A.W.) has expressed his dislike for such people.

Do not occupy the place of a person who has left the meeting temporarily. Let it remain reserved for him, and occupy it only if you know for certain that he will not come back. If two persons are sitting close to each other, do not try to separate them, as they may be sitting there for some good reason. Segregating them, would make them feel hurt.

Do not try to sit on a distinctive place in a meeting unless you are invited to do so. Take care not to sit with your legs spread and calves exposed. Do not try to sit near the master of ceremonies of the meeting and take your seat in such a way that the people coming later, are not obstructed. Incoming persons should be accommodated without any grumble.

Improper Way of Courtesy : Do not stand in front of or around somebody even if it may be as an expression of courtesy. This way of courtesy is contrary to Islamic teachings. When in a company, two persons should not whisper to each other. Others would feel that they have not been taken into confidence or that they are being talked about.

Don't Show Off in a Meeting : If you have to say anything, say it with the permission of the sir, and do not adopt an attitude in the course of discussion or questions and answers, which may indicate as if you were the Chairman or somebody important. This may be taken as if you wanted to show off. This may also be considered as an insult to the chair. One person should speak at a time, and everyone should have a chance to be heard with attention. Those present should not lose patience and start speaking simultaneously, creating confusion and chaos in the meeting.

Maintain Secrecy : If secret matters have been discussed in the meeting, they should not be discussed elsewhere. The assembly owes it to its members that its deliberations and decisions are not divulged. Another subject should not come under discussion while a subject is already being discussed. Also do not interrupt another speaker. However, if the situation demands that you should speak then and there, seek the permission of the person who is already speaking. The Chairman of the meeting should be fair in giving all the members equal chance to express their opinion freely, and he should have his eyes all over the assembly.

Prayer at the End of the Meeting : Offer the following prayer before the assembly disperses:

> *"O Allah! Grant us capacity to fear Thee which may help us to save ourselves from sin. Vouchsafe us Thine obedience which may help us to reach Thy Paradise. Give us that firm faith before which all our losses may*

the world pale into insignificance. O Allah ! As long as Thou keepest us alive, grant us the capacity to derive full benefit from our sense of hearing, and bodily energy and keep this good in operation after us, Wreak revenge upon our oppressors and grant us victory over our enemies. Do not, O Allah, test us in our faith nor make the world our goal. Make not the world as the optimum of our knowledge, nor make us over to a person who pities us not."

Principles of Business

The Best Earning : Work hard with enthusiasm to earn your living from your business and don't be a burden upon others. Once the Holy Prophet (S.A.W.) was asked as to what was the best way of earning. He said:

"The earning which is earned through one's own efforts, and the business which is free from falsehood, and cheating."

Be Truthful in Your Business : To develop your venture always speak the truth, and shun falsehood in any form.

The Holy Prophet (S.A.W.) has said:

"On the Doomsday Allah shall not speak to, nor look at, nor purify the person and admit him into Paradise who promotes his business through false oaths."

(Muslim)

He (S.A.W.) also said: "Eschew false oaths for increasing your business, for, although in the short term, they look like promotion, but ultimately it loses blessings and profit." *(Muslim)*

Be always honest and trustworthy in your dealings. Do not pollute your Halal *(Lawful) income through black -marketing or supplying poor quality goods. The Prophet of Allah (S.A.W.) has said in this context; "Allah will raise an honest and reliable tradesman with the Prophets, Siddiqs (Friends of Prophet) and Martyrs on the Day of Judgement."* *(Tirmidhi)*

Always try to supply the best possible Goods to the customer. If your are not certain about the quality of the goods, do not sell the same to the customer. If customer seeks your advice, be honest in giving him the best advice. Try to win the confidence of the customers, so that they may regard you as their well-wisher and trust you. The Holy Prophet (S.A.W.) has said:

> *"The person who subsisted on rightly-earned earnings follows my Sunnah, and did not harm the people in any way is a person destined for the heaven." The Companions said: "O Prophet of Allah; "Such people are in great number in these days." He said: "Even after me such people will abound."* *(Tirmidhi)*

Always be punctual and reach your shop or office in time, and work there patiently and steadily. The Holy Prophet (S.A.W.) has said:

> *"Go in search of your livelihood early in the morning as the business conducted in the morning brings blessings and abundance."* *(Tibrani)*

Work hard yourself and see that your employees also work hard. But they should be treated well and sympathetically. Don't treat them curtly or express anger or suspicion. The Holy Prophet (S. A.W.) has observed in this context: "Allah does not grant piety to the people among whom the poor are not given their due share." Be always polite with the customers; you should neither be harsh with them nor be inflexible when demanding return of loan.

> *The Holy Prophet (S.A.W.) has said: "May Allah have mercy upon the person who in matters of business and recovery of debts deals with sympathy and courtesy." (Bukhari)*

> *He (S.A.W.) also said: "Anyone wishing to be saved from the worry and suffocation on Doomsday, should give latitude to the debtor who is empty handed, to enable him pay his debt, or to take off the load of debt from his shoulders."* *(Muslim)*

You should avoid passing defective goods as wholesome. The buyer should be explained the defects of the product if there be any. The Holy Prophet (S.A.W.) once passed by a stock of grain. He touched it and fell moisture inside the stock. He asked the stockist what it was. The merchant said: "O Prophet of Allah (S.A.W.), rains poured upon this stock." The Holy Prophet (S.A.W.) remonstrated: "Then why did you not place the wet wheat over the rest of the stock, so people could see it for themselves. Any one practising deception has no relationship with me." Do not hold back and hoard food grains expecting a risk in price so that you may earn excessive profits. This amounts to harassing Allah's creatures. Holy Prophet's (S.A.W.) injunction on this issue is clear. "He who hoards is a sinner."

Be Fair in Measuring and Weighing : The buyer should be given full measure what he has paid. The same measure should be observed both for sale and purchase. The Holy Prophet (S.A.W.) has warned such merchants: "You have been made responsible for two such things which (if mishandled) have led earlier nations towards destruction." The Holy Quran says:

1. Woe unto the defrauders:
2. Those, who when they take the measure from mankind demand it full,
3. But, if they measure unto them, or weigh for them, they cause them loss.
4. Do such (men) not consider that they will be raised again.
5. Unto an awful Day,
6. The day when (all) mankind stand before the Lord of the Worlds ? (83 : 1-6)

Make Amends for Lying and Wrong Acts : You should make it a point to make up for the acts of omissions and commissions in the course of your business, through Sadaqah and alms as Kaffarah (expiation). The Holy Prophet's (S.A.W.) directive in this connection to tradesmen is as follows:

> *"O ye, who deal in trade! In business transaction there are chances of lying and committing wrong. Therefore, you should invariably give Sadaqah from your wealth."*

One should always bear in mind that trade, which will salvage us from dire punishment in the next world, and which gives in return not material wealth, but everlasting triumph, pleasure and tranquillity, as the Quran has said:

O, ye who believe! shall I show you a commerce that will save you from a painful doom? You should believe in Allah and His messenger, and should strive for the cause of Allah with your wealth and your lives. That is better for you, if you did not know. **(61 : 10 - 11)**

Panic and Commotion

How to Behave in Emergencies : Whether due to the fear of killing, bloodshed, looting, atrocities or widespread disturbances by the anti-Islam forces or apprehension of large scale devastation brought about by natural phenomena, in any case, as a Muslim you have to give a good account of yourself. You should try to find out the real causes of such happenings instead of wasting time on shallow measures and take steps as laid down in the Holy Quran and the Sunnah. The Quran says:

"And the mishaps that have visited you, are the results of your misdeeds. And Allah does forgive many of your misdeeds." *(42 : 30)*

And further the Holy Quran has shown the remedy in these words:

"And turn to Allah, all of you together, O Muslims, so that you may succeed." *(24 :31)*

Taubah means to 'Turn to' to 'Revert to'. When the Ummah engulfed in the whirlpool of sins feels repentant on its sins, returns to Allah with all humility, and washes its sins with the tears of repentance, renewing its pledge of faithfulness and obedience to Allah, such an act is designated as *"Taubah"* by the Holy Quran and it is this "*Taubah*" or repentance that is the best remedy against all kinds of fears and trepidation. Do not yield or surrender to the enemies of your religion, as a result of your fear of their atrocities. Do not beg for mercy from the merciless. Do not smear your national image with the spots of cowardice. Instead, we should brace up and cultivate that courage for want of which we are losing ground to the enemies of Islam.

Cause of the Downfall of the Muslims : The Holy Prophet (S.A.W.) has already anticipated that:

"A time will come when other nations shall fall upon my (Ummah) like hungry people jostling for food. Some one enquired, "O! Prophet of Allah, will our population be so small that other nations would gang up to swallow us." "No", replied the Holy Prophet (S.A.W.), "Your number will not be small : but you will be weightless like the sticks or straw carried by a river in spate. The enemies will not be afraid of you, as your hearts will be filled with cowardice. On being asked by a person as to why the Ummah would lose courage, the Holy Prophet (S.A.W.) said, "This would be due to the Muslims' love for the world and their distaste for death and avoiding to die for a just cause." (Abu Daud)

We should constantly carry on Jihad against collective maladies which cause panic and fear within the society, and poverty, famine, and bloodshed become all too common; such a situation is the ideal compost on which tyrants grow and hold the people in the vice of ear. Hadrat Abdullah-ibn-Abbas has said:

"A people among whom the habit of misappropriation becomes rampant, Allah will make them suffer from fear of the enemy. And a society in which adultery is common is doomed to perish; while persons practising short measure, shall invariably suffer from famine and starvation; and a place where judgments are unjust shall suffer from murder and killing; and a nation that betrays and turns its back on solemn affirmation, shall be subjugated by the enemy. (Miskhat)

Courage in the Midst of Ordeals : However shocking be the circumstances, we should always ,support the truth. To die in the cause of truth is better than to live a life devoid of faith and honour. Even if beset with the severest trial and danger, we should not abandon truth. If somebody threaten us with death, we should smile and, if the occasion for martyrdom comes, we should welcome it. The Holy Prophet (S.A.W.) has said:

"The wheel of Islam is in rotation. Turn to the direction shown by the Quran. Beware! The Quran and the (secular) power (state) shall soon separate. Beware! Lest

you leave the Quran. There will be rulers who would make decisions about you and if you submit to them, they would deflect you from the right path; and if you refuse to obey them, they may kill you." A companion asked: "Then what should we do?" The Holy Prophet (S.A.W.) said: "Do what the disciples of Christ did. They were sawed alive and crucified but they did not falter. It is far better to die in obedience to Allah than to live a miserable life in disobedience to Him."

Prayers for Safety from Enemies : When there is fear from enemies, the following prayer is to be recited:

"Allah! we make Thee our shield against these enemies, and seek Thy protection against their mischiefs."

"O Allah! cover my defects and grant me peace and immunity from fear and anxiety."

How to Act When Over-taken with Fear and Panic : The following prayer is to be recited when you are over taken with fear and panic.

"Pure and Sublime is Allah the real King, free from all blemishes. Lord of Angels and Jibbrail. Thou hast covered the Heavens and the Earth with glory and might."

God willing, fear will be banished and you will receive peace of mind. According to Hadrat Baraa-bin-Azib: "This prayer was prescribed by the Holy Prophet (S.A.W.) to a person who complained of dread haunting him. He recited this prayer and the dread was dispelled. (Mujam Al Tibrani)

How to React on Seeing a Hurricane : *When there is high wind or storm, it is natural that one should feel anxiety and fear.-Hadrat Aishah (R.A.A.) says that she never saw the Holy Prophet (S.A.W.) laugh so as to make his mouth open widely. He would smile only. And whenever there was a thick cloud or high wind, he used to feel anxious and started praying. He (S.A.W.) would get up and sit down, and this restlessness persisted till it rained. Hadrat Aishah (R.A.A.) says, she asked the Holy Prophet (R.A.A.) "O Prophet of Allah, I see people* *turn cheerful when they see the rain-laden clouds, but I see uneasiness and anxiety on your face, when you see thick cloud". The Holy Prophet (S.A.W.) replied "O Aishah, how can I feel immune from anxiety, when I know that the people of 'Aad were visited by similar clouds, which they thought would rain water over them, but they brought catastrophe. (Bukhari - Muslim)*

On such occasions recite *Surah Al Falaq* (Chapter 113 and *Surah An Nas* (Chapter 114) of the Holy Quran: Translation of Chapter 113 is given below:

"Say: I seek refuge in the Lord of day-break, from the evil of that which He, created, from the evil of the darkness When it is intense and from the evil of the malignant witchcraft, and from the evil of the envier when he entreth.

Translation of Chapter 114 is given below:

"Say: I seek refuge in the Lord of mankind, the King of mankind, the God of mankind, from the evil of the snacking whisperer Jinns and mankind."

According to Hadrat Aishah, the Holy Prophet (S. A.W.) recited the following prayer when he saw high wind rising:

O Allah! I ask Thee the good of this wind and the good of whatever is in it; and good for the purpose for which it has been sent. And I seek Thy protection from the evil of the wind, from the evil of that, which is in it, and from the evil of the purpose for which it has been sent. (Muslim)

When there is apprehension of danger due to heavy rains, the following prayer is to be offered:

"Allah! let it rain around us, not upon us. Let it rain over mountains, hillocks, valleys, fields, and on places where vegetation grows." (Muslim)

When there is roaring of the clouds and thunder, all conversation should be stopped and the following Ayat of the Holy Quran be recited:

"The Thunder hymneth His praise and sends the angels for awe of Him." (13 : 13)

Hadrat Abdullah Ibn Zubayr, used to stop talking on hearing the roaring of the thunder and started reciting this Ayat. *(Al Adab Al-kufrad)*

Hadrat Kaab says anyone who recites this Ayat thrice, shall be safe from the ill effects of the roaring of the clouds. (Tirmidhi)

When the Holy Prophet (S.A.W.) used to hear the roaring of thunder, recited:

"Allah kill us not with Thy wrath; destroy us not with Thy punishment and take us in Thy protection before the advent of such an adverse moment."

When fire breaks out, 'Allaho Akbar' should be recited continuously alongwith strenuous efforts to put it out. The Holy Prophet (S.A.W.) has said: "When there is a fire, recite 'Allaho Akbar', this extinguishes the fire."

During Eclipses : When there is eclipse either of the sun (kasuf) or the moon (khasuf), prayers should be offered and alms be given to the poor. As a result of these supplications, Allah will ward off all catastrophies and miseries. Hadrat Mughira ibn Shuba says that the Holy Prophet (S.A.W.) once remarked:

"The sun and moon are simply two signs of Allah. The two planets do not come under eclipse due to the death or birth of an individual. When you see them under eclipse, solicit Allah's mercy and pray till such time as the sun or the moon gets cleared."(Bukhari - Muslim)

How to Pray : When there is solar eclipse, prayers should be offered in congregation in the mosque, but there should be no call for prayers Azan or Iqamat. Only people should congregate and offer prayers. When there is a lunar eclipse, Nafils (optional prayers) should be offered individually and not collectivity.

Continuous Nafil Prayers During Eclipse : When there is a solar eclipse, two Nafils should he offered, and the recitation (during the Qiyam) should be longer than usual. Prayers are to be continued till the eclipse is cleared. Verses from the Holy Quran should be recited a bit loudly.

There was a solar eclipse during the life time of the Holy Prophet (S. A.W.). Incidentally Hadrat Ibrahim, the infant son of the Holy Prophet (S.A.W.) died on that very day. People began to attribute the eclipse to the death of Hadrat Ibrahim. When this was brought to the notice of the Holy Prophet (S.A.W.) he collected the people and offered a two-rakat prayer, with a long qirah during the qiyam, reciting Surah Al-Baqarah. He knelt (Ruku) and prostrated (Sajdah) for a longer spell. By the time the prayer was over, the sky was clear. The Holy Prophet (S.A.W.) then told the worshippers that solar and lunar eclipses are two signs from Allah and the same is not due to the birth or death of anyone. He exhorted the people to take recourse to prayers and contemplation on such occasions, and to offer prayers and charities.

(Bukhari — Muslim)

Hadrat Abdul Rahman bin Samurah has this to say about a solar eclipse.

"A solar eclipse took place during the blessed days of the Holy Prophet (S.A.W.). I was practising archery outside Medina. I threw the arrows and at once left for the city to see for myself as to what the Holy Prophet (S.A.W.) does on this occasion. As such I presented myself before the Holy Prophet (S.A.W.). I saw that with his hands cupped and raised, he was praying and supplicating to Allah. He then offered a two-rakat prayer, reciting two long surahs. He remained thus engaged till the eclipse was cleared."

Which Surahs are to be Recited : When the prayer is for the solar eclipse, Surah Ankabut (The spider) is to he recited after Surah Fatiha in the first Rakat and Surah Rum in the second Rakat. It is better to recite these Surahs although the same is not compulsory; other Surahs can also be recited. If women desire to participate in congregational prayers held for solar eclipse, they may be allowed to do so. Children should also be encouraged to join such a congregation so that the concept of monotheism takes roots in their hearts from the very beginning and no contrary impression takes root. As laid down by the Shariah prayers are not to be offered at sunrise, sunset and when the sun is at its peak. If the solar eclipse has occurred during these hours, prayers should not be offered, only recitation of supplications and verses from the holy Quran together with distribution of alms and charities be done. If the eclipse persists even after these prohibited hours prayers can be offered.

UTILIZATION OF TIME

Every lost thing can be regained. The lost game can be rewon. But the time which has passed away, it is useless to hope for its return. That is why in all the possessions of man, time is considered to be the most valuable and most precious. Man should spend his time in such a way as a greedy man spends his money. He does not show the slightest carelessness in spending even the smallest amount, and he considers everything compared to wealth insignificant and of no value. When a man thinks about his existence and contemplates over his past life to count the months and the years that have flown by, he is unable to give much time to this sort of thinking, because he cannot have the correct estimate of his correct timings.

Then days and months pass away, and the accidents and events of these days and months pass from his sight, and he feels that the whole life had been spent in one day, and all the accidents and events had taken place in a single day. An Urdu poet says:

> *"We had come with a long life of four days, which we had begged,*
>
> *Two days passed away in wishing, and two days in waiting."*

This feeling a man has in this world. What would be his feelings on the Day of Judgment, when there will be reckoning?

> *"And on the day when He shall gather them together, (when it will seem) as though they had tarried but an hour of the day, recognising one another."(Yunus: 46)*
>
> *"Murmuring among themselves, You have tarried but ten (days). We are best aware of what they utter when their best in conduct say: You have tarried but a day."*
>
> *(Ta Ha : 103-104)*

"On the day when they behold it, it will be as if they had but tarried for an evening or the morning thereof."
(Naziat : 46)

This feeling is very auspicious. And those who realize their own reality that they are made of the dust and are to mix with the dust one day, they will be uncomfortable with this feeling. This is a great and right feeling, provided the life in this world is compared with the life in the next. But this very feeling becomes a means of straying and misguidance for those who are not moved by the passage of time, being totally lost in a luxurious and sinful life. They are ignorant of their past and future, but when their last moments come, their eyes become helplessly sightless, the darkness of death is approaching, at that time they may suddenly wake up from their slumber, and may feel sorry and cry. But at such a time of what use this crying and feeling sorry would be for them. What is the use of crying over spilt milk! In this world the position of man and his affairs is very strange. He is busy in amusements and pleasure seeking, and the destiny is busy with its work. He is totally lost in his luxuries and his every act and thought is being entered in the records:

On the day that Allah will raise them all up (again) and show them the Truth (and meaning) or their conduct. Allah has reckoned its (value), though they may have forgotten it, for Allah is Witness to all things.
(Mujadla : 6)

A true Muslim values the time very dearly, because time is his life and if he loses it, he will he digging his own grave. Man is rapidly running towards Allah. Every revolution of the heaven that brings a new morning is a stage in this path, in which there is no stop-over and no staying. Is it not wise that man should not forget this reality, and that he should always keep it before his eyes. The past and the future should always be kept by him in his sight. It is only a deception of the sight that a man travelling by train should think that all the things outside are travelling or running in the opposite direction at a fast pace, and that he himself is stationary. The fact is that the time is advancing towards its destination taking man with it. It cannot leave him.

Value of Time : Islam is such a religion as recognises the importance and value of time. 'It gives to its followers this valuable advice with full emphasis : "Time is like a sword; if you will not cut it, it will cut you." It considers it a sign of faith and righteousness that man should understand this reality and in this light should lead his life

Verily, in the difference of day and night and all that Allah has created in the heavens and the earth are portents, verily, for folk who ward off (evil).

(Yunus: 7)

Those who are careless of the future, intoxicated with the present and are under the spell of the glitter of the world have been called by Islam as foolish and the losers.

Verily, those who expect not the meeting with Us but desire the life of the world and feel secure therein, and those who are neglectful of Our revelations, their home will be the Fire, because of what they used to earn.

(Yunus : 8, 9)

Islam has distributed its important forms of worship in the various parts of the day and the different seasons of the year. The five times' prayers cover the whole day, and their timings correspond with the passage of the passing day. The Archangel Jibbrail came down from the heaven so that the proper timings of the beginning and the end may be fixed, through which a firm system to regulate the Islamic life may be brought into being. Accordingly from the dawn to the dusk, the various hours have been fixed for prayers and remembrance of Allah:

So glory be to Allah when you enter the night and when you enter the morning-Unto Him be praise in the heavens and the earth! -and at the sun's decline and in the noonday. *(Rum: 17-18)*

A limited sight can only see the perceptible manifestations and the limited signs. It is confined to the world's accidents and events, the festivities and the tragedies, while Time makes the conceited tyrants eat the dust, tramples the wishes and aspirations of men, and completely destroys even such civilizations whose achievements make men gasp in wonderment.

It is Time itself that alerts the intelligent and prompts them to proceed towards righteous deeds and collecting profitable materials for the next world :

> *Blessed is He Who made constellations in the skies, and placed therein a lamp and moon giving light; and it is He Who made the night and the day to follow each other, for such as have the will to celebrate His praises or to show their gratitude.* *(Furqan: 61-62)*

The night follows the day, and then day appears with the movements of the skies. This coming and going of the day and night has not been arranged by Allah without any purpose. It will be extremely foolish if man thinks that this organised life of his is purposeless. This is a field of competition for man, and in it only that person takes part who recognises his Lord, is aware of His rights, is thankful for His gifts, and who thinks that the continuity of the months and years is for putting in efforts and labour, so that final grand relief and comfort may be obtained. Those who are ignorant of the realities, and run after their own worldly ephemeral benefits, are fools. They cannot take advice from any wise example and no lesson is beneficial for them:

> *See they not that they are tried every year once or twice ? Yet they turn not in repentance, and they take no heed.* *(Tauba : 126)*

Life is a gift given by God, about which every man will be questioned on the Day of Judgment as to where did he spend it and in what work did he utilise it ? Allah's Messenger says: "On the Doomsday no person will be able to walk a step further before answering four questions : In what acts did he spend his life ? In what did he spend his youth? From where did he get wealth and where did he spend it? And to what extent did he act on the knowledge that he attained?" In many of its do's and don'ts, Islam has taken into consideration the importance and value of time.

For example when it says that to abstain from sinful amusements is the sign of faith, in reality there is a wise move hidden in this that steps should be taken against those who invite each other for wasting time in sinful amusements. Do these idiots know that it is a game with life and that wastage of time in this way is destructive for the individual and the society both?

Time is short and Duties are Countless : The common people do not know this secret that "Duties are many and the time is short," and "The time is never impartial, either it will be the closest friend or the fiercest foe." It is a saying of Hasan Basri (R.A.): "With the appearance of the dawn a caller from God declares: 'O Son of Adam : I am a new creature and a witness for your arms.

Through me collect righteous deeds, because I cannot return again till the Doomsday." These valuable advises are extracted from the spirit of Islam and are charged with the great lesson of considering the worldly life as a sowing field for reaping the produce in the Hereafter. And this is only the favour of Allah that man spends a portion of every age in righteous deeds and gets ready for launching new acts of virtue with fresh vigour:

Of His mercy has He appointed for you night and day, that therein you may rest, and that you may seek His bounty, and so that you may be thankful.

(Al-Qasas : 73)

It is a pity that the common people are not careful about wasting their time. With this they are also guilty of committing another great crime, and that is they also waste the time of others. They interfere with the men who work and disrupt their work by making them turn to purposeless and useless amusements. How truthful had been the Prophet of Allah:

"There are two gifts about which people are mostly dishonest: one is health and the other is leisure."

(Agreed upon)

For the correct use of time, Islam has suggested that the work should be done continually, though it may be small and ordinary, and doing abundant work at one stretch should be avoided as its continuity is broken, because if the small work is done with consistency, then with the passage of time it becomes quite big, of which man had no idea in the beginning. If a desire takes hold of man for being immediately fulfilled, he is tempted to commit excesses and after the passing away of the time and subduing of the passions he feels fed up, and in this way the work he had undertaken, is abandoned by him. Islam dislikes this way of working. There is a *Hadith:*

> *"O People! Perform only those acts of which you have the strength, because Allah is not afraid of giving rewards until you are fed up. Allah likes that act best which is done consistently, even if it may be ordinary."* *(Agreed upon)*

> *Hadrat Aishah narrates that the Prophet of Allah went to her and a woman from the Banu Asad tribe was sitting with her. He inquired who she was. Hadrat Aishah replied that she was such and such lady and said that she offered prayers during the whole night. The Prophet (S.A.W.) said : "Wait, only that much quantum of work is enjoined for doing which you have strength, and Allah likes that piety which has consistency in it."* *(Muslim)*

For safeguarding time, Islam has ordained its followers to rise early in the morning, and it has induced them to start their day's work with full determination and enthusiasm. If in the beginning of the day there is a determination that full benefit is to be derived, then man will always take care to see that his time is not wasted.

The Islamic system starts its day with the dawn, and declares it compulsory that man must be fully awake before the sunrise. On the other hand that kind of night watching is disliked which comes in the way of performing the morning prayer later than its traditional time. There is a tradition of the Prophet :

> *"O Allah! Make the rising in the morning of my ummah auspicious."* *(Abu Daud)*

It is great deprivation and negligence that people should continue sleeping much after the sunrise. The sun may rise and they may sleep wrapped up in warm covers, while others may be busy going to earn their living or busy in earning for the Hereafter! Hadrat Fatima (R.A.A.) bint Muhammad (S.A.W.) narrates

> *"Allah's Messenger passed by me and I was lying. He stirred me with his foot and said : 'O my daughter! get*

up and behold the gift of your Lord, and do not be neglectful, for Allah distributes livelihood from the appearance of Fajr (dawn) to the sunrise. (Baihaqui)

This is the time when the lazy and the active persons are distinguished from one another. And Allah gives to every man from the good of the world and the Hereafter according to his capacity.

Lesson is for the Intelligent : As this worldly life is full of troubles and difficulties that befall men, similarly it is full of those decisions and commands which Allah ordains in respect of His slaves. Those who take interest in these decisions can only take a lesson from them

Verily, Allah causes the revolution of the day and the night. Verily, herein indeed is a lesson for those who see.
(An-Nur : 44)

People see the accidents and the events, but forget or are neglectful of the One who causes them. They enjoy good times and suffer during hard times, but remain unaware of the Being who is the source of everything. Therefore, if in any case they are surrounded by difficulties, they start abusing the time or the world. This is a proof of the ignorance about Allah and of being negligent of the destiny. Allah's Prophet (S.A.W.) has said:

Allah says that Adam's son hurts Him; he abuses the time, although I am Myself time, in My hand is the rein of all affairs; I cause revolution of the day and night.
(Abu Daud)

That is the time itself does not involve anybody in good or bad conditions, so that people may be pleased with it or may be sad. All this is done by the Creator of the Time and Space, the Almighty Allah.

Every soul must taste of death, and We try you with evil and with good, for ordeal. And to Us you will be returned.
(Ambiya: 35)

Allah is describing all these different conditions so that the learned men may think over them, may contemplate over them, and from that their faith may be strengthened.

> *He does regulate affairs, explaining the signs in detail, that they may believe with certainty in the meeting with your Lord.* (Raad: 2)

But those who are foolish and unintelligent, they see the good and bad conditions in the world, but do not derive benefit from them. In the *Hadith* it is stated:

> *"When a hypocrite gets ill and then recovers from his illness, his example is like that of a camel, whose master ties it to a stake and then frees it, but it does not know why was it tied and why was it freed'.* (Abu Daud)

It is correct that a person cannot be a Momin if the experiences do not make him civilised and the passage of time does not teach him anything. Difficulties and adversities befall a man so that the ignorant may become learned, the neglectful may become alert and the transgressor may become righteous

> *We have already sent to peoples that were before you, and We visited them tribulations and adversity, in order that they might grow humble. If only, when a disaster came on them, they had been humble!*
>
> (Al-dnam : 42-43)

It is human nature that man remembers God is adversity. Why he is Surrounded by various kinds of difficulties, and when all the sources of worldly support vanish, he seeks Allah's refuge. A wise man's attitude should be like this that when in difficulties he turns to Allah, in other days of comfort also he should make his relationship with Him firm and strong, because it will be sheer meanness that man should feel independent of Him and should deny His immense favours to him. Defaulters, who deny higher values and are careless of accidents and events, seek the refuge of Allah in danger, and during the peaceful days run away from Him .

> *And when his misfortune touches a man he cries to Us, (while reclining) on his side, or sitting or standing, but when We have relieved him of the misfortune he goes his way as though he had not cried to Us because of a misfortune that afflicted him. This is what they do make (seeming) fair to the prodigal.* (Yams: 13)

This is a very abominable act, which does not become a decent man.

Study of the Nations and Communities : One way of learning a lesson from the world is to study the history of the peoples, and Allah's signs should be sought in the skies and men ; the conditions of the nations should be reflected upon as to how some reached the peak of progress and how others became subject to decline and fall. What were the causes of the progress and the downfall ? Allah wants that people should see the different periods and stages of the past, and should try to derive benefit with the help of alert conscience:

> *Have they not travelled in the land, and have they hearts wherewith to feel and ears wherewith to hear? For indeed it Is not the eyes that grow blind, but it is the hearts, which are within the bosoms, that grow blind.* *(Hajj : 46)*

A man can have two conditions, either he has some specific experiences with the help of which he will correct and strengthen his faith, or he will have no knowledge. In the tatter case, he should listen to others and try to derive benefit from the experiences and learning of others. If he sees the events of the world, but does not take any lessons from them, then it is called darkness, blindness and waywardness, which does not become a Momin. Life is very short, and the condition in which a man is breathing is very straitened. Being confined to this sphere, life cannot provide to man intellect, survival and provisions for progress. It is necessary that access should be achieved to the higher spheres and everlasting times.

On consideration of the realities and the events of this world and the next, of the past, present and the future times, a vast treasure of ideas, stories and opinions would be available, which would acquaint us with the world. It will help us to understand correctly the knowledge about the Lord of the worlds. On these foundations of discussion and research, thinking and reflection, experiences and discoveries, the edifice of a strong and firm faith is built. For this reason Islam commanded its sons to undertake long journeys and distant travels and considered the covering of the distances of the east and west as an approved act. But this covering of long distances should not be for amusements and pleasure seeking but should be for deriving benefit and for acquiring knowledge. It should not be for passing away time or for sport but for research, fact-finding and discovery, and for learning a lesson from the histories of the dead and the living

> *Systems have passed away before you. Do but travel in the land and see the nature of the consequence for those who did deny (the messengers). This is a declaration for mankind, a guidance and an admonition to those who ward of (evil).* *(Al-i-Imram : 1.17-138)*

> *Have they never travelled in the earth that they might see the consequence of those who had preceded them. They were stronger than them and have left greater heritage in the earth. Then Allah grasped them for their suns, and there was home to save them from Allah.* *(Madyan : 21)*

In this way the holy Quran directs to reflect on the past civilizations and the causes of their downfall so that the coming generations may be saved from the lapses, which the earlier people had committed. How many wonders can come to light from the study of the history! The world itself is a sign, whose reality is not possible to be discovered. However we can recognise it only by studying its signs and symptoms, because the secrets of the ephemeral and everlasting life are buried in that

> *He it is Who has sown you broadcast on the earth, and to Him you will be gathered. And He it is Who gives life and causes death, and His is the difference of night and day. Have you then no sense ? (Almuminoon : 79-81)*

The thing necessary to understand is this that this life of ours is not useless, and that Allah has not made it without any purpose. When we will get to know this secret, the world will not be able to destroy us ever.

9

Duty towards Guests

When a guest arrives, receive him warmly and express your happiness on his arrival and do not express any sign of indifference or resentment. The Holy Prophet (S.A.W.) has said:

"Those who believe in Allah and the Hereafter should be hospitable to their guests." (Bukhari - Muslim)

Hospitality includes respect and cordiality, comfort and convenience to the guest; cheer him and make him happy by pleasant conversation; introduce him to your intimate friends and serve him personally. All this is known as the Ikram-e-Zaif (honour for the guest). The Sunnah of the Holy Prophet (S.A.W.) tells us that the Prophet himself used to entertain his guest and insisted on his eating till he was full.

CARING FOR THE GUEST

When the guest arrives, he should first be greeted and enquiries made about his welfare.

The Quran says :

"Hath the story of Ibrahim's honoured guests reached thee (O Muhammad) when they came unto him and said; Peace! he answered peace!" (51 : 25)

Hospitality Should be Generous : The guest should be entertained generously and lavishly with the best possible fare that may he available. When guests came to Prophet Ibrahim, he immediately set himself to arrange for their food; he picked up a well-fed and fat calf and slaughtered it to prepare roasted meat for them. The Holy Quran says :

"Then he hastened to his house and (slaughtered) a well fed and fat calf and prepared a roast for his guests."

It is also implied that Prophet Ibrahim went to his house to arrange for the food quietly, so that the guests might not know about it, otherwise considering the host's inconvenience, they might formally refuse to eat., and it would not be possible for the host to have the honour of entertaining his guests. The Holy Prophet (S.A.W.) has emphasised the importance of hospitality and this has been graphically described by Hadrat Abu Shuraih:

"These two eyes and these two ears of mine have seen and heard the Holy Prophet (S.A.W.) saying, "Those who believe in Allah and the Hereafter should entertain their guest well. The reward of entertaining the guest is the prized first day and the first night (of his stay)."
(Bukhari—Muslim)

"The First day and the first night" requires an explanation. Just as one who gives away a reward or a prize, does so with great pleasure and spiritual satisfaction, the host also feels the same way when he entertains his guest on the first day and the first night. The receiver of the award feels happy and appreciates the gesture of the giver, the same sentiments should be expressed by the guest.

Convenience of the Guest : When the guest arrives, his physical needs require looking after. Arrangements for bathroom and toilet conveniences should be made forthwith. After the guest has taken his bath and made himself easy, ask him for meal although it may not be time for a meal, and this should be done in such a way that the guest may not refuse formally. Thereafter, the room where he is to stay should be shown to him.

Allow the Guest, Time for Rest and Privacy : Keeping in view the convenience of the guest, he should be given some time to be alone and you should not be with him all the time lest he should be feeling bored or inconvenienced or may be in need of rest particularly at night when he likes to go to bed early. When guests came to the house of Prophet Ibrahim he left them alone for a while, looking after their comforts and needs. Feel happy on the arrival of guest and express your joy on his taking his meals with you, and you should not feel annoyed on his arrival. A guest is not a source of trouble, but a blessing sent by Allah. When He sends a guest to you, He also provides his food; and the guest eats at your dining table only his share of food which has been already predestined for him.

The honour and prestige of the guest should be guarded as your own and an attack upon his honour should be regarded as an attack on your honour. The guest is to be entertained lavishly and with an open heart for three days. This is the right of the guest. A Muslim should be very generous in the discharge of this duty. The first day is the special day for entertaining the guest, who should be treated very well. It does not matter if the same arrangements could not be made on the next two days. The Holy Prophet (S.A.W.) has said:

> *"And hospitality is for three days, after which whatever the host does is Sadaqah (favour)".*
>
> *(Bukhari—Muslim)*

Service of the Guest : The guest should be looked after by the host personally instead of being left to the care of the children or servants. The Holy Prophet (S.A.W.) used to entertain the guests himself. When Iman Shafi stayed as Imam Malik' guest, the latter provided him with all comforts and made him sleep in a separate room. At dawn the guest heard someone knocking at his door and said in a very affectionate voice -May Allah bless you! It, is the prayer-time." Imam Shafi got up and saw Imam Malik himself holding a water jug for ablution. Imam Shafi felt embarrassed which Imam Malik guessed, but the host said in a tone full of love: 'Do not mind this, brother. The guest has to be served."

After making guest comfortable in his room show him the toilet and the water pot. He should be furnished with a prayer mat and the place marked for prayer, and shown the direction of the Qiblah. Imam Malik's servant after having settled Imam Shafi in his room, did like this.

How to Handle the Guest at the Dining Table : At the meal time, the host should go to the dining place with his hands already washed thoroughly. He should then help the guest or guests to wash hands. When Iman Malik followed this practice,

Iman Shafi asked him the significance for this, who said: "The host should wash his hands first and then prepare to welcome the guests in the dining room. After the dinner is over, the host should wash the hands of the guests first but wash his own last, lest some guests may drop in. Make arrangements of fare, crockery, etc., a little more than the guests, so that you may not be put to embarrassment if another guest arrives. If the extra arrangement exists, the new host would naturally feel pleased and honoured. The guest should be provided with all comfort, even at the cost of your own comfort, and convenience.

Once a man presented himself before the Holy Prophet (S.A.W.) and said: "O Prophet of Allah, ! I am very much hungry." The Holy Prophet sent sword to one of his holy wives to send whatever eatable may be available with her. Her reply was: "By Allah who sent you as His Prophet, there is nothing but water with me." He then sent word to another wife and the same reply came from her. He sent word to other wives one by one, and they sent the same negative reply. Then he addressed his companions: "Who volunteers to accept this guest for this night." One Ansar companion said: "O Prophet of Allah"! 1 accept him." The companion took the Holy Prophet's (S.A.W.) guest to his house and said to his wife: "I have with me the Holy Prophet's (S.A.W.) guest, entertain him." His wife said: "I have food sufficient for the children only." The companion said: "Then put the children to sleep by some excuse. But when you place the food before the guest, put out the lamp on some pretext, and sit near him, so that he may think that we have also joined him in eating."

The guest thus ate to his fill, while the hosts passed the night without food. When the same companion presented himself before the Holy Prophet (S.A.W.) next morning, he said: "What you both did for the guest last night, has been greatly appreciated by Allah.(Bukhari—Muslim)

Hospitality to be Shown under All Circumstances : Even if your guest might have been discourteous to you in the past, you should treat him well.

Hadrat Abul-Ahwas Jashmi says that his father once asked the Holy Prophet (S.A.W.), "If a person fails to extend his hospitality to me, and later on comes to me as a guest, should I extend hospitality to him or teach him a lesson for his indifference and misbehaviour?" The Holy Prophet (S.A.W.) said: "No, you must fulfil your duty and be hospitable to him." *(Mishkat)*

The guest should be requested to pray for the host, especially if the former be a scholar or a 'virtuous and religious person. Hadrat Abdullah Ibn Busar narrates the following story in this context:

"The Holy Prophet (S.A.W.) once graced the house of my father by his stay. We offered him Haritha. He ate a little and then we offered him dates. He ate the dates and threw the stones holding them with two fingers. This was followed by a beverage, of which he drank a little, and passed it on to the person sitting on his right. When he was about to leave, my father caught hold of his bridle and requested him to pray for him. The Holy Prophet (S.A.W.) prayed for him in these words."

O Allah! Bless the food Thou hast given them. Forgive them and have mercy upon them."

PRINCIPLES OF HOSPITALITY

If you go as a guest, you should take with you, according to your financial position, gifts for the host or his children suiting to their taste and liking. Exchange of gifts and presents help increase mutual love and regard and it creates a place in the heart of the person receiving the gift for the one who presents it.

Except under special circumstances or under vehement pressure from the host, one should not stay with the host for more than three days. The Holy Prophet (S.A.W.) has said: "It is not proper for a guest to stay as long as to embarrass the host." *(Al-Adab AI-Mu frad)*

Another Hadith says: "The Holy Prophet (S.A.W.) has said that "It is not proper for a Muslim to so much prolong his stay with his brother as to render him a sinner." The companions asked, "How, O Prophet of Allah, will the guest make the host a sinner?" The Holy Prophet (S.A.W.) said: "If he stays with him so long that he has nothing to offer." *(Muslim)*

Invite Others Also to be Your Guests : You should not always be a guest of others; invite others also to be your guest and entertain them lavishly. While travelling by land or sea, the guest should make it a point to invariably take with him necessary clothes and bedding according to the season.

During winter in particular, one should not go to another's house without warm bedding. This will obviate considerable inconvenience and embarrassment to the host.

The engagements and avocation of the host should be kept in mind and the guest should see to it that he does not disturb him. Avoid making demand of different kinds from the host. He should be thanked for what he does for your entertainment and comfort.

Do Not Violate Purdah: If the guest is not related in blood with the family of the host, he should not converse with the female members in the absence of the host unnecessarily nor he should try to hear their talk. He should stay there without causing any inconvenience to them and violating their privacy.

Pray for the Host : If the guest for some reason or the other does not want to eat with the host or is on fast he should tactfully apologize and pray for the host's welfare. The guest, when invited, should pray for the abundance of means welfare, Allah's blessings and mercy for the host after the meal.

> *Hadrat Abu Al-Haysam bin Tayhan once invited the Holy Prophet (S.A.W.) and the companions. When the meal was over the Holy Prophet (S.A.W.) said: "Repay your brother! The companions asked: "What repayment should we make?" The Holy Prophet (S.A.W.) said: "When a man goes to the house of his brother and eats, he should pray for his welfare and prosperity. This is his repayment."* *(Abu Daud)*

The Holy Prophet (S.A.W.) once graced the house of Hadrat Sad bin Ubadah. Hadrat Sad offered him bread and olive, which he ate, and then said the following prayer:

> *"May those who fast, break their fasts at your place, may pious people eat here, and may angels pray for mercy upon you and forgiveness for you."*

ATTENDING THE PATIENTS

Visiting the sick is important not only from social point of view and developing mutual affection and cooperation, but it is also the religious right of a Muslim over another Muslim and an essential expression of love for Allah and a lover of Allah cannot remain isolated or indifferent with the affairs of the servants. Negligence in visiting the sick is equivalent to His neglect of Allah. The Holy Prophet (S.A.W.) has said:

> *"On the Day of Judgment Allah shall say 'O son of Adam! You did not visit me when I was sick". The servant shall say, 'O Almighty Allah! You are the Creator of the Universe, how could I visit you?" Allah shall then say; "When such and such creature of Mine fell ill, you visited him not. Had you visited him, you would have found Me there (i.e. you would have earned My pleasure and blessings)."*

That is, if a sick person is visited, it pleases Allah immensely. The Holy Prophet (S.A.W.) has further said:

> *"There are six rights which one Muslim has over the other." Some one asked to enumerate them; "O Prophet of Allah, what-sights are these." The Holy Prophet (S.A.W.) replied:*

(i) When you meet a fellow-Muslim, offer salutations to him.

(ii) If invited by him to meal, accept the invitation.

(iii) When he requests you for an advice, be good to him, and give him a sound advice to his advantage.

(iv) When he sneezes and says Al Hamdo Lillah, say Yarhamukallah.

(v) When he is sick, visit him and enquire about his health.

(vi) When he dies, participate in his funeral.

And the Holy Prophet (S.A.W.) has also said:

"He who visits his sick Muslim brother, shall have his abode in the upper chamber of Paradise."

(Al-Adab Al-Mufrad).

Hadrat Abu Hurrayrah narrates the Holy Prophet (S.A.W.) said: "When a man visits his brother Muslim, or goes to meet him, it is announced from the Paradise 'You have done a good deed; your visit has been fruitful and you have made an abode for yourself in the Heaven." *(Tirmidhi)*

When a sick person is visited, the visitor should move his hand gently over his head or body and say words of consolation and encouragement, so that his attention is drawn to the blessings and rewards of Hereafter and he may not utter any words of impatience or complaint. Hadrat Aishah bint Sad reports that once her father fell seriously ill in Mecca. The Holy Prophet (S.A.W.) graced him with visit. Her father said:

"O Prophet of Allah, I am leaving considerable property, and have only one daughter. May I will two thirds and leave one third for my daughter?" The Holy Prophet (S.A.W.) said, "No" He then asked: "can I will one-half and leave the other half to the daughter?" The Holy Prophet (S.A.W.) said, "No". He then asked. "O Prophet of Allah! Can I will one-third?" The Holy Prophet (S.A.W.) said, "Yes, will one-third, this is quite sufficient."

Thereafter the Holy Prophet (S.A.W.) placed his hand upon his forehead and, moved it over his face and stomach, and prayed for him, "O Allah! Grant health to Sad and enable him to complete his migration. Hadrat Sad said that thereafter, whenever I am reminded of that incident I feel the coolness of the Holy Prophet's hand upon my heart." *(Al-Adab Al-Mufrad)*

Hadrat Ibn Abbas says:

"Whenever the Holy Prophet (S.A.W.) visited any sick person, he used to sit near his head and recite the following prayer seven times:

"I beg Almighty Allah, the Lord of the Throne (Grand Heavens) to grant you health," And he said: "The recitation of this prayer for seven times would cure the sick, unless he is destined to die." *(Mishkat)*

How to Talk to the Patient : While visiting a sick person make enquiries about his health and pray for his recovery. Whenever the holy Prophet (S.A.W.) visited an ailing person, he used to ask him "How do you do" and then he (S.A.W.) would condole him and say, "Don't worry, Insha Allah you would be cured, and this ailment would prove a means for the condonation of your sins." And moving his right hand over the place of the pain he would recite the following prayers:

> *"Allah! Take away this ailment. O, the Sustainer of the human beings, help him recover his health. You are the Giver of health. Only You can cure him, and a cure which may completely cure him."*

You should not sit near the patient too long nor create noise near him. However. if the patient happens to be very intimate and close friend or relative and is desirous of having your company for sometime more, then only you may stay with him a little longer.

According to Hadrat Abdullah Ibn Abbas, 'Not to sit too long with a sick person and not to create noise', is a practice of the Holy Prophet (S.A.W.)

Meet the Relative of the Patient Also : The condition of the patient should be enquired from his relatives also and express your sympathies, and do whatever you can do to alleviate their difficulties, e.g., to afford medical help by bringing a doctor, securing medicines, etc., and, if necessary, financial help.

Also visit non-Muslim sick persons, and wisely request them to study and embrace Islam. When sick, a person is more inclined towards Allah and he is likely to accept Islam.

> *Hadrat Anas has it that a Jewish boy used to serve the Holy Prophet (S.A.W.). It so happened that once he fell ill and the Holy Prophet (S.A.W.) graced him with his (S.A.W.) visit. Sitting by his side, the Holy Prophet (S.A.W.) invited him to embrace Islam. The boy looked towards his father who was present, as if asking for his opinion. The father said: "Son follow what Abdul-Qasim says." The son thereupon embraced Islam. The Holy Prophet (S.A.W.) came out saying: "We are thankful to Allah, who has made safe this boy from hell."*
>
> *(Bukhari)*

While visiting a patient, you should not throw your random looks all over; and see that you sit in such a way that your eyes do not fall upon the women folk. Don't visit persons known for their atheism Persons who are known for openly insulting Islam and shamelessly violating the commands of Allah, do not deserve a visit.

Hadrat Abdullah bin 'Umar says: "Do not visit drunkards when they fall ill."

> *While visiting a sick person, request him to pray for you, the prayer of the sick is like the prayer of the angels." This means that the angels only pray when it is so willed by Allah and as such their prayers are graced with acceptance.* *(Ibn Majah)*

10

The Friendship

Deep friendships have great effect and sufficient influence in guiding a man's self and intellect, and their effects are felt on the whole society. The society advances towards economic progress or retards a few steps. Either it gains comfort and peace or pain and distress disturb it. Islam has given great importance to these connections. Through them, you have connection with some persons and you influence them, and you are influenced by them, and these people remain very near to you for a very long period. If the basis of these relationships are on sincerity and selflessness, and if they were established with a view to achieving good consequences, Allah will patronise them and bless them with prosperity, otherwise He throws them back at their faces:

Friends on that day will be foes of one another, save those who kept their duty (to Allah). O My slaves! For you there is no fear this day, nor is it you who grieve.
(Zukhruf : 67, 68)

Islam is the religion of love and collectivism. The tendency to know the people and to meet each other is the foundation of the Islamic teachings. Its development has not been based on wildness and Bedouinism, nor did it teach its sons to be aloof from the common people. It has not taught them to run away from the difficulties of life, nor has it taught a Muslim to meditate in a monastery, or to be lost in worship only. No, by no means ! Allah has not instituted high ranks for these coward and timid people. Allah's Prophet (S.A.W.) has said:

"The Muslim who lives with the people and shows tolerance for the harms received from them is better

than the Muslim who does not meet them and does not show tolerance for the harms received from them."
(Tirmidhi)

For whom the congregational prayers have been made compulsory? For whom the Friday prayers have been compulsory? Who will bear the hardships of Jihad and who have made the courage to bear the hardships experienced in the way ? This heavy burden can be borne only by that Ummah, the mutual relations of whose members among themselves are very strong and firm. Therefore, when Ibn Abbas (R.A.A.) was asked for his opinion about a man who observes fast during the day and offers prayers during the night, but does not attend the daily congregational prayers and the congregational prayers of Fridays. He said:

"Tell him that he is of the hell." *(Tirmidhi)*

It is so because Islam is ardently desirous that its symbols should prove to be the means of mutual sincerity between Muslims, deep love among them and mutual cooperation. As the collective activities of Muslims will increase Allah's blessings on them will increase in the same proportion. In the Hadith it is mentioned:

"It is better to offer prayers in company with another man than offering it alone, and offering prayers in the company of two men is better than in offering it in the company of one man, and the greater the number, the more would it be liked by Allah." *(Ahmad)*

In another tradition it is stated:

"The reward of prayers of two men, when one is Imam and another is the follower, is less than the reward of prayers of four men together, and the reward of the congregational prayers of eight men is greater than the reward of the congregational prayers of four men. The reward of the congregational prayers of hundred men is greater than the reward of the prayers of eight men, when one is Imam and others are followers."
(Tibrani)

From these traditions it appears that Islam wants to see a great collective organisation of Muslims, and does not want to see them scattered and separated. Although sometimes the coming together, the firmness in relationships and the offering of the congregational prayers become rather slack, and their importance in comparison with the other commands and rules becomes less, but this thing is certain that every attempt to live away from the Ummah would amount to run away from the responsibility of the compulsory duty of ordering of the righteous deeds and preventing the commitment of the forbidden things, or it would be a sense of weakness of defending Islam against the enemies. This is such a crime as cannot have any excuse worth considering.

People have different natures. Some people go to well-attended meetings and establish a relationship with others present there, and mix with others with the help of their smiles and friendly conversation, but there are some who avoid the meetings. They build up a wall around themselves, to cross which becomes difficult for others. They look at others with fear and suspicion, and if somebody wants to meet them they try to hide and avoid meeting him. Islam has guided persons of both these natures in a correct way. To the people of the first group it says "Keep relationship with the people and teach them the points of religion." To the other group it says: "A Muslim should be soft hearted and of good conduct. He should be sympathetic to the people and should be liked by humanity."

It is true that Islam has enjoined upon Muslims to keep away from mischief and corruption. When there is disorder in the country, and the countrymen are busy in assaulting one another for the sake of material gains and cross all the moral limits, at such a time the boycott of this mischief is the best expression of one's disapproval of such a thing, and also the last stage of fighting against the forbidden evil, to which a Hadith of the Prophet has made a reference, that is, if you can stop with hands, stop it, otherwise stop it with the use of your tongue, and if even this much you cannot do, then consider it as evil in your heart. This means that the man who has little power of criticising mischief and corruption with his tongue, to keep silent for such a man is not right. Boycotting is an effective weapon which can be used wisely during the modern times. Weak and backward rations have used this weapon against aggressive and tyrant enemies. But the position of boycott in comparison with the other weapon is the same as that of keeping away from other means and resources, that is its use is right only when other means and resources are not available. Those who have the equipment and wherewithal of extinguishing the fire of mischief and corruption, for them silence and boycott is the worst crime.

After this brief explanation the meaning of the Prophet's Hadith can be understood : When he was asked which man was better, he answered:

> *"That Muslim who strives for the cause of Allah with his life and wealth." He was again asked: "Who else?" He replied : "That man who worships his Lord in a valley secretly."* *(Bukhari & Muslim)*

It means that one's liking for seclusion or mixing up cannot be a permanent quality, therefore, a Muslim should divide his timings in such a way that his privacy as well as his company should be beneficial, so that from both benefits may be derived.

MANNERS AND ETIQUETTE

On this basis we select friends, establish relationships with them or withdraw from any relationship. The foremost condition for the best friendship is that it should be free from all selfish interests and motives, and should have been established for pure truth, and it should develop under the shadow of faith and righteousness. This is the meaning of loving Allah. When man kindles the lamp of belief and faith in his heart, his bosom is bright with the light of truth of Islam and his tongue is sweet with its sweetness, he looks at all the humans in the world in the same light which he has made his own. He makes friends for the sake of principle and not for the sake of his carnal desires, and he hates for the same principles only, and not on account of deprivation or frustration.

Different groups sometimes gather round the bitter and sweet springs, and sometimes for temporary or permanent worldly interests, and many times these develop into strong relationships, but this love, friendship or acquaintance cannot be considered as the high grade sincere friendship and selfless love which is generated as an outcome of faith. That is why Islam has given due respect to the feelings of pure friendship, and has induced Muslims to make friends purely for Allah and to keep it going only for His pleasure, and it has fixed the best reward for that. In a Hadith Qudsi it is mentioned:

> *"Those who love My Majesty will be under the shadow of My Throne, on a Day when there will be no other shadow."* *(Ahmad)*

Hadrat Umar bin Khattab (R.A.A.) says that the Prophet (S.A.W.) has said:

> *"There will be some slaves of Allah who will neither be from the Prophets nor from the martyrs, but on account of their high position before Allah Prophets and martyrs will envy them." The people asked as to who would they be? The Prophet (S.A.W.) replied: "Those persons who would have loved each other for the pleasure of Allah, even though there was no blood relation among them, nor would they give their wealth to one another. By God, from their faces light will emanate and they will be riding the light. When the people will be shuddering with fear they will have no fear, and when the people will be sad and worried they will have no sorrow." (Abu Daud)*

> *Lo! Verily the friends of Allah are (those) are whom fear comes not, nor do they grieve.* *(Yunus ; 633)*

This love for Allah is not a thing of which everybody can be capable, nor is it for making tall claims about. For this it is necessary that man should first acquire some knowledge and understanding about Allah, and this knowledge and recognition should grow so much that in his heart the value of other things should be totally reduced and he should be lost in the thought of Allah. He should prefer to do his work in every condition to say that now he loves for Allah and hates for Allah. But if he is influenced by the ability and personality of some person or somebody's life and character appeal to him, them this will be a kind of love or friendship of a different kind. This love has no relation with the one which we have mentioned above. Allah's Messenger (S.A.W.) has said:

> *"That man who has three qualities, will taste the sweetness of faith and its deliciousness: For him Allah and His Messenger are more loveable than all the world,*

he should love for Allah and hate for Allah, for him it should be preferable to jump in the fire lighted in his presence to joining any partner with Allah."(Muslim)

Accordingly, love is the last stage of faith, and its result and fruit can be achieved when the warmth of sincerity and selflessness has been completely mixed in the blood, because such a love is the proof of perfection and purity, which deserves reward. Allah's Messenger has said:

"When two men love in absence for the sake of Allah, then the man who is more liked by Allah will also be more liked by his companion." (Tibrani)

And both the loving friends remain under the security and support of Allah. A *Hadith Qudsi* has it:

"My love is certain for those who love each other for My sake, and My love is fixed for those who meet each other for my sake; and My love is definite for those who indulge in dealings (trade) for My sake, and My love is permanent for those who make friends among themselves for My sake." (Ahmad and Tibrani)

***Effects of Good and Bad Company*:** One friend exercises a deep influence over the other friend. Therefore it is necessary that a person should be very careful in selecting a friend, and he should examine them properly till he is satisfied about them. Allah's Prophet (S.A.W.) has said:

"Man is on his friend's religion. Therefore, man should see with whom he is making friend." (Abu Daud)

If the friends are such as help in performance of compulsory religious duties *(faraiz)* and in safeguarding the rights, and keep you away from committing evil and forbidden things, then they are the best friends, their company should be definitely adopted, and you should be desirous of their friendship. But those friends who embellish the paths of evil and misguidance, or are ready to help in indulging in play and amusements, and these is a fear of deception and trickery from them, then you should be careful of them.

A true friend shows the way of success in the world and the Hereafter, a misguided and tricky friend proves wicked and ominous. Th number of persons is very large who have suffered heavily the results of evil friendship, and today they are sorry for their past misdeeds:

On the day when the wrongdoer gnaws his hands, together with the messenger of Allah! Alas for me! would that I had never taken such a one for friend! He verily led me astray from the Reminder after it had reached me. Satan was ever man's deserter in the hour of need. *(Furqan: 27-29)*

One nature adopts the habits of other nature. Man very soon tries to follow the path which is liked or is approved of by his dear friend. The law which is operative in connection with the infectious diseases is also operative in connection with the conduct of men. It is observed that compared to virtue, evil spreads much faster. Many times a man who smokes cigarettes influences other persons to fall a prey to this bad habit, and it is very rare that on account of good company, this bad habit is given up by men.

Taking into consideration these bad results, and in order to safeguard good moral conduct and to give protection to good moral practices, the Prophet has commanded that a man of good conduct should be selected as a friend. He has said:

"The example of a good man is like that of a seller of perfumes; if he does not give you anything, his good smell would at least reach you ; and the example of the bad company is like the oven of the iron-monger, if you are safe from its blackness, then at least its smoke would irritate your noses." *(Abu Daud)*

When this is the position with regard to a friend with whom you come in contact for a very small time during the night or day, then what would be the position with regard to a companion who would share with you your happiness and sadness throughout the life. The friendship of pious and God-fearing men elevates men, while the friendship of foolish and idiotic persons takes to a low level.

"It is only wrongdoers that are protector, one to another; but Allah is the Protector of the righteous. These are clear evidences to men, and a guidance and mercy to those of assured faith." *(Jathiya : 19, 20)*

It is necessary that the foundation of friendship should be on the strength of beliefs and purity of conduct, and the best of men is he who is attached to his friends and who makes their love a means of success in this world and the next. About such men, the Prophet (S.A.W.) has said:

> *"He who had dealings with the people and did not ill-treat them talked to them but did not tell a lie, made a promise and kept it, then such a man is of perfect good conduct, is just and righteous, and with him friendship is enjoined."*

When the friendship will be for Allah, it will develop only if Allah is obeyed and both the friends keep away from dispute and disunity. If wickedness enters in the character of either or both, their hearts will change and their love will decrease. In the Hadith it is write:

> *"By the Being in whose hands is my life, when two friends are separated being victims of disruption, its cause is some sin which any one of them has committed."*

For this reason the honoured companions of the Prophet considered the advice to be patient and truthful and to be cooperative in righteousness, protector of love and a guarantee for the salvation as Allah:

> *Abu Qalaba (R.A.A.) narrates: "Two persons met in the market. One of them said to the other: 'Let us pray for Allah's pardon, when others are negligent.' They did so. Then one of them died, then in the dream he met the other man and informed him: 'You should know that Allah had granted us salvation in the very evening when we had met."* *(Ibn Abi Dunya)*

> *Anas bin Malik (R.A.A.) says that when Abdullah bin Rawaha used to meet somebody, he used to say: 'Let us revive our faith in our Lord.' (one day he said the same to a man, who got extremely angry, and went to the Prophet (S.A.W.) and complained : 'O Messenger of Allah (S.A.W.) Look at Ibn Rawaha he prefers to have faith in you for a short time to having faith in you all the time.' The Prophet (S.A.W.) said: 'Blessings of Allah on Ibn Rawaha. He likes those gatherings in which the angels take pride.'* *(Ahmad and Tibrani)*

Lasting Principles of Friendship : Friends should know each other well so that there is truth and firmness in their friendship. The feelings of love and brotherhood which a friend has for another friend should be conveyed to the other friend. Allah's Messenger (S.A.W.) has said:

> *When any one of you may love another person, he should inform him that he loves him.* *(Ahmad)*

> *Hadrat Anas (R.A.A.) narrates that a man was sitting with the Prophet (S.A.W.) Another man passed from there. This man said to the Prophet (S.A.W.) "O Prophet of Allah ! I love this man." The Prophet asked whether he had informed him about that. He replied in the negative. The Prophet (S.A.W.) then said: "Inform him that you love him." Therefore he addressed the sitting man and said : "I love you for the sake of Allah." In reply that man said : "I also love you for the salve of that Being for the sake of whom you love me."* *(Abu Daud)*

Allah's Messenger (S.A.W.) has said:

> *"If a man may love another man, he should try to know the name of that man, his father's name and his lineage, as this thing strengthens love and brotherhood."* *(Tirmidhi)*

Undoubtedly, similarity of thinking and temperament plays a very important role in strengthening relations and in the foundation of friendships. There is a well known saying that there are many of your brothers whom your mother has not given birth, for in this world you come across may people for meeting whom and talking with whom you are irresistibly attracted, as if you had known them for years, although actually it is not so. Same is the purport of this *Hadith*:

> *"There are thousand types of men, of them, with whomsoever you are introduced, get close to them, and shun away from the ones with whom you do not get introduction.* *(Bukhari)*

But in connection with this feeling only belief and the ruling power of that belief can give directions, and these directions become the guidance for a Momin's heart. That is why a Momin loves those persons whom he has not seen on account of distances of time and place between them, for the sake of Allah, though he had not seen their faces, and similarly he hates those persons whom he never accompanied in travels or in residence. His love and hatred are for the reasons that he loves good persons and hates wicked persons. The guidance of hearts on these lines raises men's ranks and position.

> *Abuzar narrates; that he said to the Prophet (S.A.W.) "O Messenger of Allah ! A man loves certain persons, but has no ability to work like them." The Prophet (S.A.W.) said : "O Abuzar! You will be with those whom you loved."* *(Tirmidhi)*

The tradition of Islam in connection with friendship is this that there should be mutual visits. It is necessary that the visits should be free from every interest, and purely for the pleasure of Allah. Abu Hurrayrah; (R.A.A.) narrates that Allah's Prophet has said:

> *A man went to visit his brother in a village. Allah sent an angel after him. When the angel went near him, he asked: 'Where are you going?' He replied that he was going to visit his brother in that village. The angel asked: 'Are you going to take compensation for any obligation that you might have done for him?' He replied: 'No. I love him purely for the sake of Allah.' Then the angel told him: 'I am the messenger of Allah and I have come to give you glad tidings that Allah has made you his favourite, because you have loved this man for the sake of Allah'.* *(Bukhari)*

The steps that proceed in this path are very auspicious, as are the steps proceeding in the path of Jihad for Allah, and attract similar reward. Allah's Prophet (S.A.W.) has said:

> *"When any person goes to see a sick man or visits his brother for the sake of Allah, then a caller gives a call : "to be happy, lucky are your steps ! you have made a house in the Paradise."* *(Abu Daud)*

In another tradition it is written:

> *"Whenever a person goes to visit his brother for the sake of Allah, then a caller gives a call from the heaven: "Let*

it be auspicious. Let the Paradise be auspicious for you" and Allah says on Arsh: "My slave visited for my sake and his entertainment is enjoined on Me." Accordingly He is not prepared to give any reward less than the Paradise." *(Muslim)*

If a Muslim likes that everybody should be benefited, he would like it more that his friends should be benefited more. And if they are benefited, he will be happy, and there is nothing wrong if he remembers his brethren when he is blessed by God:

And forget not kindness among yourselves. Indeed, Allah sees well all that you do. *(Baqarah: 237)*

Allah's Messenger has declared exchange of presents and gifts among friends commendable. He has said: "Give to one another among yourselves gifts, because gift vanishes heart's jealousy." *(Tirmidhi)*

"Hadrat Aishah (R.A.A.) has narrated:

Allah's Messenger used to accept gifts and in return used to send gifts." *(Bazzar)*

It is true that if in these noble practices the formalities cross the limits, they become undesirable and ignoble, for Islam has come to fight artificiality and to spread convenience and informality, and every method which has narrowness, inconvenience and formality Islam is free from that. Islam wants that for the strength of friendship and for decent behaviour such manifestations and practices be adopted which in their appearance and execution should be beautiful and which also should have their basic excellence, and they should make life easier to live and reduce the hardships of life.

"For Allah the best individuals are those who are good to their companions, and the best neighbours are those who may prove better for their neighbours." (Hakim)

Islam has permitted joining with the friends in their eating, as we join in eating with our parents, brother and relatives:

"There is no blame upon .... you even if you eat from your houses, or the houses of your fathers, or the houses of your mothers, or the houses of your brothers or the houses of your sisters,........."

so much so that it permitted to eat— (from the houses) whereof you hold the keys, or (from the house) of a friend. *(An-Nur : 61)*

And this is not surprising, because friendship is very important and has far-reaching effects, so much so that if it wire possible to provide one deliverance from the punishment of the hell, the help of a friend could be expected to do that. Allah quotes the words of the polytheists, uttered by them when they are being subjected to punishment:

By Allah, of a truth we were in error manifest when we made you equal with the Lord of the Worlds. It was but the guilty who misled us. Now we have no intercessors nor any loving friend. *(Ash-Shuara : 97-101)*

Since great rights are attached to these relationships, Allah's Messenger (S.A.W.) has said:

"Make only a Momin as your companion, and your food may be eaten only by a God-fearing man." (Abu Daud)

Love your friends and in return be loved by them. Such a man is indeed very fortunate. As against this, the man who is shunned by the people and he himself tries to avoid them, is in fact in a pitiable condition. A man without money is not poor, but a man without friends, is the poorest. A friend is an asset and adds zest in our life. He is mainstay in our long march of life and is a bounty of Allah. The Holy Prophet (S.A.W.) has said that:

"A Muslim is love and affection personified. The man, who neither loves nor is loved in return by others, has no good in him." *(Mishkat, Bab-ush-Shafqat)*

The Holy Quran says:

"Muslim males and Muslim females are friends and helpers of each other." *(9 : 71)*

The Holy Prophet (S.A.W.) used to love his companions very much, so much so that each of them considered that he was the most beloved companion of the Holy Prophet (S.A.W.). Friendship is a Test. You should live with your friends amicably and maintain sincere relations with them. Do not cultivate the 'habit of aloofness or hatred towards them. When a person moves in the circle of his friends, very often he comes across difficult and unpleasant situations; sometimes his sentiments are hurt; at other times his dignity is damaged; at times his rest is disturbed and his routine is affected; or he has to face things which are contrary to his desires and inclinations; and still at other times his patience and forbearance is put on trial or he has to suffer financial loss.

In short, he suffers a number of difficulties and torments. But when such a person puts up with these ordeals, his heart is galvanised, noble sentiments are generated and he passes through a process of self purification and spiritual development and attains greater spiritual and moral heights. He , thus gets enriched with sentiments of tolerance, love and sacrifice, sympathy and regard; fidelity and good wishes for others, courage, the faculty to cooperate and do good; chivalry and generosity, and becomes an asset for the society. The people respect him and consider him to be a blessing for them. The Holy Prophet (S.A.W.) has therefore said:

> *"The Muslim who lives among his people and puts up with worries and inconveniences created by them, is far better than one who is isolated from others and chafes at the troubles he gets from them." (Tirmidhi)*
>
> *Always cultivate friendship with virtuous persons. While selecting people for friendship, see that they are fit for association from moral as well as religious point of view. A well known adage says: "A man is known (judged) by the company he keeps." The Holy Prophet (S.A.W.) has said: "A person is supposed to follow the faith of his friends. Therefore, a person should consider as to what type of man is the person with whom he is going to forge friendship. (Musnad Ahmad, Mishkat)*

This means when somebody would associate with a person, he is bound to be influenced by the sentiments and ideas of that person, and he will have the same standard of likes and dislikes. Therefore one should be meticulously careful in making friends, and should choose only such persons for this purpose who agree with him temperamentally and have the same ideas in religious matters. The Holy Prophet (S.A.W.) has emphasised to cultivate friendship only with a Muslim and have your social contacts exclusively with him." He (S.A.W.) has said "Move in the company of a Muslim only, and only a virtuous person should join you on your dining table." Eating on the same dining table brings people closer and develops affection; and as such this relationship should exist between the true believers only; that is to say, people who are good and virtuous. Avoid the company of those who are indifferent towards Allah and are irresponsible, lethargic, and ill-mannered. The Holy Prophet (S.A.W.) has elucidated this point in a beautiful simile:

> *"The examples of good and bad friends are like those of a muskseller and blacksmith. From the muskseller you are bound to gain something. Either you will buy his musk ,or enjoy its good smell. But the foundry of the blacksmith would only burn your house or clothes or its unpleasant fume will harm your brain."*
>
> *(Bukhari; Muslim).*

In Abu Daud, however, the above hadis is recorded in these words:

> *"A good friend is like the musk-shop where even if you do not gain any advantage, you will at least feel the aroma of the musk. And a bad friend is like the fire of a furnace. Even (your clothes) are not burnt they would certainly get smeared with smoke."*

Cultivate the friendship for the sake of Allah alone. Allah's chosen servants are only those who unite with each other on the basis of his faith, and strive shoulder to should with unity of heart and soul for the establishment and protection of his religion. The Holy Quran says:

> *"Lo! Allah loveth those who battle for His cause in ranks, as if they were solid structure."* *(61 : 4)*
>
> *And the Holy Prophet (S.A.W.) has said: "On the Day of Reckoning, Allah shall ask: Where are those persons who loved people only for My sake, I shall give them protection today under My shadow."* *(Muslim)*

The Holy Prophet (S.A.W.) describing the covetous and respectable position of such persons on the Day of Judgment has remarked:

> *"There are a few obedient servants of Allah who although are neither Prophets nor martyrs, yet Allah on the Day*

of Judgment shall elevate them on such ranks, which would be envied even by the Prophets and martyers."

When the companions asked as to who would be such fortunate ones, the Holy Prophet (S.A.W.) said:

"These are the people who love each other only for the sake of Allah's religion. They were not related to each other, nor did they have any monetary transactions. By Allah! on the Doomsday their faces would be glowing with light; in fact they would be all radiant, while the other people would be trembling with fear, they would be immune from anxiety and worry. When all others would be plunged into grief, they would not be at all sad."

Then he recited the following verse from the Holy Quran:

"Listen! The lovers of Allah shall fear nothing nor grieve (over their past lives)" (10: 64). (Abu Daud)

According to Hadrat Abu Darda, the Holy Prophet (S.A.W.) said:

"On the day of Resurrection some persons shall come out of their graves, with their countenance glowing with radiation. They shall be seated upon pearl-studded pulpits, and people would look at them enviously. They shall be neither Prophets nor martyrs." A Bedouin asked: "O Prophet of Allah, who are they? Tell us how we could recognise them." The Holy Prophet (S.A.W.) said: "They are those persons who loved each other for the sake of Allah."

Consider the love of the virtuous persons as a means of Allah's pleasure and redemption in the Hereafter. Pray to Allah that He may grant you virtuous friends and their love, and to include you among good people. Hadrat Abdullah bin Masud narrates:

"A man once presented himself before the Holy Prophet (S.A.W.) and said "O Prophet of Allah, a man loves a virtuous person on account of his goodness, but he himself does not follow his good acts," The Holy Prophet (S.A.W.) said: "It matters little. A man would find himself in the company of the man he loves on the Doomsday."

(Bukhari)

The Holy Prophet (S.A.W.) one night had a vision of Allah. He commanded the Holy Prophet (S.A.W.) to ask whatever he wished. The Holy Prophet (S.A.W.) submitted the following supplication:

> *"O Lord! I request you for the capability for good deeds, and the power to leave the evil acts; love for the poor, and that You may pardon me and show mercy to me. And when You want to engulf a nation in some calamity, take me away from their midst unaffected. I ask for Your love and the love of the person who loves You. I solicit for the favour of capability for such acts which may help me to attain nearness to Your love."*
>
> *(Musnad Ahmad)*

Hadrat Muaz bin Jabal says that the Holy Prophet (S.A.W.) said:

> *"Allah has said, it is imperative for Me that. I should love those who make friendship with each other for My sake and sit together to remember Me, and do good to each other for pleasure. (Musnad Ahmad, Tirmidhi)*

The Holy Prophet (S.A.W.) draws the happy picture of friendship of two persons in these words.

> *"A man started on his way to meet a friend who lived in another village. Allah posted an angel on his way. The angel asked him: "Where are you going?" The man said: "I am going to meet my brother in the other village." The angel asked again: "Does he owe you anything which you are going to receive from him?" The man said: "No I am going thither because I love him for the sake of Allah," The angel thereupon said: "Then listen! Allah has sent me to you to convey you the happy news that He harbours the same amount of love for you." (Muslim)*

Permanent Friendship : Friendship should be cultivated with persons who are worthy of friendship from the Islamic point of view; and then such a friendship be kept up as long as you live. But it is necessary that for permanent friendship one should have good friends. The Holy Prophet (S.A.W.) has said:

"On the Day of Reckoning there will be no shade anywhere except under the throne of Allah. On that day seven kinds of people shall be under the (shadow) of the Throne. One kind shall be of those two persons who made friendship with each other for the sake of Allah; Love for Allah had brought them together, and in this state they would have been separated from each other." That is to say, their friendship was for the sake of Allah and they tried to fulfil the requirements of such friendship. When one of them was about to depart from this world he would have been in the state of friendship.

Have faith in your friends, and be happy among them. Do not be dejected nor make others gloomy. Be frank and free and be jovial among your friends and avoid being reserved and self centred so that your friends do not get wearied of your friendship. Hadrat Abdullah bin Harith says, he never saw a person more smiling than the Holy Prophet (S.A.W.). *(Tirmidhi)*

Hadrat Jabir Ibn Samurah says: "I have attended more than a hundred sittings with the Holy Prophet (S.A.W.). In these gatherings, the companions recited poems and also narrated tales of the Jahilyah *(Pre-Islamic period). The Holy Prophet (S.A.W.) used not only to listen to these attentively, but sometimes even joined in laughing along with his companions.* *(Tirmidhi)*

Hadrat Suraid says: "Once I was riding an animal sitting behind the holy Prophet (S.A.W.). I recited a hundred verses by Umayyah Ibn Assalt and he asked me to recite more after each verse, and I complied.
(Tirmidhi)

The Holy Prophet (S.A.W.) himself used to narrate stories in gatherings at his house. Hadrat Aishah reports that he once narrated a story to his family members. A woman remarked that this strange tale was exactly like that of Khurafah.

The Holy Prophet (S.A.W.) asked: "Do you know what is the story of Khurafah,?" and then he himself gave an account of the story of Kurafah in detail. Similarly he once related to Hadrat Aishah an extremely interesting story of eleven women.

Hadrat Bakr bin Abdullah describes the frank and jovial nature of the Holy Companions, that, on the one hand, in playful manner they threw feelings of water melon upon each other and on the other hand when the time for battle arrived, it was the same companions who used to be in the fore front." (Al-Adab al-Mufrad)

Hadrat Ibn Ziyad says: "I have seen that several families of the noble and virtuous people in old days lived in the same house. Many times it so happened that a guest arrived at one family's quarters, while another family would have a cooking pot ready to serve. The party having the guest, would take away the pot for his guest and the owner of the cooking pot would look for it and ask the people as to who had taken away his cooking pot. The host would then tell him, that he had taken it away for his guest; whereupon the owner of the pot would say; "May Allah bless you and increase the food in the pot." Hadrat Muhammad Ibn Ziyad says, "When people baked their bread, the same thing used to happen."
(Al-Adab al-Mufrad)

Hadrat Ali says: "At times leave the heart free. Think of cheerful titbits; because like your body the heart also gets tired." Be jovial and full of zest for life. But see that jokes should never exceed the limits, and they should not infringe upon Islamic value of self respect, balance and moderation. Someone said to Hadrat Sufyan bin Ainiyah that joking is also a curs. He said: "No it is a Sunnah, but for those who know the proper occasions and can make decent jokes." If one loves a friend, he should tell him so. This will have the psychological effect of bringing him closer, and there will be an increase in affection on both sides as a result of this exchange of mutual liking. Love will then not be a mere sentiment of the heart but will have effects on the practical side of life, and there will be a greater chance of taking personal interest in each other's personal matters and coming closer to each other.

The Holy Prophet (S.A.W.) said: "When a person harbours sentiments of love and affection for his brother, he should express them before him, and tell him that he loves him." (Abu Daud)

Once a man passed by the Holy Prophet (S.A.W.) who was then sitting in the midst of his friends; one of those present said: "O Prophet of Allah, I love this man only for the sake of Allah." When the Holy Prophet (S.A.W.) heard this, he asked him whether he had told this to the other person. When he replied in the negative, the Holy Prophet (S.A.W.) said: "Then go and tell him that you love him for the sake of Allah." He immediately got up, and expressed his sentiments to the passerby. The passerby said: "May He for Whose sake you love me, love you." In order to make friendship more firm and meaningful, and also to become closer to your friends, you should take interest in the personal affairs of friends, as much as permissible, and tell them about your intimacy to them.

> *The Holy Prophet (S.A.W.) has said: "When a person joins in friendship with another, he should ascertain his name, his father's name and his antecedents, as this would strengthen the roots of mutual love."*
>
> *(Tirmidhi)*

Friends should always observe moderation in the expression of love and in mutual dealings. Neither should you behave so coldly that your love and friendship may appear uncertain and doubtful, nor so effusive in the expression of cordiality that it may take the form of a craze, and you may have to repent later. A moderate stance that can be maintained, ought to be adopted.

> *According to Hadrat Aslam, Hadrat 'Umar (R.A.A.) once said: "Your love should never take the form of madness and your enmity should not make you adopt cruelty." Hadrat Aslam asked: "How this could be?" Hadrat 'Umar said: "As for example when you love somebody, you tend to become enamoured of him like a child and behave like children; and when you are angry with anyone, you go for his life and property."*
>
> *(Al-Adab Al-Mufrad)*

Hadrat Ubaid Kindi says:

> *"I heard Hadrat Ali saying, "Be soft and moderate in friendship towards a friend. May be, he turns to be your enemy sometime. Likewise, be on the path of moderation and just towards your enemy: It is quite possible he might become your friend later."(Al-Adab Al-Mufrail)*

Friends should be treated with fidelity and sincerity. The best act of sincerity towards a friend is that you should try to improve and better his morals and try to better his prospects in the Hereafter more than in this world. The Holy Prophet (S.A.W.) has said: "Islam is all and all wishing well for others." By wishing well we mean that we should choose for our friends what we choose for ourselves, as nobody wishes ill for himself. The Holy Prophet (S.A.W.) has said:

> *"By Allah Who has my life in His possession, no person can become a true believer unless he chooses for his brother, what he chooses for himself."*

Further, describing the six rights which a Muslim has over another Muslim, he said: "And he should do good to his brother, whether, he be present or not." And observed:

> *"Verily, Allah has made the fire of Hell obligatory upon him and debarred him from Paradise, who, in spite of his having taken an oath, has violated the rights of his fellow Muslim brother!" The Companions then asked: "And what if it is a trivial thing?" The Holy Prophet (S.A.W.) said: "Even if it be the insignificant salvadova twig."*

Join your friends in their bereavements and participate in celebrating festive occasions with them. You should try to lessen the impact of sorrow through kind and sympathetic words and increase their pleasure by participating in their happy celebrations. Every friend expects his friends to be of help to him in need and not to leave him alone and stranded. He also, similarly, expects them to add to his pleasure in celebration of happy events. The following Hadis of the Holy Prophet (S.A.W.) enunciates this point:

> *"Muslim, enforcing and supporting one another is like a brick, becoming a help for the other and reinforcing it," "having said this, he put the fingers of one hand into those of the other (and thus demonstrated with the natural relationship and strength of one Muslim with the other). He also said: "Just as when a part of the body becomes sick, the entire body feels the pain, in the same way, a Muslim will feel pain for other Muslims."*
>
> *(Bukhari-Muslim)*

Receive your friends warmly, welcoming there cheerfully. You should avoid carelessness and indifference towards them; because such a behaviour will cause ill-will between you and your friends. While meeting friends, express your pleasure and happiness. Avoid all expressions of unpleasantness, despondency and abhorrence; your attitude should make your friends thrilled with feelings of joy. They should be made to feel at ease and not as if they constitute a burden. The Holy Prophet (S.A.W.) has said:

> *"Do not regard any good as insignificant even though it may be your meeting with your friends cheerfully."* *(Muslim)*

> *"Your smile when you see a friend, is also a Sadaqah (a good deed or charity).* *(Tirmidhi)*

Soft attitude and polite manners create love and affection for each other, and these virtues help formation and development of good society. The Holy Prophet (S.A.W.) has said:

> *"I tell you the signs of the man upon whom Hell-fire is prohibited. He is the man who is gentle in temper, soft in disposition and soft-natured."* *(Tirmidhi)*

Several companions have said that, when the Holy Prophet (S.A.W.) addressed himself to someone on the occasion of a visit, he addressed himself fully attentively and when somebody spoke to him he used to listen with full attention.

> *Once the Holy Prophet (S.A.W.) was sitting in the mosque. A man came to see him; the Holy Prophet (S.A.W.) moved and collected his body. The man said: "O Prophet of Allah (S.A.W.)! The place is quite spacious. The Holy Prophet (S.A.W.) said: "It is the right of a Muslim that when a brother Muslim sees him, he should move a little.* *(Baihaqi)*

The Quran has defined a Muslim as follows:

> *" They are very merciful among themselves."(48 : 29)*

The Holy Prophet (S.A.W.) elucidated this in the following words:

> *" The faithful are just and soft-natured like the (tamed) camel who has a string in his nose which, when pulled,*

draws the animal, and if made to sit upon a stone, sits there. *(Tirmidhi)*

In the event of differences between friends, the matter should be patched up immediately. You should have no hesitation in admitting your mistake and seeking pardon.

Hadrat Abu Darda, narrates that once hot words were exchanged between Hadrat Abu Bakr and Hadrat 'Umar. Later on Hadrat Abu Bakr felt sad about it, went to the Holy Prophet (S.A.W.) and said: "O Prophet of Allah! There was some difference between me and 'Umar resulting in exchange of hot words. I felt very much ashamed later, and begged forgiveness from 'Umar, but he is not prepared to forgive me. 1 am much perturbed and in anguish. I have come to you."

The Holy Prophet (S.A.W.) said: "Allah shall forgive you." In the meantime Hadrat 'Umar also felt sorry for his mistake and ran to Hadrat Abu Baker's house, where he learnt that Hadrat Abu Baker had left the house to present himself before the Holy Prophet (S.A.W.). He also went to the Holy Prophet's (S.A.W.) and saw signs of displeasure upon the Holy Prophet's (S.A.W.) countenance. When Hadrat Abu Baker saw this, he was much frightened and falling on his knees said in an extremely submissive tone, "O Prophet of Allah: Umar is not at fault. I am to be blamed for having used strong words." The Holy Prophet (S.A.W.) remarked "When Allah sent me as His Prophet , all of you belied me and only Abu Baker believed in me. He supported me in every way with material support and personal sacrifice. Are you now bent upon causing pain and mental torture to my companion?"

There should be no delay in settling the disputes. The more the delay, the greater is the degree of animosity and ill- will. Prophet Isa (Jesus) (A.S.) has given a very faith inspiring advice in this regard:

"Thus if you are busy offering a sacrifice at the altar, I and there you are reminded hat your brother has some grouse against you, you should leave the offering there, and go to your brother to reconcile with him, and then return to complete your sacrifice."

The Holy Prophet (S.A.W.) has said:

"The muster of the acts of the people are presented on each Monday and Thursday to Allah. Every Muslim is forgiven except the one who bears grudge against his Muslim brother. They are left (out) so that they may reconcile."

Who knows whether the next moment would be that of life or death; will he be able to see next Monday or Thursday. Why then delay in reconciliation? Who would like to present himself before Allah with dark and black heart laden with a malice and animosity? Also bear in mind that when a friend confesses his fault and begs forgiveness, his explanation should be accepted and he should be forgiven.

The Holy Prophet (S.A.W.) has said: "A Muslim who refuses to accept pardon from his brother, is equal in sin like collector of illegal taxes." Show Forbearance and Patience. If you hear something from your friend that militates against your good sense, you should control your expression, and should not retaliate; instead try to ward off the topic tactfully and in a friendly way. The Holy Prophet (S.A.W.) has said:

"Prophet Moses (A.S.) asked Allah, 'My Lord! Which of your creature is dearest to You.' Allah replied, "One who has the power to take revenge, but forgives."

(Mishkat)

The Holy Prophet (S.A.W.) has also said:

"The heaviest roll which shall be placed in the scales of a Muslim on the Day of Judgment shall be his good manners; and one who talks vulgarity and insolence, shall earn Allah's wrath,"

Hadrat Abdullah bin Mubarak has defined courtesy in three ways:

(i) When a man meets another man, he should meet him with a smiling face.

(ii) He should spend upon the poor and the needy people, and

(iii) He should not cause harm to another person.

Hadrat Aishah says: "The Prophet of Allah has said that the worst person before Allah on the Day of

Resurrection will be the man whom people avoid meeting because of his foul and annoying language."

(Bukhari Muslim)

One should not neglect, reforming and training his friends on right lines, and should not allow the development if the twin faults of egoism and bride. The friends should be exhorted to realize their weaknesses and to confess them with courage; and to realize that, in not admitting their faults, they would hamper their moral development. It is in fact very easy to outwardly display humility, humbleness and suavity, but listening to one's faults patiently and to put up with the criticism from friends, is indeed a difficult task. But real friends are only those who keep an alert mind and advise their friends to desist from bride and self-esteem. The Holy Prophet (S.A.W.) has said:

There are three things which lead to grave consequences:

(i) An intense desire or infatuation that may enslave a person.

(ii) A desire that man may regard as the *sumrnum honum* of life.

(iii) Self-love is the disease that is more dangerous of all the three evils. (Mishkat—Baihaqi)

Criticism and assessment are like an operation that expels all harmful and putrid matter from the body, adds to the ethical vigour, and infuses a new life into it.

To feel irritated at the criticism of friends, and to regard oneself immune from all criticism, is very dangerous and to neglect one's duty of pointing out defects of his friends, is also full of evil consequences. All this means that one should welcome criticism from his friends and be prepared to subject himself to a strict accountability. Similarly as a sincere friend he should offer good suggestions to his friends for their improvement and betterment. In fact, the friend who is being offered advice should, instead of being puffed up, offer thanks for the kindness of his friends. The Holy Prophet (S.A.W.) has expressed this through a beautiful simile.

"Each of you is like a mirror for his brother. If he sees some thing ill in his brother, he should try to dispel it."

(Tirmidhi)

(i) The mirror shows the spots in you only when you stand before it in order to see them, and when you move away, there is nothing to see. Likewise, you should also make apparent to a friend his faults when he offers himself for criticism and provides you with an opportunity for his examination and hears them with patience. If you feel that he is not yet prepared to listen to the criticism, the advice should be postponed for a better occasion. In the meantime, not a word should be said about his weaknesses in his absence because this would amount to back-biting and back-biting instead of joining the hearts separates them.

(ii) The mirror also reflects the spots on the face that are visible not those which are hidden. It shows them as they are; it neither magnifies nor minimises. As such, a friend who is sincere should only point out to the defects he sees without exaggeration. Only defects you come across in the day-to-day life should be pointed out and you should not be curious and inquisitive about his unknown defects. Investigating hidden defects is not a service but an unethical and destructive habit. Once the Holy Prophet (S.A.W.) from the pulpit cautioned the audience in a loud tone:

"Do not go after the hidden faults of the Muslims. A person who shows inquisitiveness for the hidden faults of his fellow-Muslim brothers, shall have his faults bared by Allah, and, when Allah is determined to expose somebody, such person is sure to be disgraced even if he takes shelter within his own house." (Tirmidhi)

(iii) The mirror only presents a person's reflection as it is: It does not bear any motive nor it takes any revenge from anybody. You should as such take your friend to account, free from any selfish motive, ill-will or evil intention. The object of your criticism should be to enable your friend to reform himself.

(iv) When you see your own reflection in the mirror, you do not get annoyed and do not feel like breaking it. Instead you start making up yourself, and in your heart of hearts you begin thanking the mirror for pointing out things you knew nothing about them. In the same way, when a true friend points out to you your image as he sees it, you should not feel offended, you should rather thank him and request him to continue advising you in the future as well.

(v) As a last point, bear in mind that every Muslim is a mirror of his brother; a symbol of love for his Muslim brethren. When he sees his brother in trouble, he feels perturbed, and when he sees him happy he also feels happy. His criticism will contain sincerity, sympathy and genuine love. Only such advice helps in uniting hearts and invigorating lives.

Gifts should be exchanged among friends in order to express your loving sentiments and to cement the relationship. The Holy Prophet (S.A.W.) has said: "Exchange gifts with friends this would develop mutual love and remove ill-will." *(Mishkat)*

The Holy Prophet (S.A.W.) and his companions used to exchange gifts with each other very frequently.

While presenting a gift, you should keep your financial position in view. A gift need not be expensive; whatever you can afford may he presented. The worth of a present depends upon your sincerity and sentiments of the giver. It is the gift, and not its value that joins the hearts. The receiver should also never regard a gift with contempt but have in mind the love and affection of the giver. The Holy Prophet (S.A.W.) has said:

"If someone presents me with a leg of the goat as a gift, 1 shall accept it; and if somebody invites me and offers only a piece of cooked leg, I shall accept his invitation."
(Tirmidhi)

You must send a gift when you receive one. The Holy Prophet (S.A.W.) always did this. The gift he most liked was perfume. We should also regard this as a choice gift. In the present circumstances a book is also one of the best presents. With this end in view friends would arrange for common dinners as well. You should invite your friends on dinners given by them; such meetings go to strengthen the existing relationship and mutual affection. But instead of lavish and tasty dishes, more attention should be given to love and affection.

Each Other's Welfare : Look after the welfare of your friends and help them with man and money. Isbahani narrates that a man came to Hadrat Abdullah bin 'Umar and asked him: "Whom does Allah likes most?" Hadrat Abdullah bin 'Umar replied:

> *"The best man before Allah is one who helps and serves people most, and the deed best liked by Allah is that you should please a Muslim by solving his problems and mitigating his troubles or by satisfying his hunger. I would prefer to go with a brother to fulfil his needs, rather than sit in Itikaf in the mosque of the Holy Prophet (S.A.W.). If a man controls his anger although he had the power to carry it out, he earns Allah's pleasure. If a Muslim goes forth to fulfil the want of his brother and satisfies it, shall have his steps strengthened on the day when all others would be tottering."*

The following Ahadith of the Holy Prophet (S.A.W.) emphasize this point:

> *"He who fulfils the wants of his brother, shall have his desires fulfilled by Allah. If he satisfies a want of his friends, Allah shall mitigate one of his troubles on the Day of Judgment."* *(Bukhari — Muslim)*

> *Allah keeps on helping a person as long as he is engaged in helping his brother."* *(Tirmidhi)*

> *"Hadrat Abdullah Ibn Abbas says that the holy Prophet (S.A.W.) has said, the blessings of satisfying the want of a Muslim are more than the bliss earned by ten years of* Itikaf." *(Tibrani)*

According to Hadrat Anas (R.A.A.) the Holy Prophet (S.A.W.) has said:

> *"Allah shall please the man on the Day of Reckoning, who goes to his Muslim brother with cheerful tidings and makes him glad."* *(Tibrani)*

If your friend confides in you, you should prove as the most reliable confidant; should keep the secret in your heart and not divulge it, so that your friend may seek your advice if and when he needs and you may tender sound advice to him.

Personal Attraction : You should cultivate such a leniency, generosity, forbearance and accommodation in your character and behaviour, that persons of diverse nature and taste, may feel an extra ordinary attraction towards you. You should behave with them judiciously according to the taste and temperament of each of them. You should not try to measure others by your own standard. Diversity of taste and temperament is a gift of nature. Keep every friend in his natural place and take interest in him, and appreciate him accordingly, and thus keep him close to you.

It was the achievement of the universal genius and character of the Holy Prophet (S.A.W.) that persons of all taste and temperament could find relief in his company and were adjusted amicably. When he had love, affection and humility personified in Hadrat Abu Bakr, there was the iron road Hadrat 'Umar as well; there were Hadrat Hassan bin Sabit who hated war, and Hadrat Ali the conqueror of Khyber, as his companions. There was Hadrat Abuzar Ghifari, the great pessimist who abhorred wealth and also Hadrat Abdul-Rahman bin Auf, the wealthy and handsome person in the company of the Holy Prophet (S.A.W.). But it was the genius of the universal nature of the character of the Holy Prophet (S.A.W.) that all of them had immense and unparalleled love for the Holy Prophet (S.A.W.) and in return was so much loved by the Holy Prophet (S.A.W.) that each of them thought that the Holy Prophet (S.A.W.) loved him most. It was because of this generosity, amiability and statesmanship of the Holy Prophet (S.A.W.) which brought the opposites together. The Holy Prophet (S.A.W.) moulded together a group of companions who in spite of diversity of nature and temperament were the best organisation from all points of view that human knowledge could evolve.

Your acquaintances can be successful and permanent when you develop a sagacious flexibility, exceptional patience and forbearance. In matter of friendship give and take, generosity, sacrifice, mutual cooperation, humility, regard for each other, and selflessness are prerequisite. The following incidents from the life of the Holy Prophet (S.A.W.) show how considerate, large hearted, patient and tolerant he was, while dealing with persons around him.

The Holy Prophet (S.A.W.) once said: "I come for prayers and feel inclined to lead long prayers. But I hear a child crying, and therefore, I shorten the prayer, because I do not want to put the mother of the child to inconvenience by prolonging the prayer." (Bukhari)

Hadrat Malik Ibn Al-Huwairis narrates the following incident. "I, alongwith some other youngmen, presented ourselves before the Holy Prophet (S.A.W.), and stayed with him for twenty days. The Holy Prophet (S.A.W.) was extremely compassionate and kind towards us. After we had stayed with him for twenty days, he guessed that we had become homesick, he asked us as to whom we had left behind. Each of us told him about the situation of his home. He advised us to go back to our families and teach them what we had learnt from him, and to exhort them to do good deeds, and apprise them of proper timings for prayers; and when time for prayers comes, one of you should call the people for prayers. The most learned and pious among you should lead the prayers." (Bukhari - Muslim)

Hadrat Muawiyyah Ibn Hakam Sullami has described his own experience as follows:

"I was offering prayers under the leadership of the Holy Prophet (S.A.W.). In the course of the prayers one worshipper sneezed, and I forgetting that I was praying said "Yarhamukallah" *in the course of my prayers. Other worshippers began to stare at me as an expression of their annoyance. I said: Peace be upon you: Why you stare at me like this? Then I became quiet. When the Holy Prophet (S.A.W.) finished his prayers, may my parents be sacrificed for him, I have never seen a better teacher either before or afterwards, neither he scolded, nor beat me, nor spoke to me harshly. He only said: "It is improper to talk during prayers as they are meant for reciting His virtues, His Greatness and reading the Quran." (Muslim)*

Praying for the Friend : Friends in particular should pray for each other. I should pray for them and request them to pray for you. Prayers should be offered in the presence of the friend as well as in their absence by name. Hadrat 'Umar says that he sought permission of the Holy Prophet (S.A.W.). Giving his gracious permission the Holy Prophet (S.A.W.) said: "O My brother, remember me in your prayers." Hadrat 'Umar says that he felt more pleased at this than attainment of the whole world. The Holy Prophet (S.A.W.) has said:

> *"When a Muslim prays for his friend in absentia, Allah grants this prayer. An angel appointed by Allah by his side says, "Amen! You may have for yourself what you desire for your friend."* *(Muslim)*

In your ardent prayers, solicit the favour of Allah to clean your hearts of malice and hatred and join them with love and affection, cementing your relationship with mutual cooperation and love. The following prayer from the Quran may also be recited:

> *"Our Lord! Forgive us and our brethren who were before us in faith; and place not malice and ill-will in our hearts toward those who believe. Our Lord, You are full of pity and Most Merciful."* *(59 - 10)*

CONVERSATION AND GET-TOGETHERS

While visiting somebody you should be neatly and properly dressed. But you should not be decked in gaudy and costly dress which may give the impression as if you want to overawe the other person.

Meeting with Proper Appointment : It is better to inform the other party of your intending visit in advance and have an appointment. Doing without prior appointment is not a good habit. This interferes with the routine of the person whom you are visiting and may also cause some embarrassment to you as well.

Talk on Useful Matters : When you visit a person, talk topics which may serve some purpose, and do not waste time in random talks. This will make you an unwelcome visitor. While visiting somebody, permission to enter the house should be sought at the door, and on receiving the permission go into the house and greet the inmates with As-salam-o-'Alaikum. If no reply is received after saying As-salam-o-Alaikum thrice, you should turn back without any displeasure.

Present Gifts : Occasionally, while visiting friends or relatives take some suitable gifts to present. This exchange of gifts enhances mutual love and regard for each other. If a needy person calls, his request should be carried out as far as possible. If he requests for a recommendation, do recommend him and if you cannot do anything for him, regret your inability politely. One should never be kept on false hopes.

If you visit a person with a request, state it in a civilized manner. In case it is acceded to, thank him; and if the same is refused, greet him and return home without any grumble. You should not expect other persons always to visit you. You should also call on others occasionally. This develops mutual cooperation and regard for each other. But it should be kept in mind that the believers always meet for a noble purpose.

Removing Unwanted things from Friends' Person : If you find that there is a piece of straw or any other such thing on the person or clothes of the individual you are visiting, do remove it with your hands and if anyone does this for you, thank him and pray for him in this way. "May Allah keep you away from things you do not like."

Visiting a Person in the Night : If you have to visit someone at night, have regard for his comfort and convenience, and do not prolong your stay. If you find him asleep, return home without any grouse. If a group of persons visits somebody, the spokesman, while talking, should speak for all and should not ignore the views and interests of others, He should avoid only impressing his personal needs and importance.

11

Moral Values

People react differently to the motivations and the occasions that generate feelings of sorrow and pain. Some people are provoked by ordinary things, and they become unmindful of every thing and in haste take a very unwise step. But there are also such persons as pass through various hardships and adversities and yet do not forget to behave with seriousness, wisely, with tolerance and good manners.

It is true that the original nature of a man and his natural temperament play a very big part in a man's being hot tempered or soft-hearted, serious or hasty, righteous or wicked. But there is a very deep relation between a man's self-confidence and his solemn behaviour with others and in forgiving the errors of others. In reality, the more good-mannered and perfect a big man is, in the same proportion his heart will be big and the circle of his tolerance and forbearance will be wide. He will try to find the extenuating circumstances for the errors of others and will accept their apologies when offered. If anybody may attack him with the intention of injuring him, he will look at him as a philosopher looks at the children playing marbles on the roads, and will ignore him. We have seen that anger makes a man mad.

A man is disgraced in his own sight, when he feels that he has been put to great humiliation, and feels that this blot cannot be removed without shedding blood. Can a man who has high moral character take such a step merely because he has to pass through sorrow and pain? Never. Those who indulge in inflicting insults on others are disgraced in their own eyes before insulting others. This is what we understand from the tolerance and forbearance shown by Hud. He invited his nation to accept the belief of oneness of Allah. His nation greeted him with abuses, curses and accusations which he tolerated peacefully. The people of his nation said:

> *"Indeed, we see you in foolishness, and surely, we deem you of the liars. He said: 'O my people! There is no foolishness in me, but I am a messenger from the Lord of the Worlds. I convey to you the message of my Lord and am for you a true adviser'."* *(Al-Araf: 66-68)*

The abusing and the curses of the Nation of Hud did not provoke him, because there is a lot of difference between the two groups. On the one side is a man whom God has selected to be His Messenger. He is a representative of goodness and righteousness. On the other side are persons who are imbedded in ignorance and foolishness, and vying with each other in worshipping stones. On account of their foolishness they think that the stone idols are the masters of their destiny. How can a great teacher be disheartened by the misbehaviour of such a flock? How Allah's Messenger imbibed the qualities of tolerance and forbearance to his companions can be understood from the following tradition, which shows the foolishness of an Arab and the love and serenity of the Prophet.

It is reported that a Bedouin came to the Prophet and asked for something, and the Prophet gave him something, and asked: "Did I treat you well ?" The Bedouin replied : "No, you have not treated me well." Hearing this, the Muslims got angry and advanced towards him. The Prophet made a sign to stop them. Then he got up and went to his house and gave him some more gift, and again asked : "Did I treat you well ?" He replied : "Yes, may Allah grant prosperity to your family." The Prophet said to him : "Whatever you have said to me, is alright in its place, but my companions are angry in regard to you, if you like you may repeat before them whatever you have said to me so that the anger from their heart may be removed." He said that it was agreeable to him. When the morning came, he came again, and the Prophet pointed towards him and said : "On what this Arab had said, I gave him something more, and now he says that he is happy and pleased. Is that so?" The Bedouin replied: "Yes, May Allah grant prosperity to your family."

Then Allah's Messenger said: "My example and that of this man is like that of a man whose she-camel has been lost and the people ran after her to catch her, but the animal was more startled; so that man told his companions : 'Leave me and my she-camel alone. I know her ways more and I can bring her to the right path.' Accordingly he lifted some grass from the ground in his two hands and showed it to the she-camel, it returned and sat near his feet. He tied the 'kajawa' on her back and rode her." "If I were to leave you when he was using foul language, you would have killed him and he would have been sent to hell."

The kind Prophet was not provoked in the beginning from the misbehaviour of the Bedouin. He understood his nature and temperament, which was like that of the illiterates who are habituated to wild and foul language. If such people are summarily punished, then they will be destroyed and it would be unjust. But the great reformers do not allow the errors of people reach such a sad end. They try to remove the ignorance and emotionalism of the people by their tolerance and forbearance, so persistently that they have to turn to rigorous things, and they become all praise for them.

The wisest of the wise intellectual and the wealthiest mad cannot reach his destination, however charitable and generous he may be. Of what use is that charity which meant for making people indebted to the giver ? It is not unlikely that the Bedouin whose satisfaction was bought by giving him money might have become a wealthy man himself subsequently and he might have performed a great deed by giving his life willingly. In reality the wealth given by such great reformers is meant for such needy people, or in other words such a wealth is like the grass growing on the ground which is lifted in the hands and shown to the startled she-camel, and by means of it and by a little display of love the astray mounts are called near so that they may be used for travelling great distances.

The holy Prophet sometimes used to get angry, but he never crossed the limits of decency and the stage of pardon and forgiveness. How bright is this aspect of his character that he never took revenge for his own person, but he never hesitated in taking revenge from the man who violated the sanctity of

Allah's laws. Once when he was distributing the booty, one rough Bedouin insulted him by saying : "Deal with justice," because in the distribution of this booty only Allah's pleasure was sought. The Prophet did not say anything more than this : "Fie on you. If I will not deal justly then who else will ? If I did not do like this, then I failed, and I sustained a loss." With these words he gave an answer to his ignorance and also stopped his companions from killing the Bedouin, which they otherwise would have done.

TOLERANCE AND FORBEARANCES

Once at the time of Asr (Middle prayer) in his speech to the people he said:

> *"Adam's sons have been created of different types. There are some who get angry late and very soon return to normal. Some people become wrathful soon and soon they return to normal, and some people become angry late and are also late in returning to normal, that is the return to normalcy is according to the speed of getting angry. Be careful. Some people get angry soon and they return to normal late. Listen, the best people among these are those who get angry late and immediately repent, and the worst among these are those who get angry soon, but are very late in coming to normal. Listen, among these there arc some who repay the loan in a better way, and also demand in a good way. Some people are lazy in repaying, but good in demanding. Some demand in a bad way and repay in a good way, i.e., they have one good quality and one bad quality. Some people prove to be bad in demanding and in repaying too. Listen carefully, the best among these are those who are good in demanding and also good in repaying, and the worst are those who are bad in both the things.*
>
> *"Keep in mind, anger becomes a spark in the heart of Adam's son. Do you not see that at the time of anger a man's eyes become red, and his nostrils become enlarged. If any one sees these sign in a man, he should be glued to the earth."* *(Tirmidhi)*

That is, ne should sit in his place, he should not move so that the matter may not get worsened. Because the flames of anger and wrath burn all matters. Intelligence and consciousness disappear from it, and man is imprisoned in the magic of passions. Then these affairs do not improve. The above-quoted Hadith explains the kinds of men and their achievements and value in greatness and morality. Wherever necessary, a faithful bends himself.

An angry man indulges into various kinds of foolishness. Sometimes he abuses the door if it does not open immediately for him. In his anger he breaks whatever machine or its part may be in his hand, and abuses the animal that is not brought under control.

> *A man's sheet was flown away by the wind and he cursed it. Allah's Messenger said : "Do not curse it, because it is bound by the commands of God and it is under His control. He who curses a thing which did not deserve it then the curse returns on him." (Tirmidhi)*

There are many evils of anger, and their results are more devastating. It is therefore said that to keep the self in control at the time of anger is the proof of the praiseworthy power of control and the noble strength of toleration. Ibn Masood has narrated that Allah's Messenger had asked:

> *"Whom do you call a sandow ?" People replied : "One who is not knocked down by anybody is called a sandow among us." He said : "No, sandow is one who controls his self in his anger." (Muslim)*

One man requested the Prophet: "Give me some advice, out not such a lengthy one that I may forget. The Prophet said : "Do not be angry." (Malik). What reply could be better and shorter than this one? Allah's Messenger always gave importance to the temperament and the environment of the individuals and groups in giving them instructions and training. He used to lengthen or shorten his speech according to the demands of the occasion.

The efforts which were made to remove the jahiliya had two foundations : One was ignorance against learning and the second against tolerance. The first ignorance he removed with the help of knowledge, understanding, sermons and advice, while the second was removed with the help of suppressing the rebellious desires and preventing mischief, etc. The Arabs of the pre-Islamic days were proud of their ignorance and wickedness. As an Arab Poet of the time says:

> *"Beware! None should show any ignorance and wickedness before us, else we will prove to be more ignorant and wicked than all"*

When Islam came, it removed this intensity of feeling and emotionalism, and introduced the practice of pardon and forgiveness in the society. If one could not pardon, then one was given the command to act justly. This objective could be achieved only when anger and wrath could be kept under the control of the intellect. There are a number of sayings in which the Prophet has given directions to the Arabs leading them to this ideal, so much so that the manifestations of tyranny, aggression, anger and wrath have been declared out of the circle of Islam. The things which unite a group and do not allow it to be disturbed, abuse, etc., has been declared to be the agent which breaks this unity:

> *"Abusing a Muslim is wickedness, and his quarrelling and fighting is infidelity."* *(Bukhari)*

> *"When two Muslims meet, a curtain from Allah is hung between them. When one of the two says obscene things to the other he tears this curtain of Allah."(Baihaqi)*

> *One Arab came to the Prophet to learn the teachings of Islam. Before this he had neither seen the Prophet nor did he know about his message. His name was Jabir bin Salim. He narrates : "I saw a man whose opinions are being copied by the people. If he says anything people convey it to others. I asked them who this man was. They said that he is Allah's Messenger. I said to him : 'On you be peace (Alaik-as-Salam) O Messenger of Allah !' He said : `Do not salute like this. This is the salute of the dead ; but say Peace be on you. (Assalamu Alaik)'.*

That Arab says : "I asked : 'Are you Allah's Messenger?' He replied : `I am the messenger of that Being whom you call in adversities, and he removes your adversities, and if famine catches you and you call Him, He grows grass for you; and if you lose your mount in the arid ground, then you call Him and He causes your mount to be returned to you."

> *He says that I told him : "Advise me." The Prophet said: "Do not abuse anybody." Accordingly, thereafter I did not abuse any free man, slave, camel, goat. Then he said: 'Do not consider any virtue as mean, even if it is your brother's talking to you with a smile. This is also a virtuous act.' Then he said: 'If somebody reproaches you and makes you feel ashamed on any of your defects, do not make him feel ashamed on any of his defects, because this act of his will prove troublesome for him."*
> *(Abu Daud)*

Rebuking and Reproaching : There are also some people whose anger does not cool down. They are always in a turmoil, and this wrathfulness imprints a stamp of stone-heartedness and harshness on their face. If anybody clashes with them they spit fire like an oven. Anger, wrath, squeezing of the nostrils and reddening of the eyes, and then there starts a series of abusing and cursing. Islam is innocent of all these dirty qualities.

> *Allah's Messenger has said: "A Momin does not taunt, does not curse and reproach, does not indulge in obscene talking and obscene acts." (Tirmidhi)*

Cursing and reproaching are the signs of meanness, and it is a quality of lowliness. Those who curse others far ordinary things, they put themselves to great ruin. It is the duty of a man that he should avoid this unseemly act, even if he is harmed considerably by his opponent. As faith will be nourished in the heart, along with it will grow generosity, broad-mindedness, tolerance and forbearance, and there will grow hatred of anger for the usurpers of our rights and dislike for the desire for their destruction. The Prophet was requested to invoke God's wrath against the polytheists and to curse them. He said:

> *"I have been sent as a blessing (Rahmat). 1 have not been sent as a rebuker and reproached." (Muslim)*

A Muslim however much he would control his self, however much he would control his anger, would pardon others' errors, and however much would sympathise with others on their mistakes, in the same proportion his rank will be raised before

Allah. For this reason, the Prophet disapproved of Hadrat Abu Bakr when he cursed his slave, and said:

> *"How can it be proper for a truthful man that he should rebuke and reproach."* (Muslim)

> *In another tradition it is mentioned that the Prophet has said: "It is not possible that you indulge in rebuking and reproaching and at the same time remain* siddiqi *(truthful) and straight."* (Hakim)

Hadrat Abu Bakr, to atone for his error, freed his slave and went to the Prophet for apologising and said that he would not do such a thing again. The reason for this is that rebuking and reproaching is such an evil as is more expressive of one's blind rage than the idea of punishing others. It is not at all proper to insult others by yelling at them.

> *Allah's Messenger has said : "When a man curses somebody, then that curse rises up to the sky, but the gates of the sky shut. Then it turns to the earth. Here also the gates are found shut. Therefore it wanders to the right and to the left, and if it does not find a proper place it goes to the man who was cursed. If he deserved well and good, otherwise it returns to the man who cursed."* (Abu Daud)

Cursing and Abusing : Islam has declared cursing and abusing, exchange of vulgar and obscene words and acts as Haram (forbidden). Many clashes occur in which people's honour is attacked and a series of exchange of accusations and fault-finding ensues. The reputation of the relatives, and the female folk of the household is damaged and attempts are made to rake up the dust of centuries.

There is only one cause of all this dirty sinning, and that is man is overcome by anger and he washes his hands off all decency and good manners. The entire responsibility for committing this low and mean type of sin goes to the head of the man who first put the spark to the combustible material. It is written in the Hadith :

> *"The entire sin for mutual abusing and cursing will be on the man who first started it, except when the oppressed crosses the limit."* (Muslim)

There is only one way of escaping these intense sins, and that is that tolerance and forbearance may be allowed to have an upper hand over anger and rage, and pardon and forgiveness may be allowed to rule over the passion of taking revenge. There is no doubt that when a man's own personative or that of his relative or friends is attacked and when he is made to suffer, and he has the means and sources for taking revenge, then he wants to avenge himself immediately and does not rest till he satisfies his passion for revenge.

Hardness be Replied with Softness : But in such cases another policy can be adopted which is much nobler and is liked by Allah, which shows man's greatness and his regard for relationship and that is that he should control his anger, and should not indulge in abusing and cursing. He should restrain himself and should not be bent on taking revenge. He should consider the overlooking of the errors of the wrong-doers as a kind of gratitude to Allah, who has given him such a position that whenever he may want may take back his right. Ibn Abbas narrates that when Ainia bin Hasn came, stayed in the house of his nephew Hur bin Qais, who was greatly respected by Hadrat Umar, because the readers of the Quran were the members of the Consultative Committee of Hadrat Umar, whether they were old or young. The uncle asked the nephew to take him to the Amir-ul-Mominin, Umar bin At-Khattab. Accordingly permission was sought, and when both of them went in the presence of Umar, he very harshly said to the Khalifah:

> *"A pity on you, O son of Khattab! because you neither give us gifts nor do you deal with us justly." Hadrat Umar was enraged on this and wanted to punish him.*

The nephew, Hur, immediately intervened and said : "Amirul Mominin! Allah says to his Prophet : `Adopt the method of softness and forgiveness, advise for doing righteous deeds and do not clash with uneducated. This man is uneducated, he may be forgiven.'

> *Accordingly, the Amir of the Faithfuls forgave him and did not deviate slightly from the teachings of those verses when it were recited before him and he was the true follower of the Book of Allah."* *(Bukhari)*

Hadrat Umar was enraged because that Arab had come merely to provoke him. The idea of punishing him came to his mind because he had not gone there with the intention of giving right advice or reform. The only purpose of his going there was to rebuke the Amirul Mominin and to receive rich gifts without working for them. But when he was told that the man was uneducated, he controlled his anger and allowed him to go scot free.

> *It is written in a* Hadith *: "He who controls his anger though he had the power to act on it, Allah will call him first of all on the Day of Judgment and will give him the authority to select whatever houri he likes."*
>
> *(Abu Daud)*

Ibada bin Samit says that the Prophet has said:

> *"May I not tell you those qualities for which Allah will give you tall buildings in the Paradise and He may raise your rank?" The people said: "Certainly, tell us O Messenger of Allah!" He said : "He who behaves with you in the manner of an uneducated person, you behave with him with tolerance, forgive the oppressors, and give to those who deprive you, and he who cuts away from you, try to join him."* *(Tibrani)*

Quran has declared these decent habits and qualities as the path of welfare by which a man can enter the Paradise.

> *"Be quick in the race for forgiveness from your Lord, and for a Paradise whose width is that (of the whole) of the heavens and of the earth, prepared for the righteous,-those who spend (freely) whether in prosperity or in adversity; who restrain anger, and pardon (all) men ; for Allah loves those who do good."*
>
> *(Al-i-Imran : 133-134)*

The Excellent Example : The way in which the Prophet ignored Abdullah bin Ubay, the leniency which he showed him, and the manner in which he overlooked his crimes, are instances whose example cannot be found in the entire human history. Abdullah bin Ubay was the worst enemy of the Muslims. He used to be always in search for finding out ways of inflicting injuries and damages to Muslims and he was in league with the devil against the Muslims. He never let slip any opportunity of harming Muslims, of defeating them and spreading a network of conspiracies against them. He cast aspersions on the chastity of the Mother of the Faithfuls, Hadrat Aishah, and he incited some people to indulge in the whispering campaign against her and thus weaken the foundation of the Islamic society, as from the ancient times the eastern traditions had given a very high position of decency and nobility to women. For this reason the Messenger of Allah and his dear companions were terribly distressed and were in great mental anguish. They were in a great dilemma on account of this blatant false accusation, till at last the verses of Surah Noor were revealed which refuted the charges of the hypocrites, vouchsafed the chastity and purity of Hadrat Aishah and exposed the machinations of the enemies :

> *"Those who brought forward the lie are a body among yourselves ; think it not to be an evil to you ; on the contrary it is good for you ; to every man among them (will come the punishment) of the sin that he earned and to him who took on himself the lead among them, will be penalty grievous."* *(Noor : 11)*

In this tragedy, those who had openly accused the Ummul Mominin were punished, but the germ which had spread this disease was not touched, so that he might further go on with his nefarious activities of harming Muslims. Allah blesses His Prophet and his armies with victory and glory. Islam refined the disorderly government of the centuries and reformed the corrupt society.

The enemies of Islam were then found within the limits of the Islamic society. Abdullah bin Ubay was pining within himself till he fell ill and died, after leaving the bad and deadly odour of disruption behind him. His sons went to Prophet seeking his pardon for their father. He forgave him. Then the son requested for the Prophet's shirt for the shroud of his father. He gave it to them. Then they requested him to lead his funeral prayer and to pray for their father. The gracious Prophet did not refuse even this request of theirs. He stood up to pray for the salvation of the person who in the past had attacked his honour and reputation. But Allah denied to grant all these concessions, and this verse was revealed:

"Whether you ask for their forgiveness or tot, (their sin is unforgivable); if you ask seventy times for their forgiveness, Allah will not forgive them ; because they have rejected Allah and His Prophet; and Allah guides not those who are perversely rebellions. (Tauba : 80)

In this tragic event of false accusation was also involved a near relative of Hadrat Abu Bakr, who was living on his help. This man did not hesitate to falsely muse the pure and chaste lady, whose father was giving him help and was sustaining him. He forgot the right of Islam, and did not care for the relationship, and tore to pieces the old custom. Hadrat Abu Bakr was deeply stirred and he swore that he would not give anything to this near relative of his and would not show any kindness to him as in the past. Thereupon the following command from Allah was revealed

"Let not those among you who are endued with grace and amplitude of means resolve by oath against helping their kinsmen, those in want, and those who have left their homes in Allah's cause ; let them forgive and overlook; do you not wish that Allah should Forgive you ? For Allah is Oft-Forgiving, Most Merciful."

(Noor: 22)

Accordingly, Abu Bakr restarted helping his relative saying: "I like that Allah may pardon me."

MODESTY

Modesty is the true symbol which indicates human nature. It gives an idea of a man's faith, virtue, etiquette and morals. If you see a man hesitating or restive at the time of performing some improper act, or he is sorry on doing some wrong work and the colour of his face is changing, then you can consider him to be a man with a living conscience. He is a man of simple nature and right temperament. But if his face does not show any colour, no trace of modesty or shame is seen on it, his mind does not take any notice of the wrong act being performed by him, he is totally careless about what he is taking up and what he is leaving, then there is no virtue in him, there is not an iota of modesty and shame in him which can prevent him from committing sin and from living a sinful life. Islam has taught its children modesty, and it has considered it its most distinguishing quality. Allah's Prophet (S.A.W.) has said:

> *Every religion has its moral, and the moral of Islam is modesty.* *(Malik)*

In the time of Prophet Moosa (Moses) (A.S.) the special element of the Jewish teachings was courage and bravery. In the time of Isa (Jesus) (A.S.) the Christian teachings gave a special place to charity and generosity. And the distinguishing feature of Islam is modesty and sense of shame, when all religions and nations give importance to all the good qualities and take a reckoning of them.

The sense of loving virtue and hating wickedness found in a Muslim has been said by the Prophet (S.A.W.) to be the foundation of adopting virtues and rejecting evils, in order that before the final requital the feeling of love for the good and hate for the evil should be generated in every man. How truly Ibn Qayim has said:

> *"Suppose the Messenger of Allah (S.A.W.) had not brought Allah's Message and the fire of Hell had not been kindled, then was it not incumbent upon the slaves to display modesty before their Benefactor."*

The Prophet (S.A.W.) was the softest of men, most virtuous, decent and the most considerate for giving the dues of Allah and others. He was the farthest away from evil.

> *Abu Saeed Khudri (R.A.A.) says : "Allah's Messenger was (S.A.W.) more modest than the maiden staying behind the veil. If he saw any unpleasant thing, we could see its sign on his face."* *(Muslim)*

Modesty and Faith : Faith, in fact, is the name of the best relationship between the slave and his Lord. It affects the human life primarily in this way that it purifies the self, morals are improved, and actions are corrected. This so happens when there is an awakening in the self which would keep it away from errors and induce man to hate even the smallest of sins. If a man does not keep away from small errors and goes on committing them without any care, then it is the symbol of the fact that there is no modesty in him and his faith has been shaken.

Allah's Messenger (S.A.W.) has said : "Modesty and Faith are one another's companion. If one goes, the other will also not remain." (Hakim)

The reason for this is that when a man gives up modesty, he gradually moves from a smaller coil to a deadly evil and from a smaller sin to a bigger sin, till he reaches the lowest of the low. One Hadith of the Prophet (S.A.W.) takes off the veil from this fall of man. It begins with lack of modesty and consequently reaches the worst of the sins.

"When Allah wants to destroy a man, He takes away modesty from him. When he is deprived of modesty, he becomes the most detestable man. And when he becomes detestable, he loses trust. When he loses trust and honesty, he becomes extremely fraudulent. Allah's blessing is snatched away from him. He becomes extremely cursed, and when he becomes reproachable, then the yoke of Islam comes out from his neck." (Ibn Majah)

The explanation of the psychological sickness and how it advances, stage by stage, has been very dexterously shown. It has been explained how an evil progressively leads to the commitment of the worst sin. When a man tears the raiment of modesty and does not keep an account of his acts, nor does he care for she reproaches of others, then he extends his hand of aggression to others, he subjects his subordinates to tyrannies. A man of such a character cannot show mercy to any one. He will nourish rancour and jealousy in his heart and will encourage them.

A man who becomes so aggressive with the public, can a quality like modesty prevent him from sins ? When a man falls so low, he cannot be trusted with people's valuables in his trust. How can he be made a trustee, when he is not ashamed in misappropriating the property of others or how can he be considered a watchdog of honour, when he is ever ready to make an assault on any body's honour, or how can his promises be relied upon when he does not care to keep his promises ? No responsibility can be entrusted to him, as the fear of negligence and defection will always be there. Nor can he be given a high office, because there is no guarantee against deception and trickery. When a man loses his modesty and is deprived of trust and honesty, then he is like a mad dog and runs after his desires and in his way tramples upon the righteous and pure feelings. Then he misappropriates the wealth of the poor and the beggars, and no softness is felt by him in his heart for those unfortunates ; he observes the weak and the meek, but no waves of kindness is generated in his heart. And if at all some delicate feeling is engendered in his heart, he blindfolds himself. Then he seeks knowledge about those things, which go on throwing him in further darkness and misguidance. When a man falls down so low, then be sure that he has become free of the restrictions of the religion and he has thrown away the yoke of Islam from his neck.

There are different occasions when modesty is desirable. In conversation decency demands that man should avoid obscene talk, back-biting and fault-finding of others, and he should avoid touching upon the personal matters of the people. It is extremely disrespectful that a man should irrelevantly blurt out obscene and lewd words.

Allah's Messenger (S.A.W.) has said :

"Modesty is faith, and the faithful will go to Paradise, and obscene talk is tyranny and the place of a tyrant is Hell." *(Ahmad)*

It is also included in modesty that Muslims should talk in a balanced way in their gatherings. Some people have the habit of making lengthy speeches in big meetings; they fret and fume and their saliva drips from their mouths, but they are not ashamed. Islam has disliked this bad habit. The Prophet (S.A.W.) has said:

He who has learnt the art of conversation for the purpose of turning the hearts of the people, then on the Day of Judgment Allah will not accept his eloquence."

(Abu Daud)

In another tradition he has said:

Allah does not like those eloquent men who move their tongues as cows chew the cud. *(Tirmidhi)*

The reason for Allah's dislike and hatred of these people is on account of the fact that their talk is full of exaggeration and falsehoods, their affairs are never devoid of hypocrisy and exhibitionism, their gatherings are a prey of various moral diseases. If these people adopt modesty, then they can get rid of all these diseases completely. For this reason in some Hadith it is mentioned that weakness and helplessness is better than eloquence. Here helplessness is of the tongue and not of the heart. Modesty also demands that a man should feel ashamed if he is adversely criticised any where ; he should be desirous of being introduced as a person who shuns sins and keeps away from evil.

It is forbidden (Haram) to speak ill of those absent persons whose defects are hidden, but those who display their own faults and themselves show their own evils, then other people cannot spread it so speedily as they themselves spread it far and wide. Therefore, the Prophet (S.A.W.) has said that one, who has committed sin, walks hiding from the people. When the companions of the Prophet (S.A.W.) saw him with one of his wives in a corner of the mosque, he stopped them and told them that he was not with any strange woman.

There is a man who wants, more than anything else, name and fame, and there is another man who turns away the eyes of others from his fame. Their difference is quite distinct. The meaning of a Muslim's hiding from the people is not that he should indulge in the evil of hiding his evil and displaying his good points, but it means that he should not go on advertising his defects and evils and that he should feel ashamed of committing any sin openly.

A man who feels ashamed to disclose his defects has some element of good in him, and the man who feels proud to show his good points has some element of wickedness in him. As a man feels ashamed in the presence of others, he should have the similar feeling of being ashamed even from himself. If he dislikes that others should find any defect in him, then he should also feel hateful towards having any defect in himself. There is a well-known saying : "Whoever has done a thing secretly which he would have been ashamed to do openly, he has no respect for himself in his own eyes." Therefore it is essential for every Muslim that he should be free from all sins, open or secret, whether they may be known to him only or disclosed to all the people. A well-known saying is: "Adopt a thing which both your ears may like to hear, and keep away from the thing which your ears may not like to hear."

Foundation of Virtue

Modesty is the foundation of virtue. This is the only criterion of decency in all acts. Allah's Messenger (S.A.W.) has said : "The thing, which has obscenity in it, will be spoilt by it, and the thing in which there will be modesty, it will adorn it." (Tirmidhi)

If a man puts on the raiment or modesty, he becomes the symbol of welfare and goodness. Hadrat Aishah (R.A.A.) narrates that the Prophet (S.A.W.) has said:

"If modesty were to appear in the form of a man, then it would have appeared in the form of the best and virtuous man, and if obscenity takes the form of man, it would be of the worst man." (Tibrani)

Modesty also demands that man should pay the rights of the right claimants and should give them their proper place. He should treat every man of talent in a respectable way. The relationship of the slave with his master and of the student with his teacher is that of respect and honour. It is not proper that they should raise their voices in their presence, or should walk ahead of them. In a Hadith it is written : "Treat them well from whom you learn." (Tibrani)

"O Allah! Do not show me the time when the learned men of the religion are shunned and men of tolerance and forbearance are not treated with modesty." (Ahmad)

Abdullah bin Yasar (R.A.A.) says:

"I have been hearing a Hadith for a long time: 'When you go to a nation, and from their faces you realise that there is none among them who is afraid of Allah, then know that the matter is extremely delicate'."(Ahmad)

Modesty is not cowardice. A modest and respectable person would rather sacrifice his life than tolerate disgrace and immodesty. Sometimes an element of fear creeps in modesty, but this fear is for safeguarding the honour lest morality and modesty may suffer in the straitened circumstances. The borders of modesty meet the limits of bravery and valour, which is praiseworthy. When the Jews avoided taking up cudgels against the invaders of the holy land :

> *Then outspoke two of those who feared (their Lord, men) to whom Allah had been gracious : Enter in upon them by the gate, for if you enter by it, surely you will be victorious.* *(Maida : 23)*

These people feared Allah. They feared disgrace and infamy. They were ashamed to take the course of running away. If there were fighting, then these people only led the people in the fight and brought victory nearer.

Undoubtedly perfect modesty is given to man by nature, while there are some people in whose very nature there is shamelessness and immodesty. On the other hand there is no dearth of the people in whom the substance of modesty, sense of shame and consciousness for honour is much more. But in spite of the fact that shyness is a distinct element of modesty, it is displayed at both good and bad occasions, and sometimes a shy person commits a very serious mistake. Modesty appears within the religious limits only.

A man who is cowed down by the threats of the followers of Falsehood can not be called modest or respectable. Modesty or respect will not be displayed before falsehood, and it is not required to be shown before the people who have gone astray, when helping Truth and giving assistance to the right is the need of the time. The polytheists accused Islam that its followers were abusing their gods, saying that they have no power to create anything, that they are unable to whisk away flies from their faces. They said that it is not modesty that their gods should be so insulted. This was answered by Allah thus:

> *Allah does not feel shy of using similes of the lowly things, be it a mosquito or a still lower being. Those who are believers know that it is truth from their Lord. But these who are rejectors of Faith, they say: What does Allah mean by such a simile?* *(Baqarah: 26)*

The picture drawn of the false gods is correct and Allah has no shyness in saying what is true, and a Muslim should not be afraid of proving what is truth and what is falsehood, nor should he care about it.

Modesty before your Lord : The highest peak of modesty is to be modest before the Lord Almighty, Allah, the Creator of the Universe. We eat from the provision given by Him. We breathe in His air. We grow up on His land, and we are under the shadow of His blue umbrella, the vast sky. A man does not pay his fellowman for his kindness and favour by some evil or unkind act. But it is surprising how his dealing with God is different while he is under his obligation and burden of favours from the cradle to the grave, and even after this his life is at the mercy of the Gracious Lord. Allah has great rights on his slaves. If people appreciate this, they will rush towards righteousness and virtue without any pressure or delay, and will run away from evil and shameless acts. Hadrat Abdullah Ibn Masood (R.A.A.) has narrated that the Messenger of Allah (S.A.W.) has said:

"Be modest before Allah as it is proper to be modest." We said : "We are modest before Allah, and for this we thank Him." The Prophet (S.A.W.) said:

> *"This is not modesty. The modesty that should be before Allah demands that you keep your head and all the parts safe from falsehood, keep your belly and your foods safe from the forbidden things, and remember the condition of death and that of the grave ; and he who wants to love the life of the Hereafter, he should give up the embellishments and grandeur of the worldly life, and should prefer Hereafter to the world. He who has done so, he has, as if, fulfilled the right of being modest before Allah."* *(Tirmidhi)*

This advice contains a majority of Islamic principles of etiquette and virtues. It is the responsibility of a Muslim that he should not let any wrong word to come out from his mouth, his eyes may not be directed towards any forbidden thing or things exciting sexual feelings, his ears should not hear wrong things ; he should not accustom his stomach to accept forbidden food, but that it should be content with permissible and clean things. Then it is also his duty that he should spend his time in seeking Allah's pleasure, and should employ all his efforts and resources and capabilities in earning sawab (reward). Carnal desires should not misguide him.

If he does all these things with the consciousness that Allah is watching him, and if he hates to be lax and defective in matters concerning Allah, then he has fulfilled the right of being modest before Allah. In this sense modesty comprises the whole religion. When it is applicable on so many acts then it has become a part of faith. The Messenger of Allah (S.A.W.) has said:

> *There are more than seventy aspects of faith. The highest among them is the confirmation of the words that there is no god, except Allah, and the lowest is to remove some harmful thing from the road, and modesty is an aspect of faith.* *(Bukhari)*

Man tries to display good conduct and behaviour in the presence of those whom he considers great and whom he wants to please. Before them he speaks only when necessary. Every step that he takes before them is with caution and fear. A Muslim, whose religion teaches him that he is never away from the sight of Allah, because he is in his presence day and night, feels more awe from the wrath of Allah, and he should be very cautious and careful in obeying His commands. The meaning of this Hadith is also the same: "Be modest before Allah, as you are in the presence of the powerful people of your nation."

> *On some occasions a man's feeling of hesitation and the changing colour of his face is the proof of the fact that there is a streak of virtuousness and purity in him, and "modesty is the name of perfect virtue."* *(Muslim)*

If the colour of modesty goes out from the face, then life becomes free to adopt a sinful line, and becomes the fuel of the hell. For this reason it is said: "If you have no modesty, do whatever you like."

GENEROSITY

Islam is a religion whose foundation has been kept on charity, generosity, and philanthropy. Narrow mindedness, greed and miserliness are evils that shake its edifice. Therefore Islam likes that its followers should be generous and charitable. It has advised them to treat others kindly, to act righteously, to help their kinsmen and to do all kinds of good and virtuous deeds. It has stressed on its followers to make righteous living a permanent policy .

> *"Those who spend (in charity) their wealth by night and by day; in secret and in public, have their reward with their Lord; there is no fear for them, nor shall they grieve."* *(Baqarah: 274)*

It is the responsibility of every Muslim that in meeting his needs he should act in a balanced way, so that he may not spend all his wealth on his personal needs only, but that it is his duty that he should let others also partake of the blessings which Allah has bestowed on him, and that he should allot a part of his wealth for the help and assistance of the poor and needy persons.

> *Allah's Messenger has said: "O Adam's son! Spend your wealth, it is good for you. And do not block it, it is bad for you, and the wealth according to the need cannot be reproached. Spend first for your family and dependents, and the raised hand is better than the lowered hand."* *(Muslim)*

Quran has very clearly hinted at this subject when it has commanded the Muslims to spend for their kinsmen and the needy persons and prevented wasteful spending. A spendthrift wastes his wealth and indulges in foolishness. He spends his excess wealth for his personal pleasures, then what can remain with him for payment of the rights of others and the necessary assistance to the needy persons? Allah has commanded:

> *"And render to the kindred their due rights, as (also) to those in want, and to the wayfarer ; but squander not (your wealth) in the manner of a spendthrift. Verily, spendthrifts are the brothers of Satans, and the Satan is to his Lord ungrateful."* *(Bani Israil: 26, 27)*

And after this, advice is given to be mindful of the sentiments of the needy and the people in want, and their feelings should not be hurt. If there is nothing that can be given to them, they should be refused softly and in a decent way:

> *"And even if you have to turn away from them in pursuit of the Mercy of your Lord which you do expect, speak to them a word of easy kindness:"* *(Bani Israil: 28)*

Islam's call to its followers to spend in the cause of Allah and for charity is famous and well-known. Similarly its war against miserliness, greed and narrowmindedness is as clear as the day.

> *One* Hadith *has it : "A giver of charity is near to Allah, is near to humans, and is near to Paradise and away from hell. And a miser is away from Allah, is away from humans, away from the Paradise and is near to hell. An uneducated giver of charity is liked more by Allah than a miserly worshipper."* *(Tirmidhi)*

There does not exist any system in this world, and there is also no possibility of its existence, in which all the people may be indifferent to and not in need of mutual cooperation. As long as there are power and weakness, wealth and poverty side by side in the human society, it is necessary for achieving peace and satisfaction and for ensuring the success and security of the society that the strong should be kind to the weak, and that wealthy should favour the poor and needy with gifts and donations. If wealth and property are amassed as a result of the capabilities and striving of the people, then some people amass lot of riches and some people get only the bare necessities. And this cannot be objected to. The question regarding misfortune and ungratefulness arise when these people live a life away from the society, when they are concerned only with meeting their own personal needs and for providing for their own pleasures and luxuries, when Allah has caused the people to live together, and has declared this togetherness of theirs, instead of differences in their circumstances, a severe trial for them. This provides a test for their faith and an opportunity for proving their worth.

> *"We have made some of you as trials for others. Will you have patience? For Allah is One Who sees (all things)."*
> *(Furqan : 20)*

A community can be successful in this field of life only when the relationship among its individuals is strong and firm. No individual of the community should be so deprived that he may be facing a life of starvation and no wealthy man of the community should be so greedy that he may be spending his wealth only for his own personal pleasures and luxuries. To achieve this high objective Islam has framed very strong laws. Peoples' hearts have been prepared to indulge in righteous and virtuous deeds, and they have been tempted to cooperate with each other, help each other and act righteously. It explained to them that the benefit of spending in the cause of Allah is not only derived by the poor and needy persons but the givers of charity also achieve the invaluable riches of peace and satisfaction; their hearts are protected from the earthquakes of rancour and jealousy, and they are saved from the adverse consequences of selfishness and narrow mindedness:

> *"Behold, you are those invited to spend in the way of Allah ; but among you are some that are niggardly. But any who are niggardly are so at the expense of their own souls. But Allah is free of all wants, and it is you that are needy."* *(Muhammad : 38)*

Poverty Destroys all Charm : Poverty and want is a condition which causes a lot of trouble for men. It throws him down from the position which Allah had given him, and there is always a lurking fear that it may deprive him from that nobleness for which Allah has declared him the best of all the creatures. Human nature does not like to see any person in dirty, torn and tattered clothes, that would expose a man's defects ; there should be no footwear to cover his feet, or his heels and fingers are dragging on the road, or he is hungry for a number of days ; he may be looking greedily at tasty and luscious food and be unable to taste it.

Those who see such sad and sorrowful scenes and are not moved by them at all, they are not humans : they are not Muslims. To feel disturbed and sorry by seeing the plight of the unhappy men is common human nature. One who is bereft of this basic quality is not a human ; he is a stone. As an Urdu poet says:

> *"Man was created for sympathy (by Allah),*
>
> *Otherwise there was no dearth of angles for worshipping Him."*

The question before faith is that it should frighten men from their Lord in relation to the condition of such helpless and poor people. Once the Prophet of Islam saw such a scene the tears rolled out from his eyes, and he was very much perturbed.

He gathered all the Muslims and delivered a very effective speech. He reminded them of the rights of men on men and their duties.

He warned them of the punishment from Allah and the consequences in the Hereafter. His speech was so effective that the people who were present there, freely donated whatever they could, with the result that so much money was collected that the man whose condition had so moved the Prophet became a wealthy man from this spontaneous help from the companions of the Prophet, and all his defects were covered.

Jarir has narrated : "We were in the company of the Prophet in the morning. Some people came in his presence. They were ill-clad. Their sheets were torn from various places. Many of them belonged to the tribe of Bani Madhar. When the Prophet saw their starving condition, his face changed colour. He went into his house and then came out and asked Bilal to give Azan. He called the faithful to prayer and the Prophet led the prayer. Then he delivered a speech, and said

> *"O People! Fear your Lord, who created you from a single person, created, of like nature, his mate ; and from them twain scattered (like seeds) countless men and women;-fear Allah through Whom you demand your (rights) of one another, and towards the womb (that bore you). Verily, Allah ever watches over you."*
>
> *(An: Nisa:1)*
>
> *"O People who believe ! fear Allah, and every person should see what he has prepared for his future."*
>
> *(Hashr: 18)*

Then the Prophet said: "Every one should give in charity dinar, dirham, cloth, dates, wheat, etc." He went on till he urged : "Give, even if it is a stone of a date." The narrator says that after this a man from Ansar brought a bag so full that it was slipping from his hand and it fell to the ground before he reached the Prophet. Other people also brought things to be given in charity, till there were two big heaps of eatable goods and clothes. At that time I saw that the face of the Prophet glowed with joy as if it was gold. Then he said:

> *"Anybody who inducted a good Sunnah in Islam, he will get its reward (sawab) and then also the reward*

of others acting on it, without there being any reduction in the reward of these who act on that Sunnah.

And anybody who inducted a bad system in Islam, he will get the punishment for it and also the punishment of all those who will act on it, without there being any reduction is the punishment of those who act on it."

(Muslim)

These eloquent words invite us to compete in matters of righteousness and we should try to vie with each other in performing virtuous deeds, e.g. social welfare work during inclement weather, or relief work after natural calamities, etc. On the other hand these words warn those who introduce bad practices in the society, and by this they increase the problems and complications of the society, and they leave their successors to face the ill consequences of their acts.

Charity : It is human nature to love wealth and to be greedy to get it. For this a man travels long distances and bears various kinds of troubles. The disease of selfishness and a tendency of giving preference to his own benefits over all other things are there in a man from the first day. He thinks about himself more and cares little for others. If he is given the entire wealth of the earth, nay, even if he gets the treasures of the blessings of his Lord, he will not be prepared to spend from it willingly, and different kinds of diseases of selfishness will tie his hands.

"Say (O Prophet!) If you get the treasures of my Lord in your possession, you would have blocked it from fear of it being spent. Verily, man is narrow-minded."

(Bani Israil: 100)

Islam has considered this kind of thinking and mentality as very cheap and mean, and it is to be resisted vehemently. It is to be counted with alertness and cleverness. Islam has very clearly stated that only that man can be successful in achieving the rewards in this and the next world who removes the motivations of narrowmindedness and niggardliness and nourishes charity and generosity

"So fear Allah as much as you can ; listen and obey; and spend in charity for the benefit of your own souls; and

those saved from the covetousness of their own souls,- they are the ones that achieve prosperity."

(Taghabun : 16)

Heaps of silver and gold from which the rights of poor and needy persons are not met become the causes of their owner's punishment and disgrace in this world and in the next. Such wealth is like the snakes which are hiding in their holes and are waiting to bite men.

Islam has clarified that this wealth will be turned into living snakes on the Doomsday, and this snake will be chasing for attacking and biting its owner.

"The wealthy man who has not paid the rights of others from his wealth, his treasure will become a snake on the Doomsday, which will chase him with open mouth, then a voice will be heard: 'Catch hold of your wealth which you had concealed, and I am unconcerned with this.' When he will see that there is no escape, he will put his hand in its mouth, and it will bite him as a bull eats the grass." *(Bukhari)*

Islam explains to the man that his love for wealth leads him near destruction, and that if he ponders over the reality of wealth and its consequences he will realise that charity is better than selfishness and that gift is nobler than miserliness.

"Man will say: my wealth, my wealth, although his wealth, was of three kinds: whatever he ate, drank and finished it ; or had spent on clothes and they were torn ; or he gave to others and stored for the Hereafter, and what was other than this has been finished or has been left for the people." *(Muslim)*

It is strange that what a man leaves for others, he expresses harshness in that? He will not use his wealth for bettering his own economic condition and for the welfare in the Hereafter, then from what else will he try to derive benefit?

The holy Prophet disclosed this reality, when he said: "Who is there among you that likes the wealth of his inheritor more than his own wealth ?" The Companions replied: "O Messenger of Allah! We like our own wealth." The Prophet then said: "The wealth of each one of you

is what he has sent to God, and the wealth of the inheritor is what each one of you leaves behind."
(Bukhari)

In spite of this when the Prophet declared that he would collect the Zakat, he treated leniently and with softness the greed of men to hoard money and tackled them with great dexterity. He said:

"Soon to you will come the collectors of Zakat. When they come, welcome them. Give them full liberty to collect whatever they want. If they act justly, they will do good to themselves. And if they are unjust, its evil will be on them. Keep them pleased, for the payment of your zakat will be completed by their pleasure, and they should pray in your favour." *(Abu Daud)*

If a man is successful in removing the obstructions that miserliness and narrow mindedness place in the path of righteous feelings, then it is a perfect achievement in the eyes of Islam. Ordinarily a man is hopeful about his life, and his relationship with it is strong and firm, provided he is healthy and energetic and courageous about future. At such a time man spends his money moderately and he is always thinking of increasing his wealth, so that he may be reassured about his future and that of his children. If in these circumstances a man controls all the factors, and keeps his hands open, spends his money openheartedly and generously, he neither worries about poverty or want, nor is he afraid about his ruin, then such a man performs the act of great good. One man went to the Prophet and asked him:

"O Messenger of Allah ! What charity is the best reward-winning ?" The Prophet said : "That you give in charity, although you may be healthy and in need of money ; you may be afraid of getting poor so also you may be hopeful of getting wealth and being free from want. Let it not happen that you should go on postponing to give in charity, till your last breath, then you start making a will to give this much in charity to this man and that much to that man." *(Bukhari)*

"If you give charity openly even so it is good, but if you give it secretly to the needy, it is much better for you,

and He will remove some of your ill-deeds. And Allah is well aware of what you do." *(Baqarah: 271)*

"If you loan to Allah a beautiful loan, He will double it to your (credit), and He will grant forgiveness ; for Allah is most Ready to appreciate (service), Most Forbearing-Knower of what is hidden and what is open, Exalted in Might, Full of Wisdom"(Taghabun : 17, 18)

When a man commits a sin and he realises that there has arisen distance between him and his Lord, then the thing that brings back cleanness light and gets him a shelter under the benevolence and pleasure of his Lord is spending his most loved wealth and property in the cause of Allah, and he should gladden the hearts of the poor and the needy with its help, and should try to achieve rank before the Most Gracious Being. Hadrat Abuzar has narrated that the Prophet has said: There was a worshipper in the Bani Israil, who had worshipped Allah in a monastery for sixty years. One day there was rainfall and the whole area became green. When he saw from his hillside—monastery he felt—would it that he went down in the valley and recited Allah's praises and collected more virtue. Then he went down from the monastery. He had one or two loaves. In the meanwhile he met a woman, and talked to her and the woman also enjoyed, and suddenly he covered the woman and then slumber overtook him.

Then he came for taking a bath to a lake, and a beggar asked him for alms. The monk then gave him both the loaves, and then he suddenly died. His sixty years' worshipping was weighed against the act of illegal sex, then the scale of the sin was heavier. Then in the scale of his virtue the two loaves were put, then the scale of the virtue became heavier, and he achieved salvation." (Ibn Habban)

The effect of and the role that charity and generosity play in salvation and deliverance can be found in the best example that Allah taught to His Prophet so that he may convey it to his followers : "I command you to give charity. Its example is like that of a man who has been held by his enemies, his hands have been tied to his neck, and he has been drawn near with the intention of being beheaded; suddenly he inquires of the possibility of saving his life by giving money. Then he began giving whatever valuable things of little or more value that he had, till he was able to get himself free." *(Hakim)*

Zakat, charity and other generous acts are of great importance in this life and in the Hereafter. On its basis alone a Muslim's relationship with his religion either becomes strong or weak. There is nothing more depriving than miserliness in paying others' dues and nursing misgivings against God. And there is nothing more helpful for success and glory than confidence in Allah's favours and a man's charity and generosity.

Allah's Messenger has said: "The acts of righteousness and virtue save a man from the adverse consequences of the wicked acts. The charity that is given unobtrusively cools down Allah's anger, and kindness to kinsmen increases a man's age." *(Tibrani)*

Another tradition has it:

"Arrange for the cleanness by taking zakat out of your wealth. Arrange for the treatment of your sick by giving in charity, and fight the waves of adversity by praying to God meekly and humbly." *(Abu Daud)*

The heaviest blow to Satan, the most successful method to counter his tricks and the greatest shield against his distrusts is that man should give his wealth in charity, and spend his money in the cause of Allah. For this reason the devil inspires man to be weak and narrow-minded so that he may be prevented from giving generously and be involved in the entanglements of the material world:

"The devil threatens you with poverty and bids you to lewd conduct. Allah promises you His forgiveness and bounties. And Allah is All-Embracing, All- Knowing." *(Baqarah: 268)*

It is mentioned in the Hadith:

"When a man decides to give something in charity, a group of seventy devils clings to him and tries to put him off it." *(Ahmad)*

When a man distributes his salary or allots it to different items of expenditure, he allots its major portion to such items as are perishable. He thinks of them as if they are the dues from which there is no escape. Islam has informed that a man may consider the expenditure on his food and medicine as on perishable items, but the wealth which he spends in the cause of Allah is such that never perishes.

> *Hadrat Aishah narrates that they slaughtered a goat, and the Prophet asked: "How much of its flesh has remained?" They replied: "Nothing remained except the shoulder piece." The Prophet said: "Everything has remained except the shoulder piece."* *(Tirmidhi)*

This *Hadith* is in accord with these words of Allah

> *"Whatever is with you is perishable, and whatever is with Allah is permanent."* *(Nahl: 96)*

In a *Hadith-Qudsi* it is written

> *"O son of Adam! Spend your treasure in the cause of Allah. With me there is no fear of its getting burnt, drowned or stolen. In its place whatever you would need, I will give it to you."* *(Baihaqi)*

Philanthropy: Sometimes a thought enters the mind that charity, reduces the wealth, and brings a man nearer to poverty, and takes away from him that peace and reassurance that is available to him under the shadow of wealth. Such a thought is generated by Satan, who puts it into the minds of the hoarders of low and mean nature. The fact is that charity is the means of nourishment and development. Donation of wealth is a long and wide road. A man who spends the gifts of Allah generously with his two hands, his hands are always full with the gifts of Allah. He is always surrounded by the favours and blessings of Allah. In a *Hadith* it is mentioned:

> *"There are three men about whom I can take an oath. No man's wealth can be reduced by charity. Any man who shows patience in the face of oppression, Allah honours him. And a man who opens the door to begging, Allah opens on him the door of poverty and want."*
> *(Ibn Majah)*

Man should display charity and generosity and should try to fill up the gaps found in society. Those poor and needy persons who may come to him for succour should not be returned by him disappointed, but instead he should satisfy them and should deal with them in such a way that he himself reaps rich benefits for the next world. If today a little is spent in charity, tomorrow or day after tomorrow great advantages will accrue from that.

Allah has termed this generosity or donation as 'excellent loan,' which will be repaid in increased quantities, not two or three times-but many more times. He has encouraged His slaves to spend money in His cause and has very clearly informed them that this spending in the cause of Allah enables them to deservingly get limitless favours and blessing of Allah, which are everlasting. It is mentioned in a *Hadith Qudsi*:

> *"O My slave ! spend, spend, it is your duty to spend. Allah's hand is full. The charity of the day and night cannot reduce it. What do you think, how much has He spent since He created the earth and the heavens? He never closed His hands, when His throne was on the water, in His hands was the balance which went down and went up."* *(Bukhari)*

Allah says:

> *"And whatever you spend (for good) He replaces it. And He is the Best of Providers."* *(Saba: 39)*

Spenders in the cause of Allah remain in his sight and in his shelter in both the states of plenty and adversity. The angel sent Darud on them, and wish for increase in their wealth. As regards those who hoard money very miserly, they wish their loss and ruin. And will they remain with their wealth or will the wealth remain with them for all time? The wealth has come to us from others, and will again go to others. Then why this pride and conceit about it? And for this reason why should one forget his position and manners.

The things with which man is attached in this world, will be left by him for the real inheritor of those things, and he will appear before his Lord in such a condition that he would have no wealth nor would he enjoy any rank or position. He will be totally empty-handed, as he had first come to the world. The wealth and property about which he had acted miserly will become a load in his neck on the Day of Judgment. And it is not surprising because Allah will take revenge on such persons who forgot these realities and lived in this world unmindful of their duties. The only thought that troubled them was that whether a thing was beneficial for them or not they were thoroughly self-centred and in their selfishness they forgot what was really good for them.

> *Allah's Messenger says : "Every morning two angels come down to earth. One of them says 'O Allah'. Give full recompense to the spender (for good cause).' The other one says : 'O Allah ! Ruin and destroy the miser'.* *(Muslim)*

Remove Poverty Movement : A man is greedy for Wealth because he wants that he should leave behind him plenty of wealth and property for his children, so that they may be safe and secure after him. This is a good and virtuous intention. Islam considers it a duty of a Muslim that he should take care of his family and dependents, and keep them away from want and penury. If Islam wants you to be helpful in removing poverty and want from the homes of others, it also dislikes you to bring poverty and want in your homes. It is mentioned in the *Hadith:*

> *"To leave your inheritors rich and wealthy is much better than leaving them poor and needy, and being forced to beg before others."* *(Bukhari)*

Provision for the children and a guarantee for their future are duties of accepted importance. But how can it be proper if a man stakes his religion and character after these things? It is sheer foolishness if a man sacrifices his position, decency and Allah's pleasure only for the purpose of leaving his income for his children. Islam shows that like all other good things a man's wealth and children are a trial for him. If he is entangled in their love and forgets his duties and does not offer the expected sacrifices, then these good things and gifts become a trouble for him, nay, they become more dangerous and destructive.

> *"O you who believe! Truly, among your wives and your children are (some that are) enemies to yourselves; so beware of them ! But if you forgive and overlook, and cover up (their faults), verily, Allah is Oft-Forgiving, Most Merciful. Your riches and your children may be*

but a trial; but in the presence of Allah, is the highest reward." (Taghabun: 14, 15)

Yes, the man who does not go to *Jihad,* because he likes the proximity of his wife, or the man who restrains his head from giving in charity because he wants to save his wealth for saving more and more for his children, he is showing ungratefulness to Allah for the good things of life that He has provided, and he thinks that they are really 'gifts' white actually they are a trial for him.

Khaula Bint Hakim says: "One day the Prophet came out carrying his grandchild and he was saying: 'You (children) become the means of miserliness, cowardice, ignorance and foolishness. And you are also the fragrance of Allah." (Tirmidhi)

It means that the person who preferred to be a miser, coward and fool on account of his child, he was in a loss, and a person who paid the dues of Allah and His slaves, he became successful. However, being niggardly in paying the dues and for hoarding for the children, a man's poverty and need do not end, it also does not guarantee his becoming a wealthy person; and such a man will not be able to proffer any excuse which will be acceptable.

Abdullah bin Masood narrates that the Prophet has said : "Allah has blessed two types of persons with plenty of wealth, property, and children. He will ask the persons of one of these groups: 'O Such and such man!' He will reply: 'We are present, O our Lord! we are present.' He will ask: 'What have you done with the wealth and property with which I had blessed you?' The slave will reply: 'That I have left for my sons, for I was afraid of his poverty'. The Lord will say : 'If you know the reality you will laugh less and cry more. The thing which you fear, I have sent it down on them."

He will ask another person , 'O Such and such man!' He will reply: 'I am present, O My Lord! I am present.' He will ask: 'Had I not blessed you with plenty of wealth and property?' The stave will reply: 'Certainly, my Lord!' He will ask: 'What have you done with those blessings? 'He will reply : 'I spent it in the path of your obedience, and I left my children to your Mercy, Kindness and

Benevolence.' Then God will say: 'Listen, If you know the reality, you will laugh more and cry less. The things on which you relied, I provided him with them'."

(Tibrani)

Islam advises that man should first be kind to himself, then with his home people, then with his relatives and with all humans. A man's being kind with himself means that he should meet all his permissible and proper needs by halal or permissible means, and should avoid *Haram* or forbidden means. He should keep himself safe from the manifestations of poverty and starvation, for a man loses his dignity because of these conditions. The necessary standard of Muslim's honour is not maintained. But all these things should be done in between miserliness and wasteful spending. Muslims are allowed to keep so much wealth with them that it may suffice to meet their needs, and if they have not these swans then they are poor and needy.

Abu Saeed Khudri narrates: "A man in a poor condition entered the Masjid-i-Nabavi *(Prophet's Mosque). At that time the Prophet was commanding the people to give charity. When the people collected the donations, he gave two items of clothing to that man in poor condition. When for the second time the Prophet advised the people to give in charity, that needy looking man threw one item of clothing. The Prophet said in anger: 'See this shabby looking man, I had given him two pieces of clothing, and when I again advised people to give in charity, he threw his one piece.' The Prophet reproached him considerably,"* *(Abu Daud)*

The holy Prophet wanted to remove poverty, penury; to end want and obscenity from society, while some people did not care whether they were moving about without clothes or without footwear. If the people of this kind consider their such appearance as a manifestation of religious teachings, then it is not correct, because Islam makes it a duty for every Muslim to strive for so much wealth as may make him able to raise his head with dignity in society.

Jabir has reported : "A man came to the Prophet with a piece of gold with him and said to the Prophet that he got it from a mine and requested him to accept it ; that it was in charity and that he had nothing else which he could give in charity. The Prophet turned his face away. So he came from the right side, and again requested. This time also the Prophet turned his face away. So he came from the left side and pleaded. This time also the Prophet did not pay any attention. So he came from behind and repeated his request. The Prophet took it and threw it towards him so forcefully that had it touched him it would have been painful.

Then he said : 'Some of you come to give the entire property in charity. After this they go on begging before others, and the best charity is that which comes from a wealthy person'."

Who Deserves First to Partake of your Wealth? : It is the duty of the Head of the family to find out what are the reasonable needs of his household-people, and he should meet them with generosity. It is not religiousness that a man should let his wife and children suffer for want of means and should spend his wealth for other purposes, however important they may be. Family relationships deserve more attention and preferable treatment over others.

The Prophet has said : "One dinar is that which you spend in the cause of Allah, and one dinar is that which you spend for freeing a slave; and one dinar is that which you spend on your family. But of all these, the greatest reward will be given for the dinar which has been spent on the family." *(Muslim)*

In the discussion on Sincerity this Hadith had been quoted:

"What a Muslim spends on his family, for seeking the pleasure of Allah, is also counted as charity."

(Bukhari)

By this clear guidance Islam wants that the allotment of the expenditure should be in proportion to the benefit to society; for family is the foundation of a great society and the first brick of its edifice. Therefore, it is necessary to pay attention to it first and to pay its dues fully. In this teaching there is a warning for those who spend heartily and squander money carelessly outside their homes among their friends while at home they become a picture of poverty and helplessness.

The people who deserve more to be benefited from the excess wealth of a person are his relatives and kinsmen. It is their right that when the hand should be raised for giving in charity it should first be extended towards them.

It also appeals to a sound intellect that when there are needy and poor persons in the vicinity of a person, then where is the sense, in leaving them uncured for and extending the helping hand towards others? Such an action might generate a feeling of hatred and rancour in the hearts of the deprived persons, and they may feel that the ignorance shown in their respect is with a view to harming them and putting them to great loss. And if giving of pain and dissatisfaction is done consciously, then this kind of charity becomes troublesome for the giver.

> A Hadith *has it: "O Community of Muhammad ! By the Being Who has sent me with Truth, Allah cannot accept the charity of those persons whose relatives are in want of his kindness and help, and he is distributing it among others, lowing them. By the Being in Whose power is my life, on the Day of Judgment Allah will not look at such a man."* *(Tibrani)*

The wife of Hadrat Abdullah bin Masood, Zainab Saqafiah says : "Allah's Messenger has said: 'O Group of ladies! Give in charity, even if you have to sell ornaments." She says: 'I went to Abdullah bin Masood and told him : 'You are a poor man and the Prophet has asked us to give in charity. You go to the Prophet and ask him whether this thing can be an alternative for charity, if so it is well, otherwise I will give in charity to others instead of to you.' Abdullah Ibn Masood said: 'You go and ask him.'

She says that on her way to see the Prophet, she met a woman from Ansar, who was also troubled with the same thoughts. They went together. As a precautionary measure they had to stop outside his room. When Hadrat Bilal came out of the room, she said to him: 'Go and ask the Prophet and tell him that two women have come to ask you whether looking after the husbands and nourishing their children can be an alternative to charity or not ? And do not tell him who the women are.'

She says that Bilal went in the presence of the Prophet and asked him about her problem. The Prophet asked who the women were. He answered that one was a woman from the Ansar and another was Zainab. The Prophet asked: 'Which Zainab ?' He replied: 'The wife of Abdullah bin Masood.' The Prophet said: 'These two will get the reward of the relationship and also the reward for the charity.' *(Bukhari)*

Allah's Messenger has said: "To spend on the poor is charity, and to spend on the relative gets the reward for double charity, one is charity itself, and another for kindness to relatives." *(Tirmidhi)*

KINDNESS

Kindness is a basic quality of the human nature, which softens the heart when informed about the sufferings of the fellow creatures and makes one restless for providing relief to them. This quality makes a man feel sorry for the mistakes of others and causes him to guide them properly. This is a natural quality, because if this feeling of kindness dies, and it is not at all moved on occasions of happiness and sorrow, then a man falls to the level of animals, and all his virtues are vanished. This feeling is created by love and sympathy. Some times some vague feelings are created in animals too, on account of which they show some kindness to their offsprings, and for this reason hard-heartedness or cruelty is a trend which is lower and meaner than the tendency found in the animals. Nay, a cruel person is like the inanimate objects that have no feelings and no consciousness, and they are not moved by anything.

Kindness, in its highest and vast sense, is the attribute of the Almighty, God. His kindness is for all the existing things and covers the entire universe, wherever the ray of His knowledge (which encloses the entire universe) falls. The angels, in his praise, pray to him—

Therefore, grant salvation to those who have repented and have followed Your path, and save them from the punishment of hell. *(Momin:7)*

It is narrated by Hadrat Umar bin Khattab (R.A.A.) that in the presence of the Prophet (S.A.W.) a female-slave was brought along with other prisoners. This woman was running here and there and trying to expel milk from her breasts. If she saw any child, she embraced it and suckled it. The Prophet (S.A.W.) saw this condition of the woman and said:

"What do you think, can this woman throw her child into the fire?" They replied: "No, by God, this woman cannot throw her child into the fire." The Prophet (S.A.W.) then said: "Allah is more kind to His slaves than this woman is kind to her child." (Bukhari)

Most names of Allah carry the meaning of Kindness, Graciousness, Favour, Forgiveness and the like. A *Hadith Qudsi* states:

"My kindness surpasses My anger." (Muslim)

That is, to forgive humans for their lapses and errors is liked by Him more than to punish them, and therefore, He is more kind than the other people.

O Prophet! Say : 'My Lord, pardon, and be kind, and You are the Most Kind of all the kind people'.
(Muminoon : 118)

Today on this earth the blooming flowers of mutual love, good conduct, graciousness, and virtue that we see, are the reflections of the Divine Graciousness, only a small part of it He has placed in the hearts of His creatures. The most soft-hearted man among men is he who has received the greater portion of this kindness, and who has more sympathy with the life of the weak persons.

The cruel, the hard-hearted tyrants and the conceited persons of the nation will find their abode in the lowest part of the hell.

The man who is cruel and hard-hearted will be the farthest away from Allah. (Tirmidhi)

Allah's Messenger (S.A.W.) considered the dryness of the eyes and hardness of the heart as signs of ill-luck.

When Allah wanted to be gracious in view of the bad conditions on the earth and to send down a person who would remove the sorrow of the people of the world, who would tend to their wounds, who would sympathise with them on their lapses, who would inconvenience himself for their guidance, who would cause the strong to give the rights of the weak, who would fight for their rights and for their protection, who would convert the rebellious and tyrant men into kind-hearted human beings, He sent down, for all these purposes, Muhammad (S.A.W.) He placed treasures of knowledge and forbearance in his heart. He instilled in his character the light of virtue and righteousness. He made softness and kindness his second nature. He embellished his character with the qualities of charity and generosity. All these excellent qualities made Muhammad (S.A.W.) the most soft-hearted, kind, broad-minded and generous of all the men in the world:

> *It was by the mercy of Allah that you were lenient with them (O Muhammad), for if you had been stern and fierce of heart they would have dispersed from round about you.* *(Al-i-Imran : 159)*

This quality was also seen in action it the Battle of Uhud when the polytheists were poised to kill him. He was thrown into a pit so that he may die there. He saw his companions dying around him. His remaining companions looked at him and found that there were scratches on his cheeks and some of his teeth were broken. On this crucial occasion, they pleaded with him to subject them to a curse. He prayed: "O Allah! Give guidance to my community, they know not what they are doing." Pious men act in this manner only. The motivations of cruelty and tyranny do not excite their hearts. In the face of wrath and rage, tyranny and revenge, they always show mercy, forgiveness and kindness.

Cruelty is a very wicked thing for an individual to have. In the history of nations it has caused great upheavals. We should not be surprised to learn that Islam has warned us against it, and has declared it as a rebellion against God and deviation from the right path.

> *Has not the time arrived for the believers that their hearts in all humility should engage in remembrance of Allah and of the Truth which has been revealed to them and that they should not become like those to whom was given Revelation aforetime, but long ages passed over them and their hearts grew hard ? For*

many among them are rebellious transgressors.

(Hadid : 16)

Islam has commanded Muslims to be kind to all creatures and all humans, and has considered it a proof of perfect faith. A Muslim meets all Muslims. For them he has a feeling of love, sympathy and kindness in his heart. For them he extends his hand of cooperation and tries, as far as it is in his power, to remove their troubles and difficulties.

Allah's Messenger (S.A.W.) has said:

"You cannot be a Momin until you are not kind among yourselves." The companions said that they were all kind. He said: "Kindness is not this that you sympathise with your companion, but kindness is this that you should think all men deserving of it." *(Tibrani)*

When a man meets his friends, sympathy is naturally created. When a man looks at his children, feelings of love and kindness are generated. This is a common thing. Bat for a Muslim it is certain that the sphere of his kindness is widest. He treats all humans with kindness and love and meets them with a smiling face. There are many traditions in which this general kindness has been recommended for Muslims. The Prophet (S.A.W.) has said:

He who does not show mercy to the people, Allah also does not show mercy to him. *(Bukhari)*

In another tradition it is said : "He who does not forgive others, Allah also does not forgive him." Yet another *Hadith* says:

"How lucky is that man who adopts humbleness without having scarcity, who considers himself inferior without having to beg for anything, who spends his own earned money in the right causes without disobeying Allah, who is kind to the inferior and mean persons, and remains in the company of the learned men and the intellectuals." *(Tibrani)*

Allah has stated that the characteristic of the Muslim Society is that it is humble towards its own people and stern towards the others.

Humble towards believers, stern towards disbelievers.
(Maidah : 54)

At another place it is said:

Hard against the disbelievers, kind among themselves.
(Fath : 29)

Humble towards their Own People and Stern towards Others : Here a question can be raised: What is the relevance of discussing hardness and sternness when the talk is about Rahmat and kindness? The fact is that Islam talks of general kindness and does not keep out any person, animal or bird from it, and the authorities quoted above, all support the exhortation for the general kindness. But some men and animals are such as are a cause of danger and a source of terror for others. In their cases the demand of the public benefit is that their evil should be cut short and their menace should be put a stop to. Sometimes sternness with a person proves to be beneficial to him and serves as a whip against his going astray.

Islam is entirely a religion of peace. It commands its followers to be gracious and kind to all mankind. Allah addresses His Messenger (S.A.W.) and says:

"We sent you not save as a Mercy for the peoples."
(Ambiya : 107)

All the Quranic Surahs are commenced with this verse:

In the name of Allah, Most Gracious, Most Merciful.

But the human wolves act as obstructions in the path of this general Islamic kindness. They place rocks in its way so that the humanity may not derive benefit from its springs, and may die in the valley of bewilderment and ignorance by keeping away from it. It is necessary to remove these obstructions and it is inevitable that stern attitude should be adopted towards these social wolves.

The day when their harassment would end their transgression and rebellion will be subdued, they will also come under the shadow of its kindness. Therefore, the fault does not lie with the kindness of Islam, but with these people, that they have kept themselves away from it. Allah's graciousness covers every thing, but a polytheist or an apostate cannot derive benefit from it:

My Mercy embraces all things, therefore I shall ordain it for those who ward off (evil) and pay the poor-due (zakat) and those who believe Our Revelations, those who follow the Messenger, the Prophet who is unlettered. *(Araf : 156-157)*

It can be illustrated in this way : A public hall has a capacity to seat one thousand persons, but there is a condition, of obtaining permission for admittance. If somebody refuses to get the required permission then he has deprived himself of admittance into the hall. The capacity of the hall is not affected by that. The same sense is conveyed in this *Hadith* in which the Prophet (S.A.W.) has said:

"Every person of my Ummah will go to Paradise, save who denies." The people asked "Who can deny?" He said: "He who obeyed me will go to Paradise, and he who disobeyed me, denied." *(Bukhari)*

Sometimes kindness takes the mantle of sternness, but the reality does not change. Children are sent to school forcibly, and they learn their lessons after a little harsh treatment. If they are allowed to carry on according to their own sweet will, then they will never turn out to be good students or good citizens.

The doctor treats a patient in a similar fashion, and while performing a surgical operation has to cut the flesh, or sever the bones, and sometimes has to remove away a part of the body. This cannot be called unjust or harsh, on the contrary he is doing a favour to the patient by showing kindness to him.

Therefore, kindness does not only include comfort and convenience, it covers all rights and aspects. If a man is hanged, his body dangles from the gallows, his eyes become sightless, and his tongue protrudes. If on seeing this terrible sight, a feeling of sympathy is aroused in our hearts and the murderer is set free, then this whole world will be filled with anarchy and lawlessness. At such a time the real kindness demands that these kind of feelings should be suppressed.

O you men of understanding! There is life for you in Qisas, so that you may fear to break His law (against murder). *(Baqarah : 179)*

The hard-heartedness which is considered objectionable and despicable in Islam is the name of dryness of the self and of the heart, which has no connection with intellect and logic, with justice and fairplay. It is the worst desire, which begins with pain-giving and trouble and spreads with selfishness and blind desires, but graciousness is a factor of the Divine Beauty, which is enshrined in the human heart. It induces them to be righteous and virtuous, and keeps their lives fresh and their breasts open in the hardest of times. Allah's Messenger (S.A.W.) has said:

> *"Allah has made hundred parts of kindness and has sent down only one part on the earth. With the help of that part the creatures sympathise with one another, even an animal removes away its hoof so that it may not hurt its calf.* *(Bukhari)*

In another *Hadith*, it is stated:

> *"The day when Allah created the earth and the skies, He created hundred kindnesses. Every kindness or Rahmat is equal to the layer that is between the earth and the sky. Out of this, one layer of Rahmat He sent down on earth, as a result of which a mother loves her child, and animals and birds show kindness to one another."* *(Muslim)*

As the intellect improves and develops due to various causes, similarly this Rahmat too grows and develops due to various causes. If it is allowed to die, then man will be liable to go to hell. Hadrat Abu Hurrayrah (R.A.A.) has narrated that he has heard the True and the Most Tustworthy Abul Qasim, the Prophet (S.A.W.) saying: "Rahmat (kindness) is snatched away from the cruel-hearted only."

The Foremost Deserving of Kindness : Islam has shown that there are some who are the foremost among those who deserve our kindness and safeguard from us. These are our kinsmen (Zawil Arham), who deserve our attention and our kindness more than others. Allah's Prophet (S.A.W.) has said:

> *"Allah shows mercy to those who show mercy to others. Be kind to the people on the earth, the Master of the Skies will be kind to you. Kindness to the kinsmen is among the laws ordained by Allah, He who united the*

relations, Allah unites with him, and he who cuts them, Allah is separated from him. *(Tirmidhi)*

Every Muslim has a duty to fulfil his responsibility towards his relatives, pay their dues, to strengthen the mutual relations with love, sympathy and kindness.

One's own parents are the most deserving of one's love, good treatment and favours.

And lower to them the wing of submission through mercy, and say: 'My Lord I Have mercy on them both as they did care for me when I was little.'

(Bani Israil: 24)

Then his own children are deserving of his mercies : Barwa has narrated that Hadrat Abu Bakr (R.A.A.) came to his daughter, Hadrat Aishah (R.A.A.) who had fever. He asked:

"How are you my dear?" And he kissed her cheek.

(Bukhari)

Rough and coarse people do not have much softness and kindness in their behaviour and their conduct expresses bitterness and meanness. Abu Hurrayrah (R.A.A.) has narrated that the Prophet (S.A.W.) kissed his grandsons Hasan and Hussain (R.A.A.) . There, Aqra' bin Habisul Tamimi was also present, who said: "I have ten children, but I never kissed any one of them."

The Prophet looked at him and said: "He who does not show mercy, will not to be shown mercy." In another tradition it is written: "May I understand that Allah has snatched away mercy from you heart?"(Bukhari)

Anas (R.A.A.) narrates: "We went with the Prophet (S.A.W.) to Abu Saiful-Quin (R.A.A.) who used to feed milk to the Prophet's (S.A.W.) son, Ibrahim. The Prophet lifted his son and kissed him. Then again when Ibrahim was about to die we went with him for the second time. Owing to excess of sorrow, the Prophet (S.A.W.) shed tears, Ibn Auf was astonished and said: "You are crying O Prophet (S.A.W.) of Allah!" The Prophet replied: "O Ibn Auf ! This is a sign of mercy." Then again he said: "The eyes are shedding tears, the heart is bursting, but we will say whatever is liked by our Lord: O Ibrahim! we are sorrowful from your separation." *(Muslim)*

It is not permissible for a Muslim to close his heart, mind and his house to his relatives and to lead his life keeping away from them and severing relations with them, not to express sympathy in their difficulties, and to abstain from extending the hand of cooperation in their hour of need. Unconcern deprives a man of the Divine suspiciousness, and invites His wrath.

Abu Hurrayrah (R.A.A.) narrates that he has heard the Prophet (S.A.W.) as saying: "Kindness to kinsmen is within the commands of the Gracious God; it says: O My Lord! I have been treated with unconcern, and I have been maltreated, O my Lord ! I have been wronged." Then Allah replies: "Is she (kindness) not pleased that I unite with the person who unites with her and I separate from the person who cuts her off." (Ahmad)

Graciousness for the Orphans: Orphans are also included in the list of those with whom dealing with mercy and kindness is enjoined. To treat them in an excellent manner, to be kind to them, to meet their needs, and to safeguard their future from ruin is an extremely purified kind of worship. Even the astray natures, by adopting these qualities, follow a policy of justice and moderation, and come to the right path.

Abu Hurrayrah (R.A.A.) narrates that a man complained to the Prophet (S.A.W.) about the hardness of his heart. The Prophet (S.A.W.) said : "Pass a hand of kindness over the head of an orphan and feed a needy person." (Ahmad)

The words of another tradition are like these: "A man went to the Prophet (S.A.W.) and described the hardness of his heart. Then the Prophet (S.A.W.) said:

"Do you like that your heart should be soft and you should achieve your objective? Be kind to the orphan, pass a hand over his head, feed him your food, then your heart will be soft and your need will be fulfilled." (Tibrani)

The reason for this is that the heart becomes insensitive and dead in a society in which there is ample provision for pleasure and happiness; days and nights may pass but the people may not be able to see beyond their own luxuries and amusements. The men of wealth and power remain unaware of the difficulties and troubles of the common people, because the luxuries available to them close the gates of their hearts, so that they may not hear the sighs of the oppressed people. They veil their eyes so that they may not see the helplessness of the orphans and the needy. The common men are able to experience purified sensations and delicate feelings because they have to pass through hot and cold circumstances, and they taste both the happy and unhappy times. After this only they are able to know what is the meaning of helplessness and loneliness. How terrible is their defenselessness? And what is the plight of the wretched people?

Relief for the Stricken People : The sick and the stricken people should be shown the best expression of kindness and mercy, because the means of livelihood are very limited for these people, for which reason they cannot take part in the race for life, and cannot meet the needs of their life. Allah Himself has declared them helpless and has forgiven them. It is not permissible for us to criticise them:

> *No blame is there on the blind, nor is there blame on the lame, nor on one ill (if he joins not the war); but he that obeys Allah and His Prophet. —(Allah) will admit him to Paradise, beneath which rivers flow; and he who turns back, (Allah) will punish him with grievous penalty.* *(Fath : 17)*

The sick person is in difficulties because of his sickness, and his life becomes very unpleasant and painful. If he shows patience, he achieves nearness to Allah and deserves to receive Allah's mercies. When on the pain of pricking with a twig a Momin's sins are forgiven, then what to say of the purification of the person who is constantly in pain in the form of sickness, and the worst types of pains are troubling him. This is the reason why such a person is directly under the protection of God. Therefore, we should abstain from ill-treating, insulting and jeering at the sick persons, because it is the worst crime.

Kind Treatment of the Employees : Our servants and employees are also deserving of our mercy and kindness. We should give a proof of our good treatment of them. They should be entrusted with the work according to their capacity, and we should forgive their lapses. We should not make them conscious of our superiority over them, nor should we ridicule them, because when a man with the property and wealth granted by God adopts an attitude of cruelty and tyranny, then God takes back his property and wealth and makes him face adverse circumstances. Abu Masood Badri (R.A.A.) narrates that he was whipping his slave, then suddenly he heard a voice from behind "Beware! Abu Masood!" He could not recognise the voice on account of his anger. When the voice came from near, he recognised it to be that of the Prophet (S.A.W.) , who was saying:

> *"Listen O Abu Masood! The power you exercise over this slave, Allah exercises more power over you than that." He immediately replied: "For the sake of Allah's pleasure, I free this slave." The Prophet replied : "Had you not done this, the hell-fire would have burnt you."*
> *(Muslim)*

Another *Hadith* says:

> *"The best wealth is that for which arrangement to develop it are made and ill-treatment of the creatures is a misfortune."* *(Abu Daud)*

One man asked the Prophet (S.A.W.) : "How many times should we forgive a slave?" The Prophet (S.A.W.) replied: "Daily, seventy times." There are many men and women who never lose an opportunity to take advantage of the weakness of the servants. They hurl them in different ways. Islam has warned against this misfortune and has declared definite punishment for such behaviour.

Kindness to Animals : Islam desires kindness to animals. Hadrat Umar (R.A.A.) saw that a man was dragging a goat by its feet for slaughtering it. He reproached him and said: "Fie on you, carry it properly."

> *One man told the Prophet (S.A.W.) : "O Messenger of Allah! When I slaughter a goat, I try to be kind to it." The Prophet (S.A.W.) said: "If you will show mercy on it, Allah show mercy on you."* *(Hakim)*

Islam is very severe on those who are cruel to animals, and who have no hesitation in hurting them. It has been declared that if a man, however great he may be, ill-treats the dumb animals, he can even earn the punishment of the hell-fire. Allah's Messenger (S.A.W.) has said:

"A woman was thrown into the hell, because she had tied a cat, which she neither fed nor set free, so that it could roam about and feed itself on insects, etc." (Bukhari)

He further clarified that the feeling of kindness generating in the heart, even if it is for a dog, washes away major sins. The Prophet (S.A.W.) has said:

"One man was travelling in a desert. He got terribly thirsty. He saw a well, descended down it and drank to his heart's content. In the meanwhile a dog came to the well, thirsty, its tongue hanging out on account of the thirst. The man said to himself : "On account of thirst the plight of this dog is the same as was mine." Then he descended into the well, and filled his sock with water, and holding it with his teeth came out of the well. He made the dog drink that water. Allah appreciated this act of his and granted him salvation." The people asked "Is there reward for good treatment to the animals?" He replied: "There is reward for good treatment to every animate thing."

In one tradition it is stated:

"A disobedient woman saw a dog looking down the well in extreme heat, and his tongue was hanging out on account of severe thirst. She felt kind towards it and she made it drink water by bringing it in her sock. Accordingly for this act of hers, she was granted salvation. (Muslim)

If this act of kindness of a disobedient woman with a dog can be the cause of her salvation, then surely the treatment of the humans with kindness can achieve wonders !!

Bibliography

Abbas Hashmi : *Rasul (PBUH),* Adam Pub., New Delhi, 2001.

Abdali, M.R. : *Scientific Thought in Islam,* Pious Publications, Hyderabad, 2001.

Abdul Qadir : *Criminal Law of Islam,* Kitab Bhavan, New Delhi, 1999.

Abdul, H.S.: *The Life of Muhammad (PBUH),* Islamic Pub., New Delhi,1997.

Abdullah Enan : *Decisive Moments in the History of Islam,* Islamic Book Company, Delhi, 1996.

Adil, H. M. : *Letters of Hadrat Usman Ghani (R.A.A.),* Kitab Bhavan, New Delhi, 1992

Ahmad, Ilyas : *Sovereignty, Islamic and Modern,* Allies Book Corporation, Karachi, 1965.

Ahmad, Imtiaz : *Ritual and Religion among Muslims in India,* Manohar Publishers, New Delhi, 1984.

Ahmed, Hasanuddin : *Islamic Economics,* Goodword Books Pvt. Ltd., New Delhi, 1991.

Ali, Ameer : *Muhammadan Law,* Kitab Bhavan, New Delhi, 1986.

Arnold, T. W. : *The Caliphate,* Routledge & Kegan Paul Ltd., London,1965.

Asghar, Ali : *Islam : Women and Gender Justice,* Gyan Books Pvt. Ltd., New Delhi, 2001.

Ataur-Rahim : *Jesus a Prophet of Islam,* Idara Ishaat-e-Diniyat Pvt. Ltd, New Delhi, 1995.

Azam, Zaki : *The Ideas of Arab Nationalism,* Cornell University Press, New York,1956.

Baral, Raj : *Regional Migrations : Ethnicity and Security,* Popular Prakashan, Bombay, 1995.

Beverly, Milton : *Islam and Politics in the Contemporary World*, Blackwell, New York, 1987.

Bosworth, C.E. : *The Legacy of Islam*, Oxford University Press, New York, 1979.

Carl, W. : *Teaching of Sufism*, Deep & Deep, New Delhi, 2000.

Charles Howard : *The Constitutionalism*, Great Seal Books, New York, 1947.

Chave F. : *Islamic Histroriography*, Cambridge University press, New York, 1990.

Daniel, N.A. : *Islam and the West : the Making of an Image*, University Press, Edinburgh, 1962.

De, Laet : *The Political Systems of Empire*, Oxford, New York, 1963.

Edwin, Elliot : *Worship in Islam*, University of Madras, Madras, 1925.

Fauzi M. : *The Islamic State : a Study in Traditional Politics*, Oxford, New York, 1967.

Gardet, Louis : *Mystique Musulmane*, Allen & Co., Paris, 1961.

Gellner, E. : *Post-Traditional Forms in Islam : the Turf and Trade*, Oxford, New York, 1982.

Ghulam Sarwar : *Muhammad (PBUH) the Holy Prophet*, Dar-ul Ishaat, Karachi, 1997.

Gibb, H.A.R : *Studies in the Civilization of Islam*, Beacon Press, Boston,1962.

Glubb : *The Story of Arab Legion*, Feroz Pub., Lahore, 2000.

Gulzar Ahmed : *The Prophets (PBUH) Concept of War*, Aziz Pub., Islamabad, 2000.

Herbert, Friedman : *The Amazing Universe*, National Geographic Society, Washington D.C., 1980.

Husaini, S.A.Q : *The Pantheistic Monism of Ibn al-Arabi*, Feroz Pub., Lahore, 1970.

Hussain, Ahanger : *Customary Succession among Muslims*, Uppal Publishibng House, New Delhi, 1997.

Hussain, M. : *Imam Abu Hanifah : Life and Work*, Kitab Bhavan, New Delhi, 2001.

Hussain, S. : *Human Rights in Islam*, Kitab Bhavan, New Delhi, 2001.

Ikbal Ali : *Islamic Sufism,* Idarah-I-Adbiyat-I-Delhi, Delhi, 1979.

Ikram, S.M. : *Muslim Civilization in India,* Oxford, New York, 1981.

Jafar Sharif : *Islam in India,* Atlantic Publishers, New Delhi, 1999.

Jafar, Sharif : *Islam in India,* Oxford, New Delhi, 1972.

James, Piscarton : *Islam in the World of National States,* Macmillan, New York, 1982.

Jean-Baptiste : *Travels in India,* W.Crooke, London, 1925.

Jha, V. : *Indian Society: Historical Probings,* Rawat Pub., Delhi, 1974.

John L. Esposite : *Islam in Transition,* Oxford, New York, 1969.

John Surowiecki : *The Pulse of the Planet,* Crown Publishers, U.S.A. 1972.

Kalim Bahadur : *Domestic Conflicts in South Asia,* South Asia Publishers, New Delhi, 1986.

Kalim, M. Siddiq : *Studies in Pakistan Culture : an International Perspective,* Manohar Publications, New Delhi, 1993.

Karnal, A. : *Islam : Today and Tomorrow,* Deep & Deep Pub., New Delhi, 1989.

Katharine, Scarfe : *Perception of the Islamic Word,* Cambridge University Press, New Delhi, 1992.

Kaur, R. : *Islamic Co-operation and Unity,* Deep & Deep Publications, New Delhi, 1993.

Kazim Munishi : *Alamgir-Nama,* A.B.C. & Co., Calcutta, 1865.

Khaduri, M. : *War and Peace in the Law of Islam,* Hopkins Press, Baltimore, 1955.

Landau, R. : *The Philosophy of the Ibn Arabi,* Century Pub., London, 1959.

Lewis, Richards : *Universe,* Harmony Books, New York, 1973.

Mac, Closky : *Pacts for Peace,* New Century Pub., London, 1980.

Margery Milne : *The Nature of Life,* Crown Publishers, New York, 1995.

Mathew, Thomas : *Political Economy of Etimic Conflict,* School of International Studies, Jawaharlal Nehru University, New Delhi, 2003.

Mayne, P. : *Saints of Sind,* New Century Pub., London, 1965.

Meer, Ali : *Observations on the Musulmauns of India,* Macmillan & Co., London, 1832.

Mohiuddin, Ahmad : *Saiyid Ahmad Shahid,* Modern Pub., Lucknow, 1975.

Moreland, W.H. : *From Akbar to Aurangzeb,* MacMillan & Co., London, 1923.

Mualana, Taqi : *Fundamentals of Ijtihad,* Idaara-I-Adabiyat, Delhi, 1986.

Muhammad, Asad : *Islam at the Crossroads,* Kitab Bhavan, New Delhi, 2003.

Murtaza, G. : *Judicial System of Islam,* Kitab Bhavan, New Delhi, 1994.

Muslehuddin, M. : *Islam : its Political System,* Kitab Bhavan, New Delhi, 1999.

Nabith, A. : *The Foundations of the Articles of Faith,* Feroz Pub., Lahore, 1963.

Nicholson, R.A. : *Studies in Islamic Mysticism,* Cambridge, New York, 1967.

Nikki, R. : *Saints and Sufis, Muslim Religious Institutions since 1500,* University of California Press, California, 1972.

Noomi, Kurtha : *Prisoners of War and War Crimes,* Deep Publications, Lacknow, 1980.

Padwick, C.E. : *Muslim Devotions,* MacMillan & Co., London, 1960.

Palamer, E.H. : *The Quran,* Atlantic Publishers, New Delhi, 1996.

Peter Lambron Wilson : *Traditional Modes of Contemplation and Action,* University Press, Tehran, 1977.

Qazi A. Qadir : *The Changing World of Islam,* Royal Pub., Lahore, 1992.

Richards, J.F. : *Mughal Administration in Golkonda,* Oxford, New York, 1975.

Robert, D. : *Exploring our Living Planet,* National Geographic Society, Washington, 1989.

Rodinson, Maxime : *Islam and Capitalism,* Penguin, London,1974.

Rosenthal, E.I.J. : *Islam in the Modern National State,* University Press, Cambridge,1965.

Sardar, Ziauddin : *The Future of Muslim Civilization,* Croom Helm, London, 1979.

Sarton, George : *Introduction to the History of Science,* Carnegie Institute, Washington, 1950

Saxena, K.P. : *Human Rights: Perspective and Challenges,* Lancers Books, New Delhi, 1996.

Saxena, V. K. : *Muslims and the Indian National Congress,* Discovery Publishing House, New Delhi, 1985.

Scarman, Leslie : *Law : the New Dimensions,* Stevens and Sons, London, 1974.

Schacht, J. : *The Origins of Muhammadan Jurisprudence,* Clarendon Press, Oxford, 1953.

Schwartz, E. : *Science and Civilization in Islam,* Cambridge, London, 1966.

Seervai, H. : *Constitutional Law of India,* N.M. Tripathi & Co., Bombay, 1967.

Setalvad : *War and Civil Liberties,* Feroz Pub., Lahore, 1992.

Sharif, M. : *Islamic Social Framework,* Islamic Book Foundation, Dacca, 1980.

Sharma, S.R. : *Women's Education in Ancient and Muslim Period,* Discovery Publishing House, New Delhi, 1996.

Siddiqi, M.Z. : *Hadith Literature,* Deepali Pub., Calcutta, 1961.

Singh, Nagendar : *Human Rights and International Cooperation,* S. Chand & Co., New Delhi, 1969.

Sir William : *The Caliphate, its Rise, Decline and Fall,* Oxford, Edinburgh, 1915.

Sir, Richard : *Sind and Races that Inhabit the Valley of the Indus,* Allen & Unwin, London, 1851.

Sir, Thomas : *The Caliphate,* MacMillan, London, 1965.

Smith, M. : *An Early Mystic of Baghdad,* Cambridge, New York, 1920.

Smith, M.: *The Mystic and her Fellow Saints in Islam,* Cambridge, London, 1929.

Smith, W. C. : *Modern Islam in India : a Social Analysis,* Manohar Publishers, New Delhi, 1985.

Suhrawardi, Umar : *Awarif al Maarif bin Muhammad*, Sheikh Ghulam Shahabuddin Ali & Sons, Lahore, 1964.

Syed Husain : *Three Muslim Sages*, Cambridge, New York, 1959.

Syed, Amir Ali : *The Spirit of Islam*, Royal Pub.,Lahore, 1979.

Taqi Muhammad : *An Introduction to Islamic Finance*, Idara Ishaat-e-Diniyat Pvt. Ltd., New Delhi, 1999.

Thompson, H.R. : *Sculptures and Inscriptions of Darius the Great on the Rock of Behistan*, Oxford, London, 1907.

Valliuddin, Mir : *The Quranic Sufism*, Motilal Banarsi Das Publishers, New Delhi, 1989.

Wahed, Husain : *Administration of Justice during the Muslim Rule in India*, Ashish Publishing House, New Delhi, 1977.

Waheed, Akhtar : *Sufi Approach to the Problem of Alienation*, Wilson & Co., New Delhi, 1975.

Waheed, Mirza : *The Life and Works of Amir Khusrau*, Kaveri Pub., Calcutta, 1935.

Walker, Benjamin : *Foundation of Islam : the Making of World Faith*, Rupa & Co., New Delhi, 2001.

Watt, M. : *The Faith and Practice of Al-Ghazzali*, MacMillan & Co., London, 1953.

Watt, W.M. : *Islam and the Integration of Society*, Routledge, London, 1961.

Yazbeck, Haddad : *Islamic Values in the United States*, Oxford, New York, 1997.

Yezbeck Haddad : *Islamic Values in the United States*, Oxford, New York, 1999.

Zafeeruddin, M.M. : *System of Modesty and Chastity in Islam*, Idara Ishaat-e-Diniyat Pvt. Ltd, New Delhi, 1995.

Zahid, Malik : *Subjects of Quran*, Kitab Bhavan, New Delhi, 1998.

Zahurul Hasan : *Tarikb-i-Sufiya-i-Gujarat*, Jamil Academy, Ahmadabad, 1981.

Zaydan, Jurji : *Umayyads and Abbasides*, Luzac & Co., London,1907.

Index

G

H

I